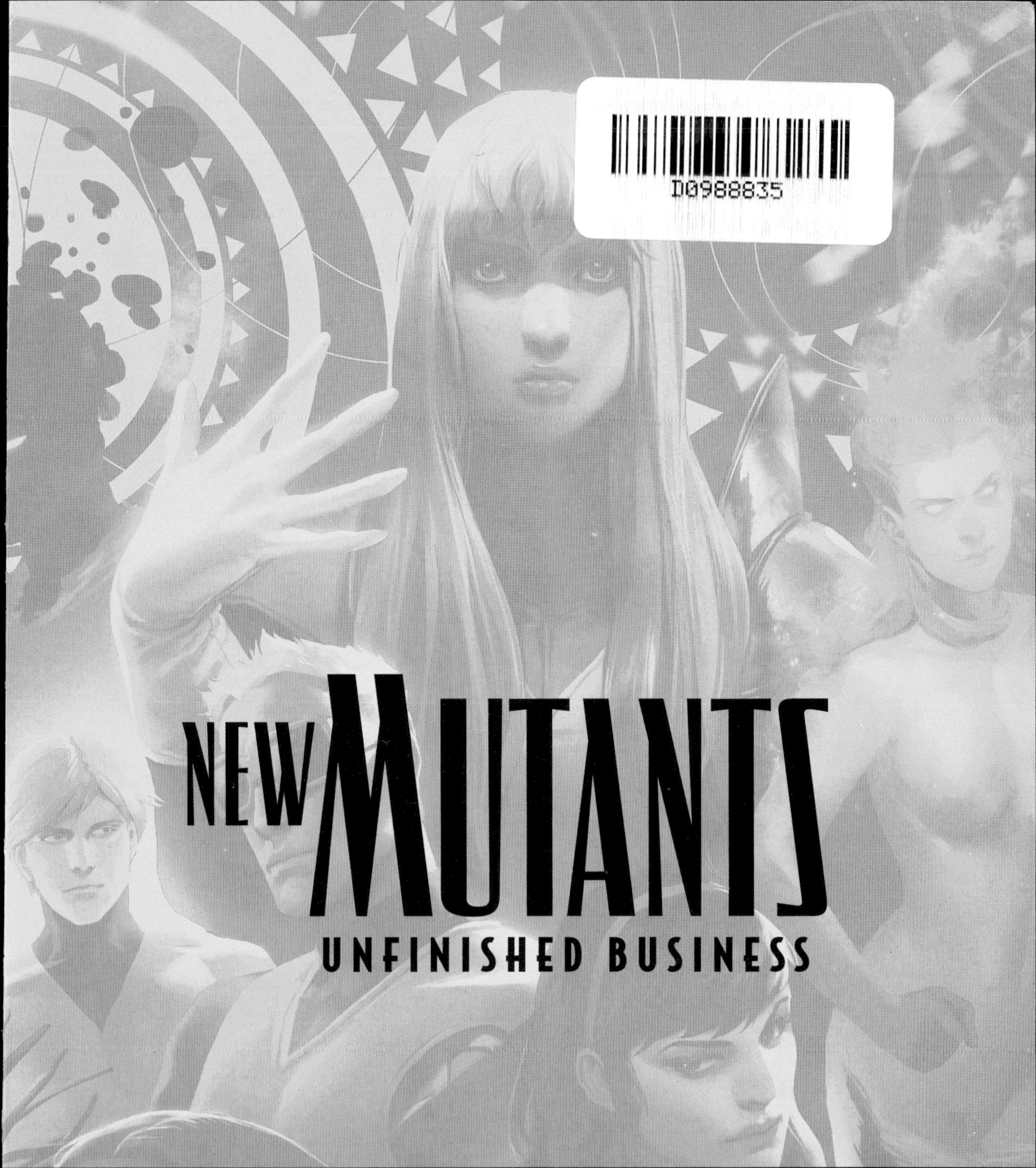

NEW MUTANTS
UNFINISHED BUSINESS

WRITERS
DAN ABNETT & ANDY LANNING

ARTIST, #25-27
LEANDRO FERNANDEZ

PENCILS, #28
MICHAEL RYAN

INKS, #28
NORMAN LEE

COLORS, #25-27
ANDRES MOSSA

COLORS, #28
DAVID CURIEL

LETTERER
VC'S JOE CARAMAGNA

COVER ART
MARKO DJURDJEVIC (#25-27) **& JORGE MOLINA** (#28)

EDITOR
SEBASTIAN GIRNER

SENIOR EDITOR
NICK LOWE

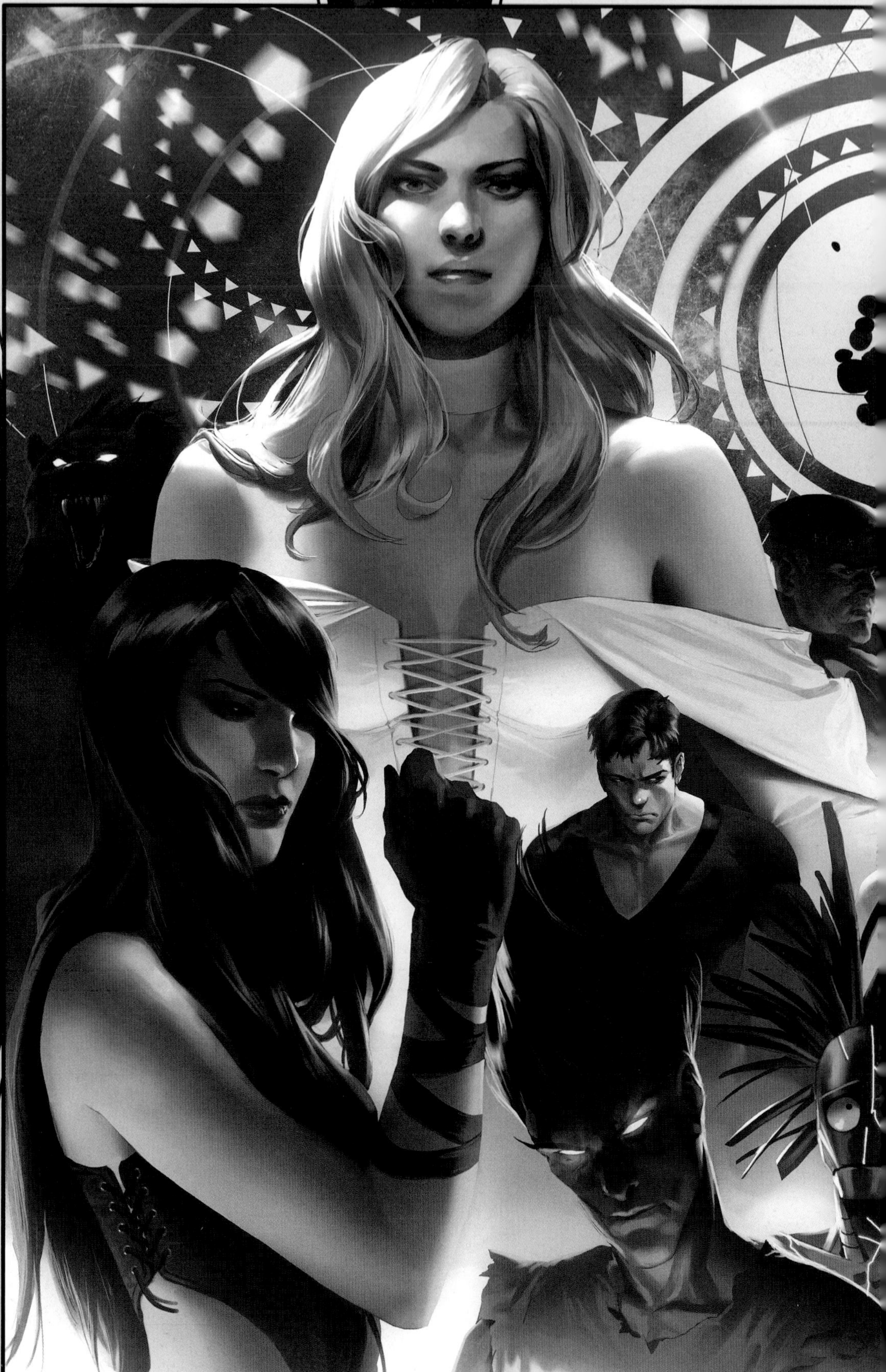

NEW MUTANTS
UNFINISHED BUSINESS

COLLECTION EDITOR
JENNIFER GRÜNWALD
EDITORIAL ASSISTANTS
JAMES EMMETT &
JOE HOCHSTEIN
ASSISTANT EDITORS
ALEX STARBUCK &
NELSON RIBEIRO
EDITOR, SPECIAL PROJECTS
MARK D. BEAZLEY

SENIOR EDITOR, SPECIAL PROJECTS
JEFF YOUNGQUIST
SENIOR VICE PRESIDENT OF SALES
DAVID GABRIEL
SVP OF BRAND PLANNING & COMMUNICATIONS
MICHAEL PASCIULLO
BOOK DESIGN
JEFF POWELL

EDITOR IN CHIEF
AXEL ALONSO
CHIEF CREATIVE OFFICER
JOE QUESADA
PUBLISHER
DAN BUCKLEY
EXECUTIVE PRODUCER
ALAN FINE

NEW MUTANTS: UNFINISHED BUSINESS. Contains material originally published in magazine form as NEW MUTANTS #25-28. First printing 2011. Hardcover ISBN# 978-0-7851-5230-9. Softcover ISBN# 978-0-7851-5231-6. Published by MARVEL WORLDWIDE, INC., a subsidiary of MARVEL ENTERTAINMENT, LLC. OFFICE OF PUBLICATION: 135 West 50th Street, New York, NY 10020. Copyright © 2011 and 2012 Marvel Characters, Inc. All rights reserved. Hardcover: $19.99 per copy in the U.S. and $21.99 in Canada (GST #R127032852). Softcover: $16.99 per copy in the U.S. and $18.99 in Canada (GST #R127032852). Canadian Agreement #40668537. All characters featured in this issue and the distinctive names and likenesses thereof, and all related indicia are trademarks of Marvel Characters, Inc. No similarity between any of the names, characters, persons, and/or institutions in this magazine with those of any living or dead person or institution is intended, and any such similarity which may exist is purely coincidental. **Printed in the U.S.A.** ALAN FINE, EVP - Office of the President, Marvel Worldwide, Inc. and EVP & CMO Marvel Characters B.V.; DAN BUCKLEY, Publisher & President - Print, Animation & Digital Divisions; JOE QUESADA, Chief Creative Officer; JIM SOKOLOWSKI, Chief Operating Officer; DAVID BOGART, SVP of Business Affairs & Talent Management; TOM BREVOORT, SVP of Publishing; C.B. CEBULSKI, SVP of Creator & Content Development; DAVID GABRIEL, SVP of Publishing Sales & Circulation; MICHAEL PASCIULLO, SVP of Brand Planning & Communications; JIM O'KEEFE, VP of Operations & Logistics; DAN CARR, Executive Director of Publishing Technology; SUSAN CRESPI, Editorial Operations Manager; ALEX MORALES, Publishing Operations Manager; STAN LEE, Chairman Emeritus. For information regarding advertising in Marvel Comics or on Marvel.com, please contact John Dokes, SVP Integrated Sales and Marketing, at jdokes@marvel.com. For Marvel subscription inquiries, please call 800-217-9158. **Manufactured between 8/29/2011 and 9/26/2011 (hardcover), and 8/29/2011 and 3/26/2012 (softcover), by R.R. DONNELLEY, INC., SALEM, VA, USA.**

10 9 8 7 6 5 4 3 2 1

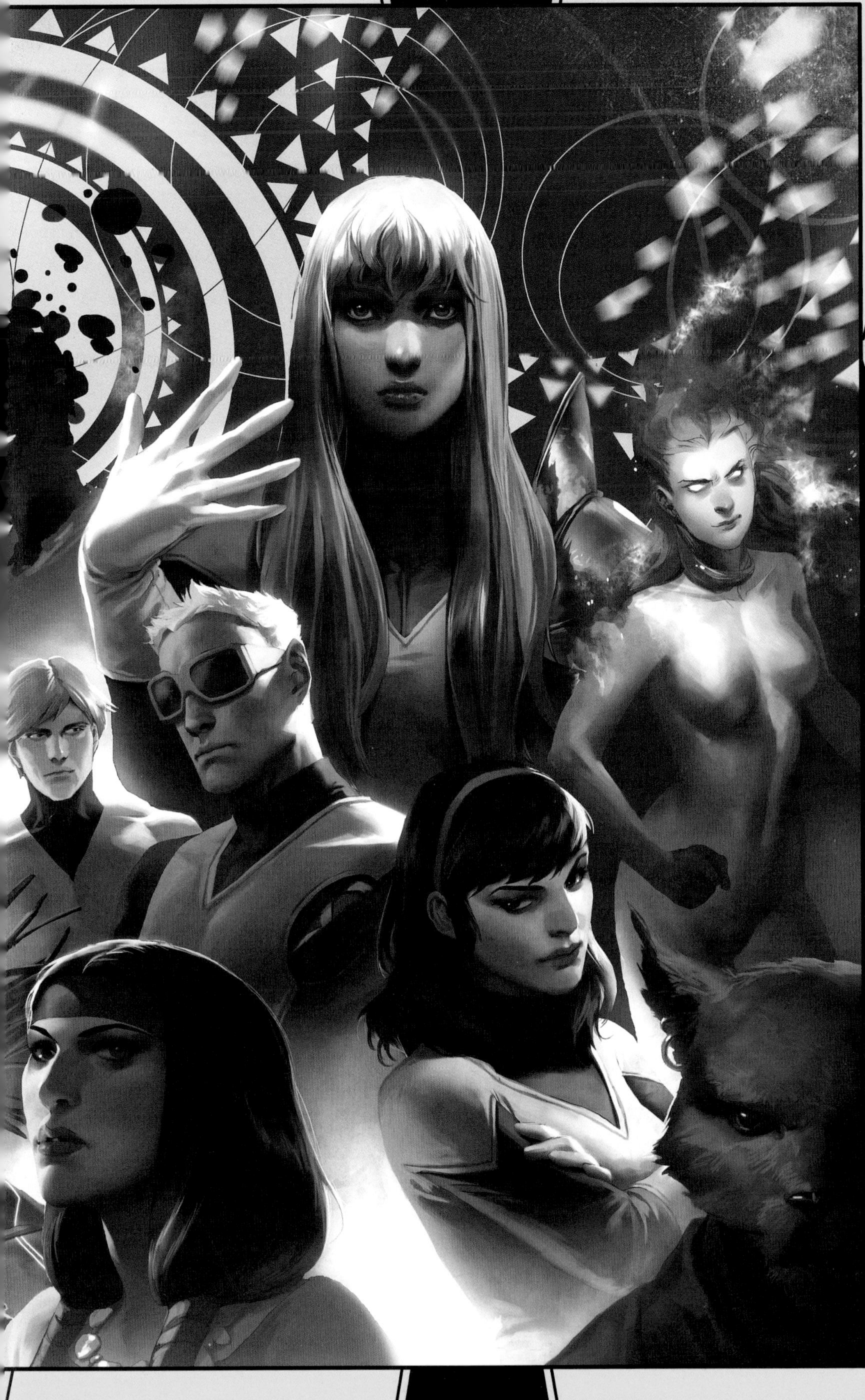

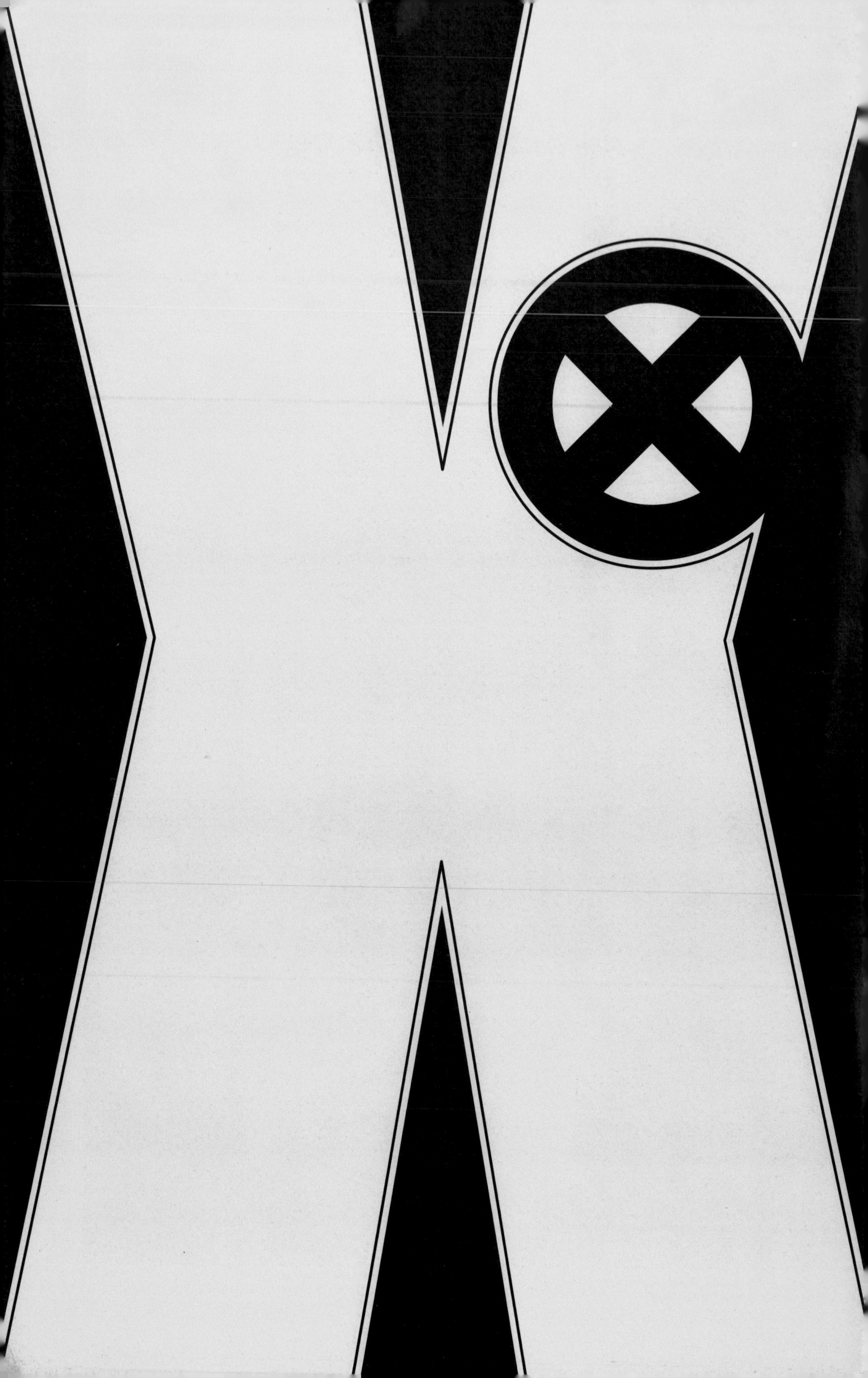

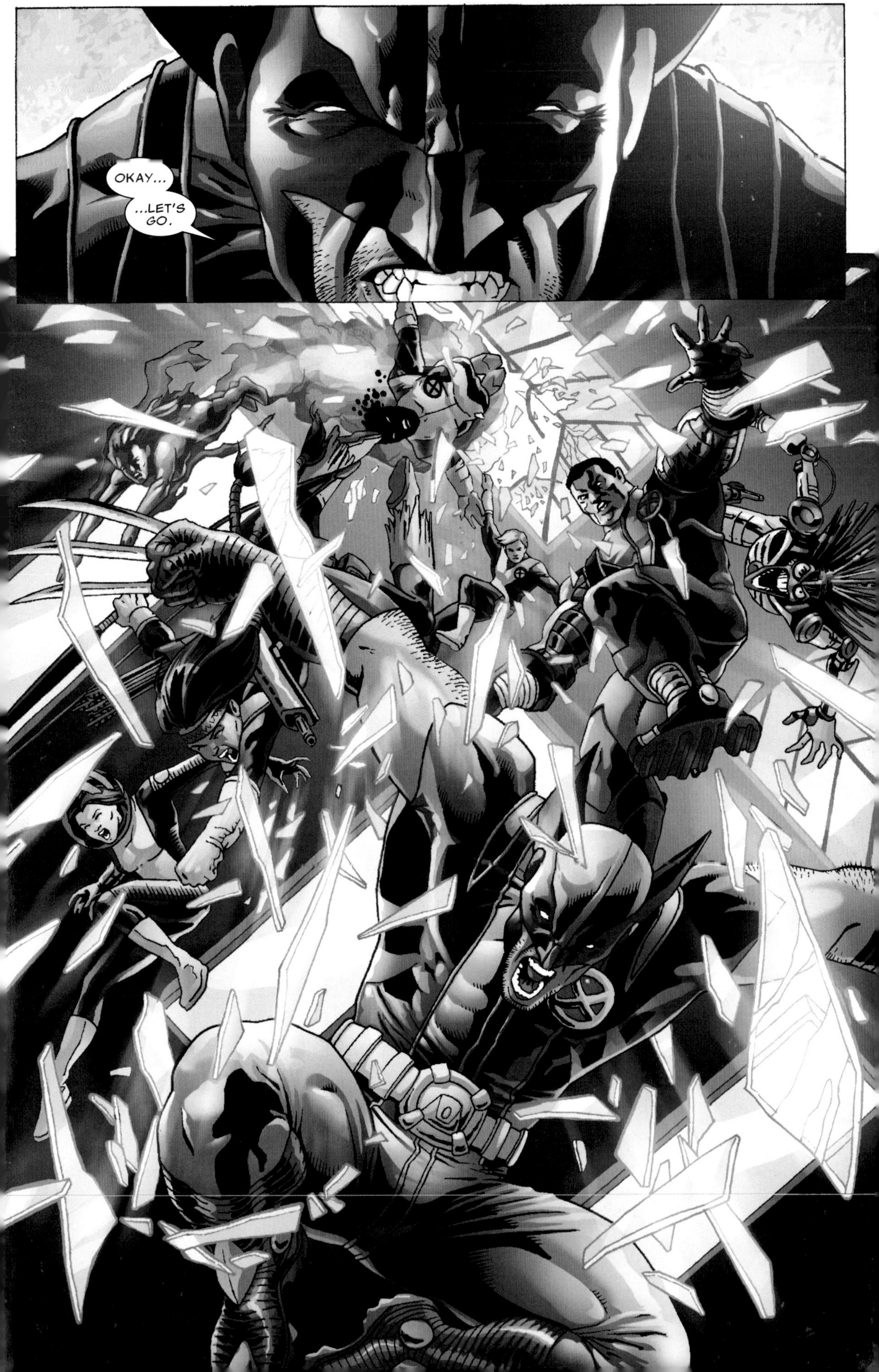
OKAY...
...LET'S GO.

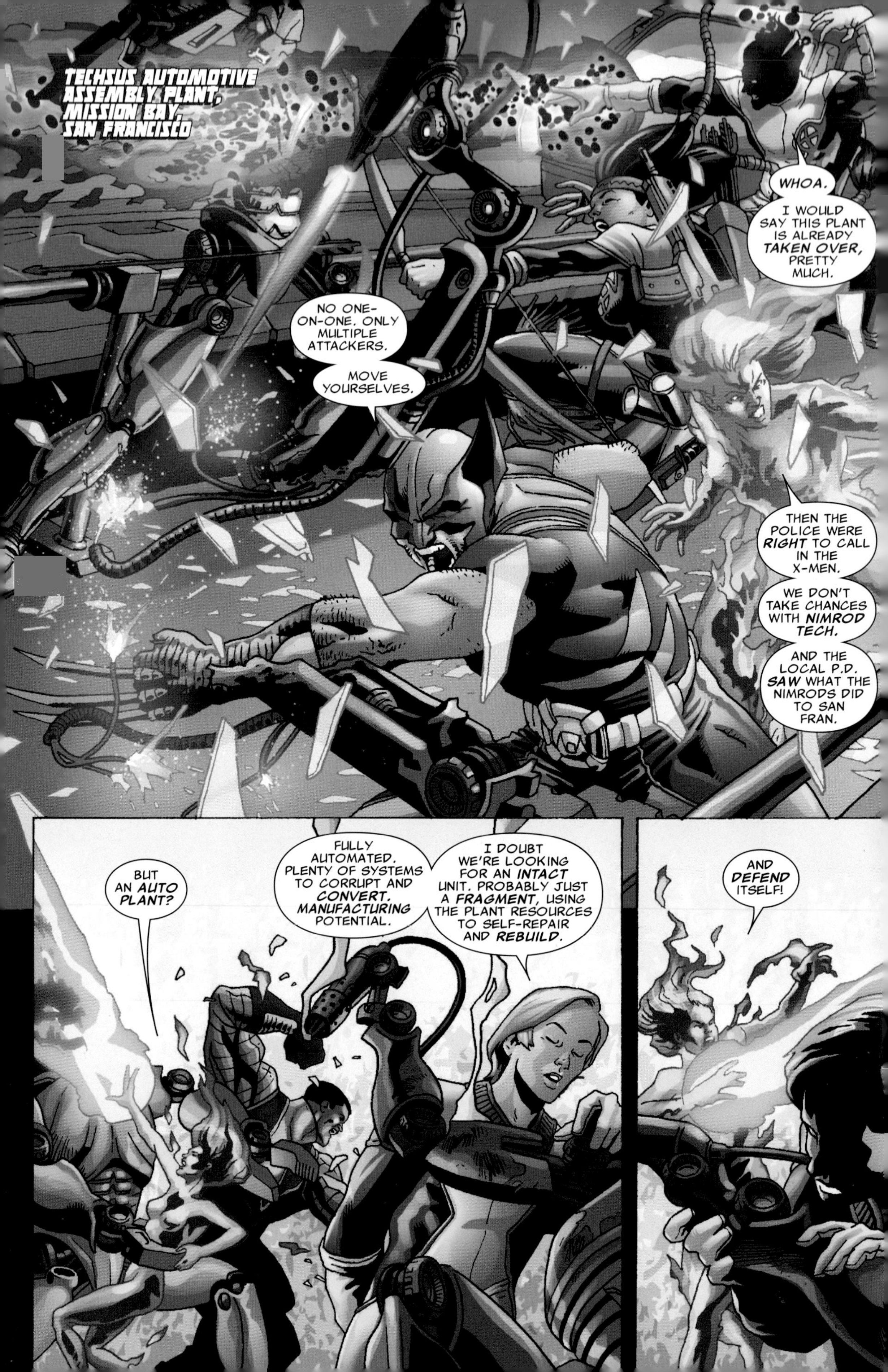
TECHSUS AUTOMOTIVE ASSEMBLY PLANT, MISSION BAY, SAN FRANCISCO
WHOA.
I WOULD SAY THIS PLANT IS ALREADY TAKEN OVER, PRETTY MUCH.
NO ONE-ON-ONE. ONLY MULTIPLE ATTACKERS.
MOVE YOURSELVES.
THEN THE POLICE WERE RIGHT TO CALL IN THE X-MEN.
WE DON'T TAKE CHANCES WITH NIMROD TECH.
AND THE LOCAL P.D. SAW WHAT THE NIMRODS DID TO SAN FRAN.
BUT AN AUTO PLANT?
FULLY AUTOMATED. PLENTY OF SYSTEMS TO CORRUPT AND CONVERT. MANUFACTURING POTENTIAL.
I DOUBT WE'RE LOOKING FOR AN INTACT UNIT. PROBABLY JUST A FRAGMENT, USING THE PLANT RESOURCES TO SELF-REPAIR AND REBUILD.
AND DEFEND ITSELF!

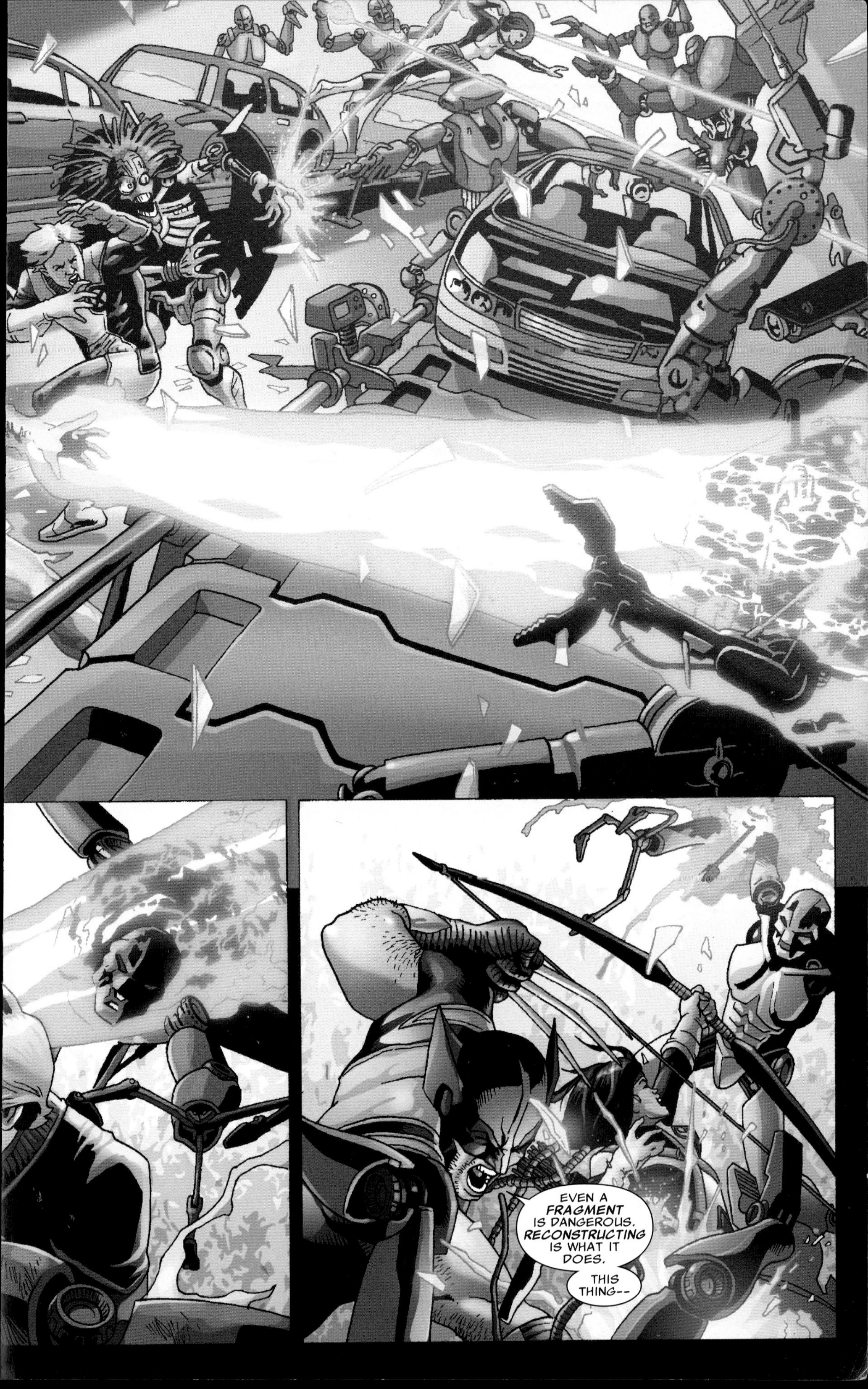
EVEN A FRAGMENT IS DANGEROUS. RECONSTRUCTING IS WHAT IT DOES.
THIS THING--

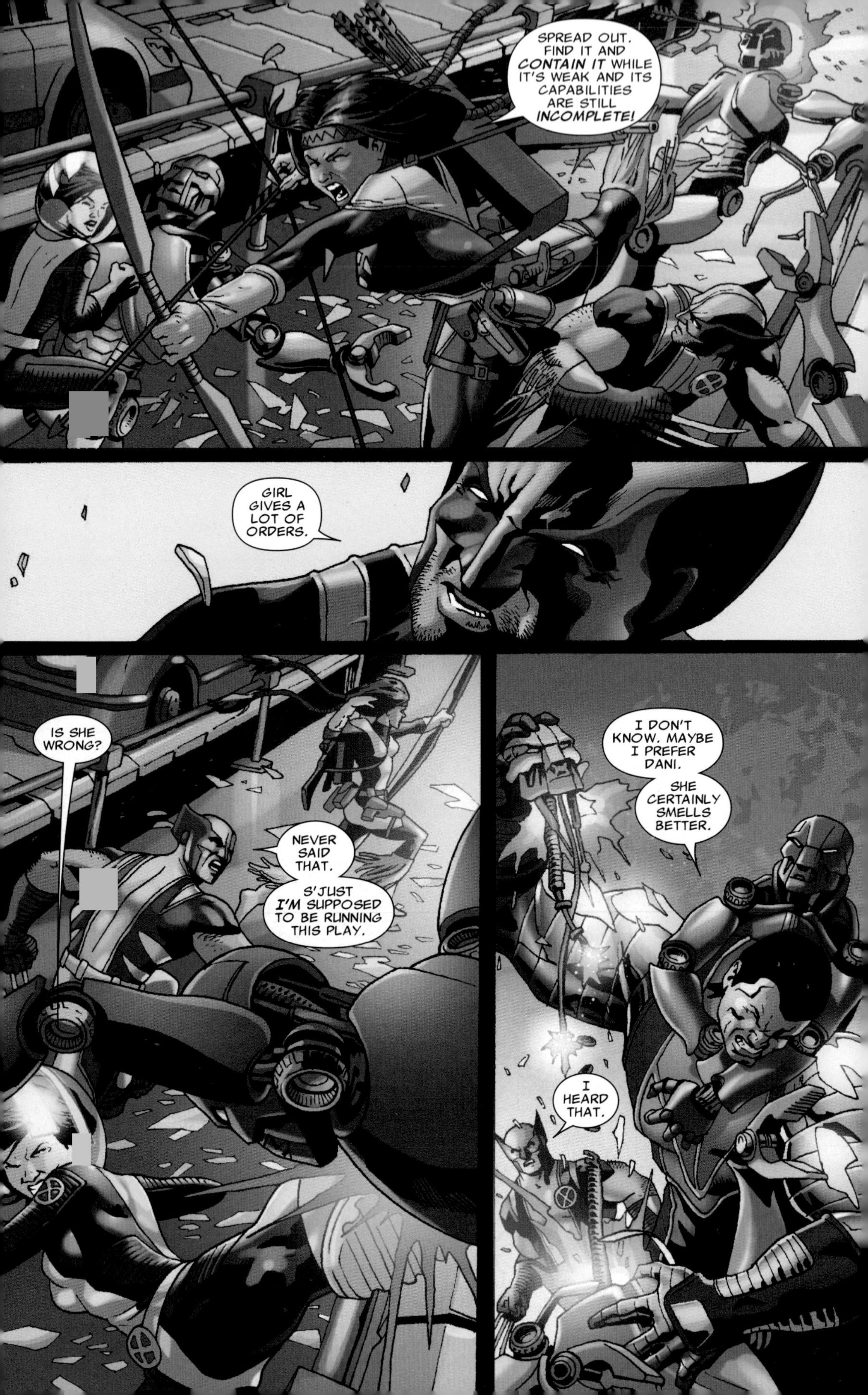
SPREAD OUT. FIND IT AND CONTAIN IT WHILE IT'S WEAK AND ITS CAPABILITIES ARE STILL INCOMPLETE!
GIRL GIVES A LOT OF ORDERS.
IS SHE WRONG?
NEVER SAID THAT.
S'JUST I'M SUPPOSED TO BE RUNNING THIS PLAY.
I DON'T KNOW. MAYBE I PREFER DANI.
SHE CERTAINLY SMELLS BETTER.
I HEARD THAT.

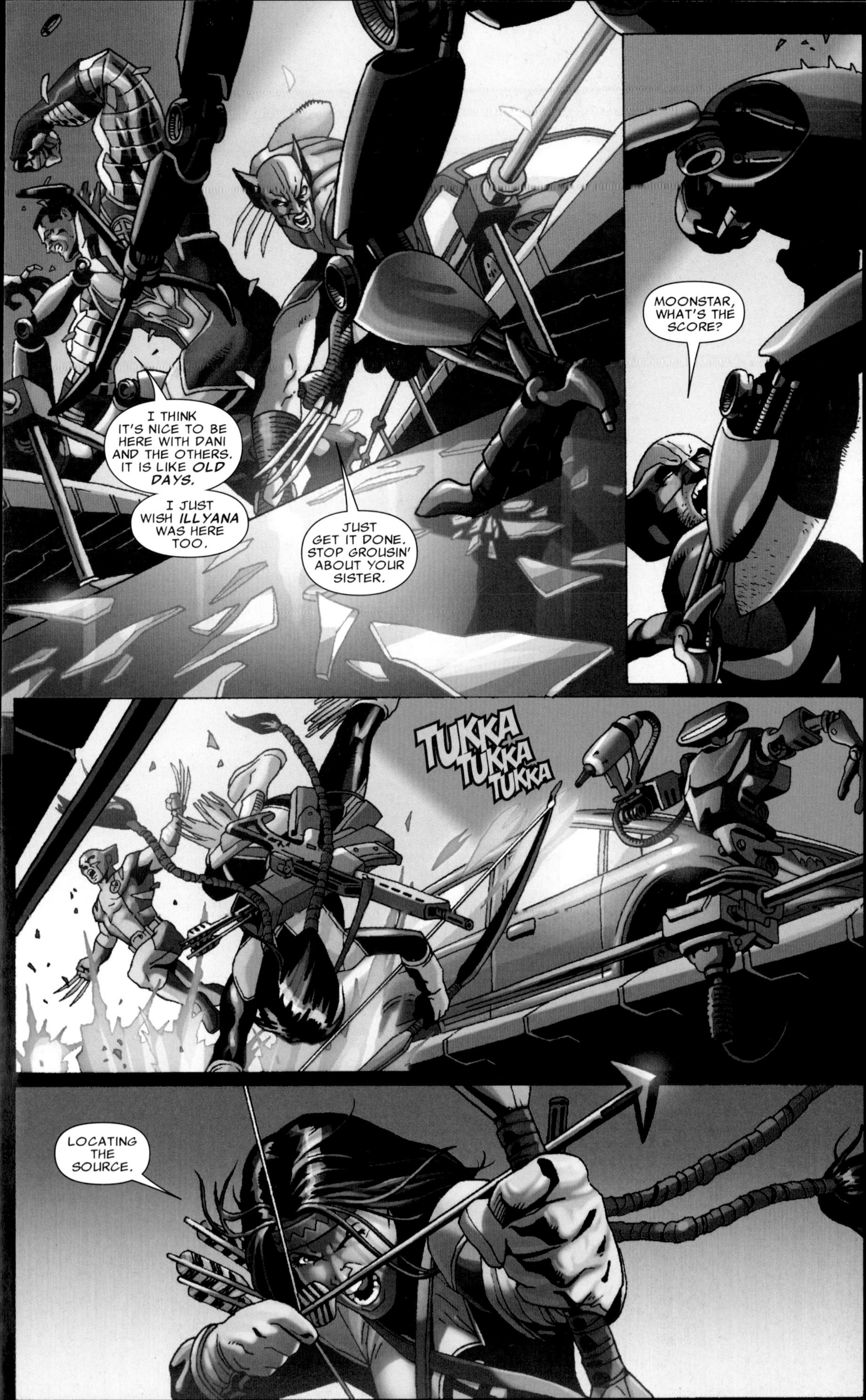
I THINK IT'S NICE TO BE HERE WITH DANI AND THE OTHERS. IT IS LIKE OLD DAYS.
I JUST WISH ILLYANA WAS HERE TOO.
JUST GET IT DONE. STOP GROUSIN' ABOUT YOUR SISTER.
MOONSTAR, WHAT'S THE SCORE?
TUKKA TUKKA TUKKA
LOCATING THE SOURCE.

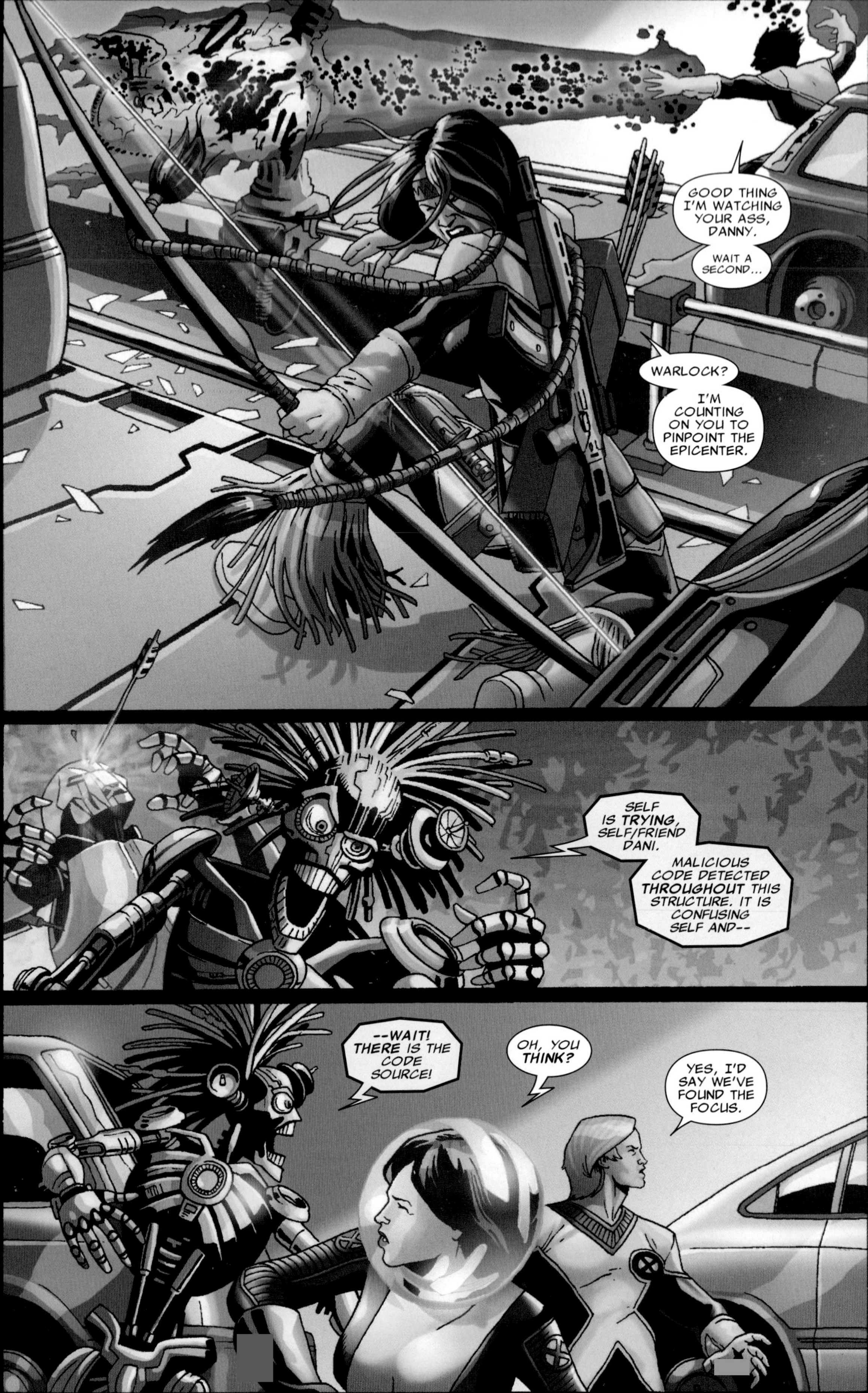
GOOD THING I'M WATCHING YOUR ASS, DANNY.
WAIT A SECOND...
WARLOCK?
I'M COUNTING ON YOU TO PINPOINT THE EPICENTER.
SELF IS TRYING, SELF/FRIEND DANI.
MALICIOUS CODE DETECTED THROUGHOUT THIS STRUCTURE. IT IS CONFUSING SELF AND--
--WAIT! THERE IS THE CODE SOURCE!
OH, YOU THINK?
YES, I'D SAY WE'VE FOUND THE FOCUS.

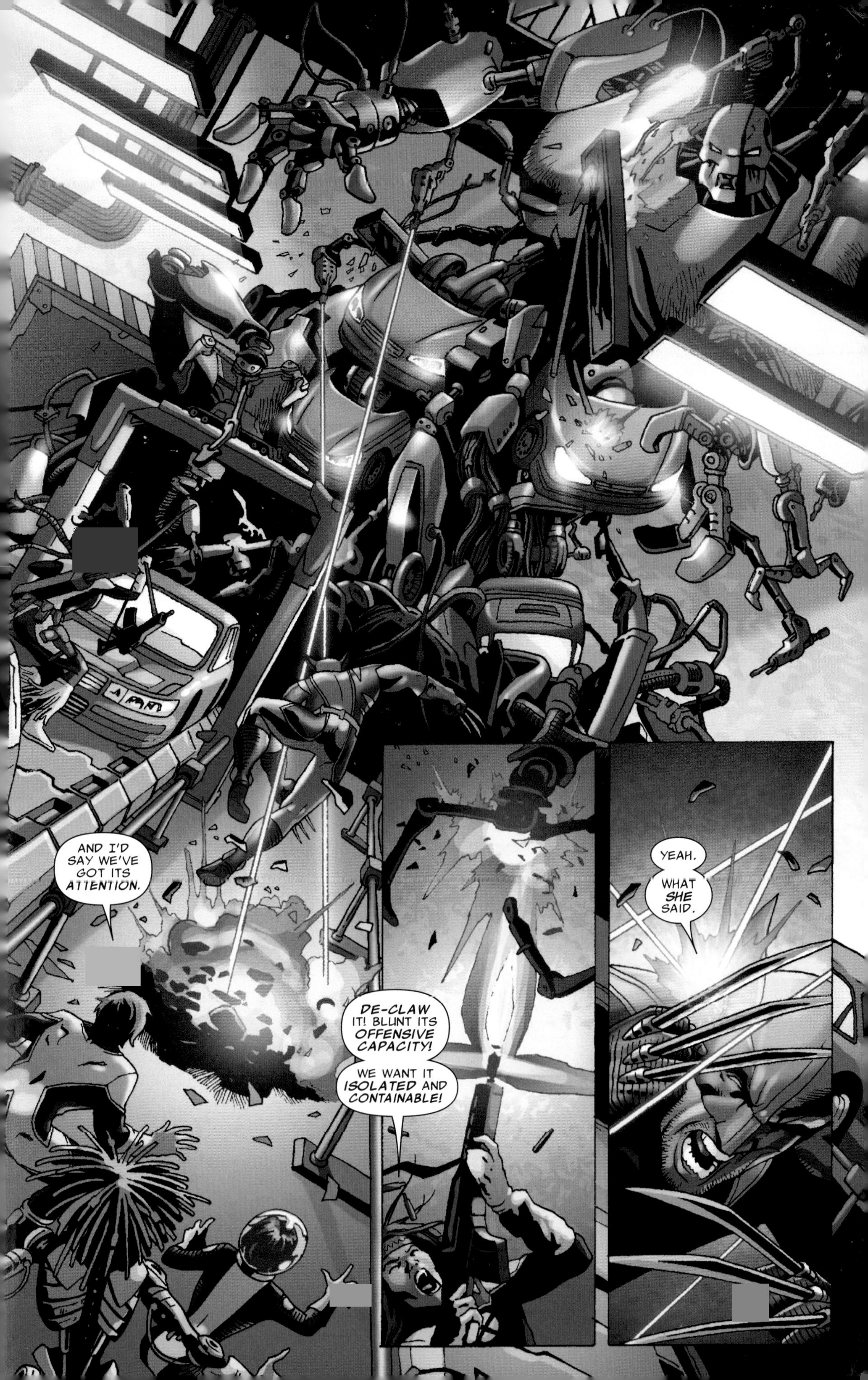
AND I'D SAY WE'VE GOT ITS ATTENTION.
DE-CLAW IT! BLUNT ITS OFFENSIVE CAPACITY!
WE WANT IT ISOLATED AND CONTAINABLE!
YEAH.
WHAT SHE SAID.

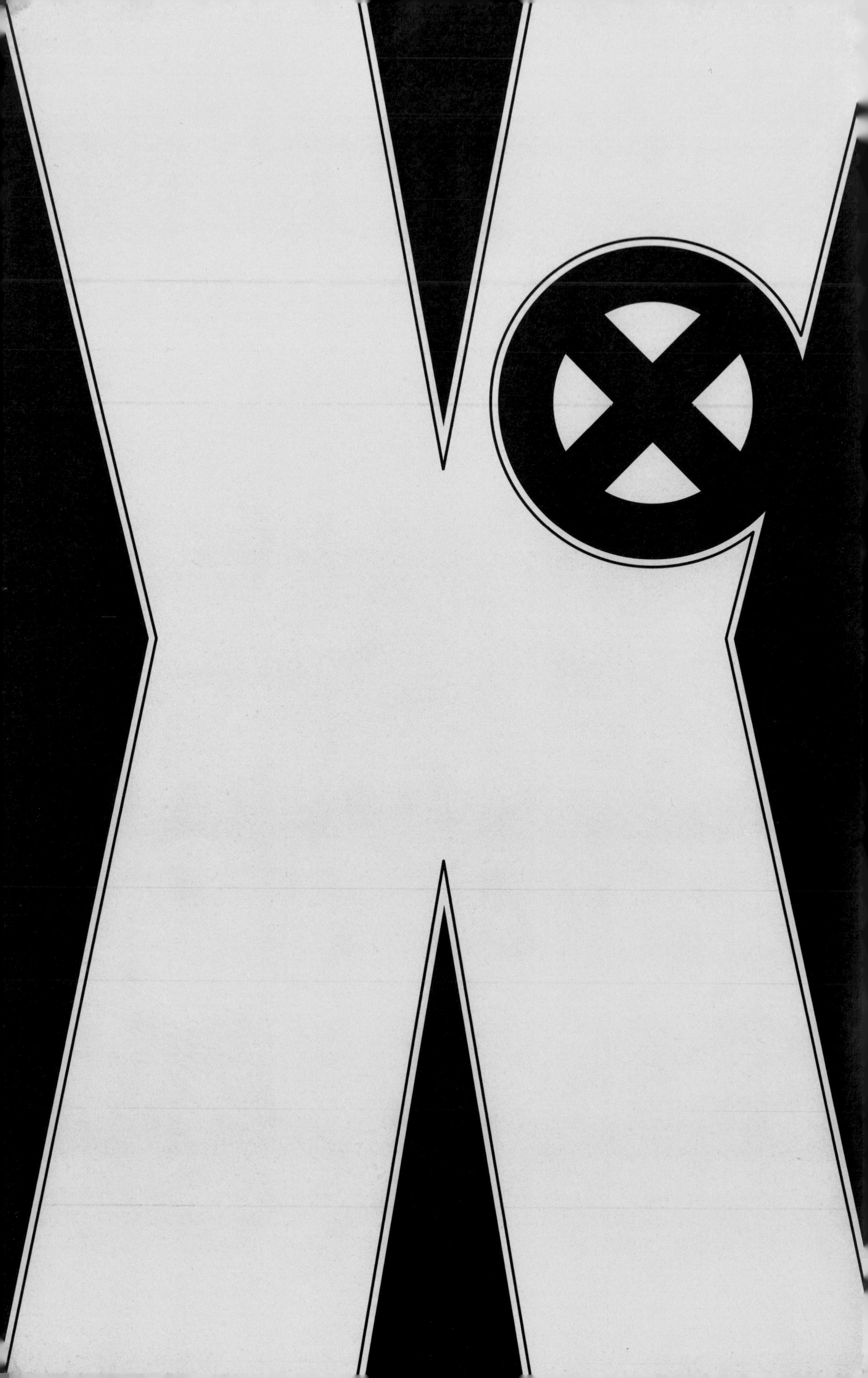

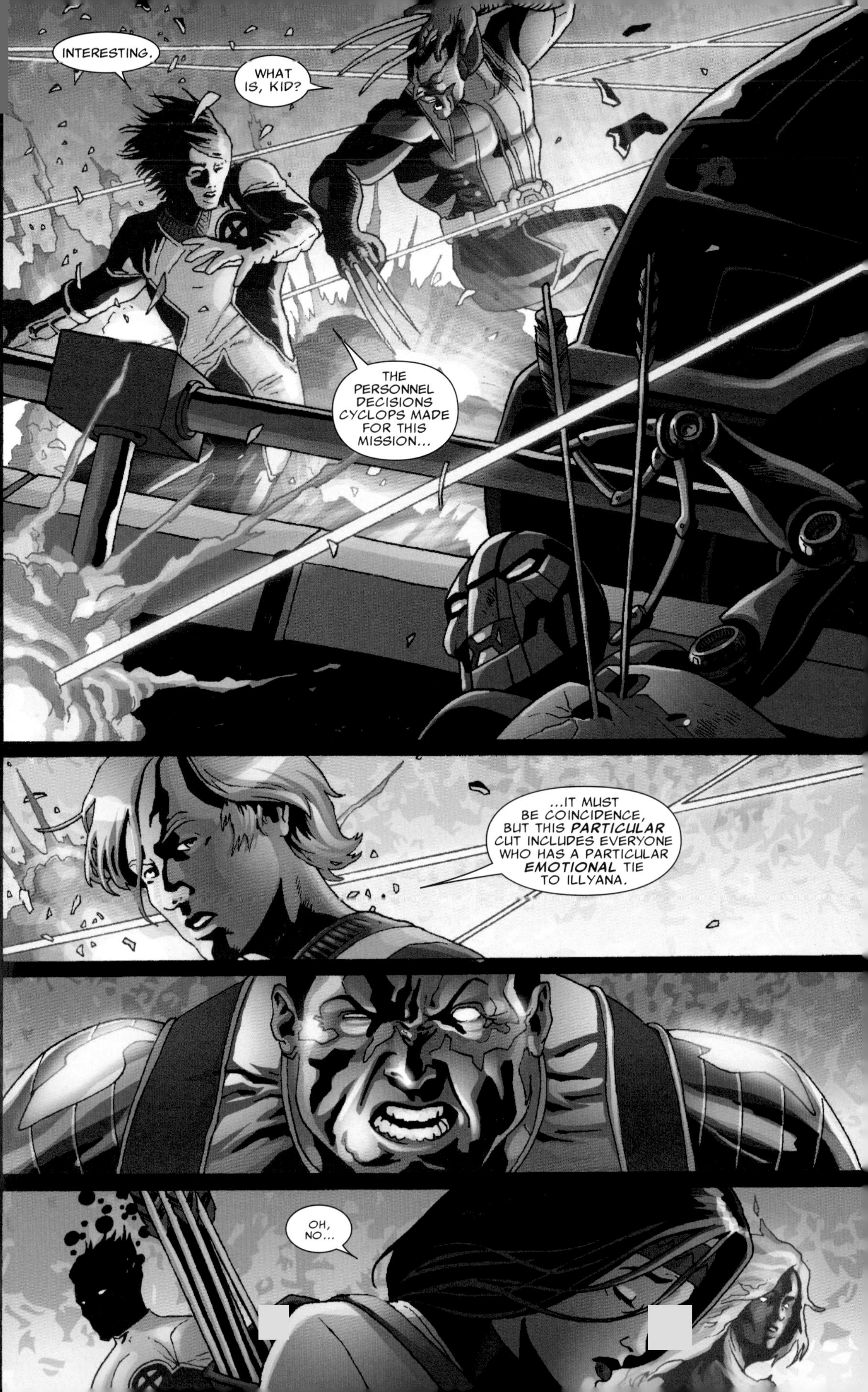
INTERESTING.
WHAT IS, KID?
THE PERSONNEL DECISIONS CYCLOPS MADE FOR THIS MISSION...
...IT MUST BE COINCIDENCE, BUT THIS PARTICULAR CUT INCLUDES EVERYONE WHO HAS A PARTICULAR EMOTIONAL TIE TO ILLYANA.
OH, NO...

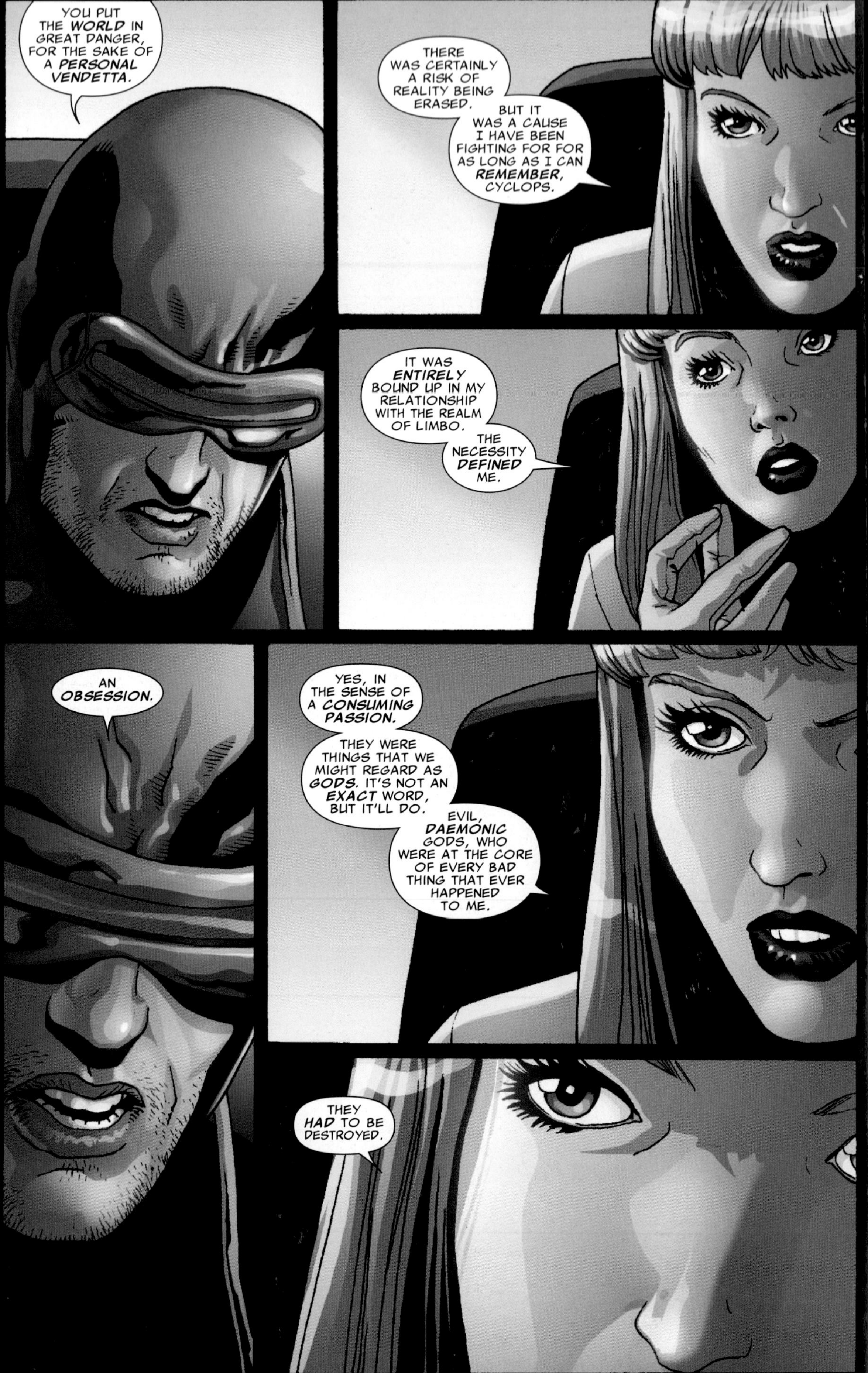

YOU PUT THE WORLD IN GREAT DANGER, FOR THE SAKE OF A PERSONAL VENDETTA.
THERE WAS CERTAINLY A RISK OF REALITY BEING ERASED.
BUT IT WAS A CAUSE I HAVE BEEN FIGHTING FOR FOR AS LONG AS I CAN REMEMBER, CYCLOPS.
IT WAS ENTIRELY BOUND UP IN MY RELATIONSHIP WITH THE REALM OF LIMBO.
THE NECESSITY DEFINED ME.
AN OBSESSION.
YES, IN THE SENSE OF A CONSUMING PASSION.
THEY WERE THINGS THAT WE MIGHT REGARD AS GODS. IT'S NOT AN EXACT WORD, BUT IT'LL DO.
EVIL, DAEMONIC GODS, WHO WERE AT THE CORE OF EVERY BAD THING THAT EVER HAPPENED TO ME.
THEY HAD TO BE DESTROYED.

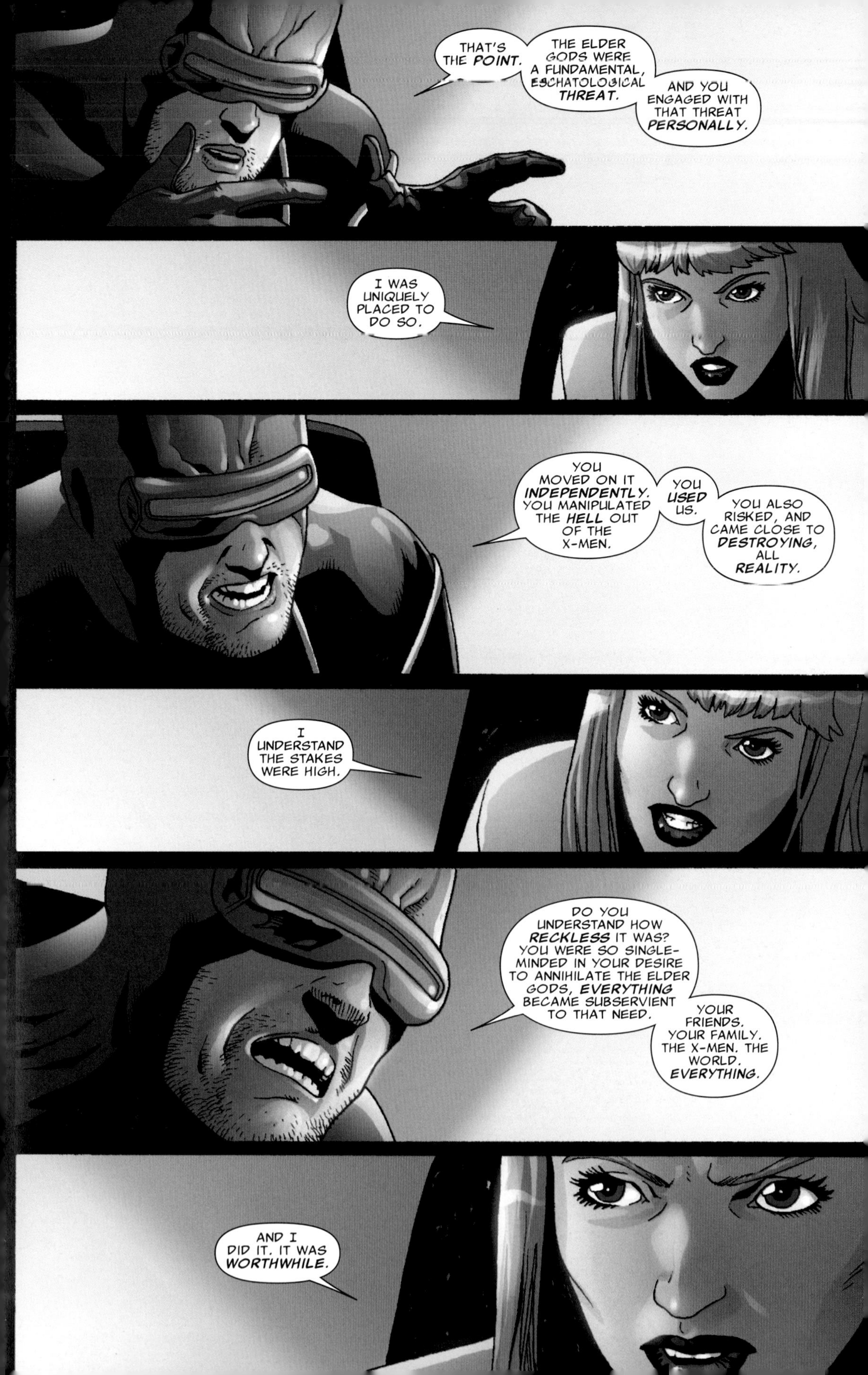
THAT'S THE POINT.
THE ELDER GODS WERE A FUNDAMENTAL, ESCHATOLOGICAL THREAT.
AND YOU ENGAGED WITH THAT THREAT PERSONALLY.
I WAS UNIQUELY PLACED TO DO SO.
YOU MOVED ON IT INDEPENDENTLY. YOU MANIPULATED THE HELL OUT OF THE X-MEN.
YOU USED US.
YOU ALSO RISKED, AND CAME CLOSE TO DESTROYING, ALL REALITY.
I UNDERSTAND THE STAKES WERE HIGH.
DO YOU UNDERSTAND HOW RECKLESS IT WAS? YOU WERE SO SINGLE-MINDED IN YOUR DESIRE TO ANNIHILATE THE ELDER GODS, EVERYTHING BECAME SUBSERVIENT TO THAT NEED.
YOUR FRIENDS. YOUR FAMILY. THE X-MEN. THE WORLD. EVERYTHING.
AND I DID IT. IT WAS WORTHWHILE.

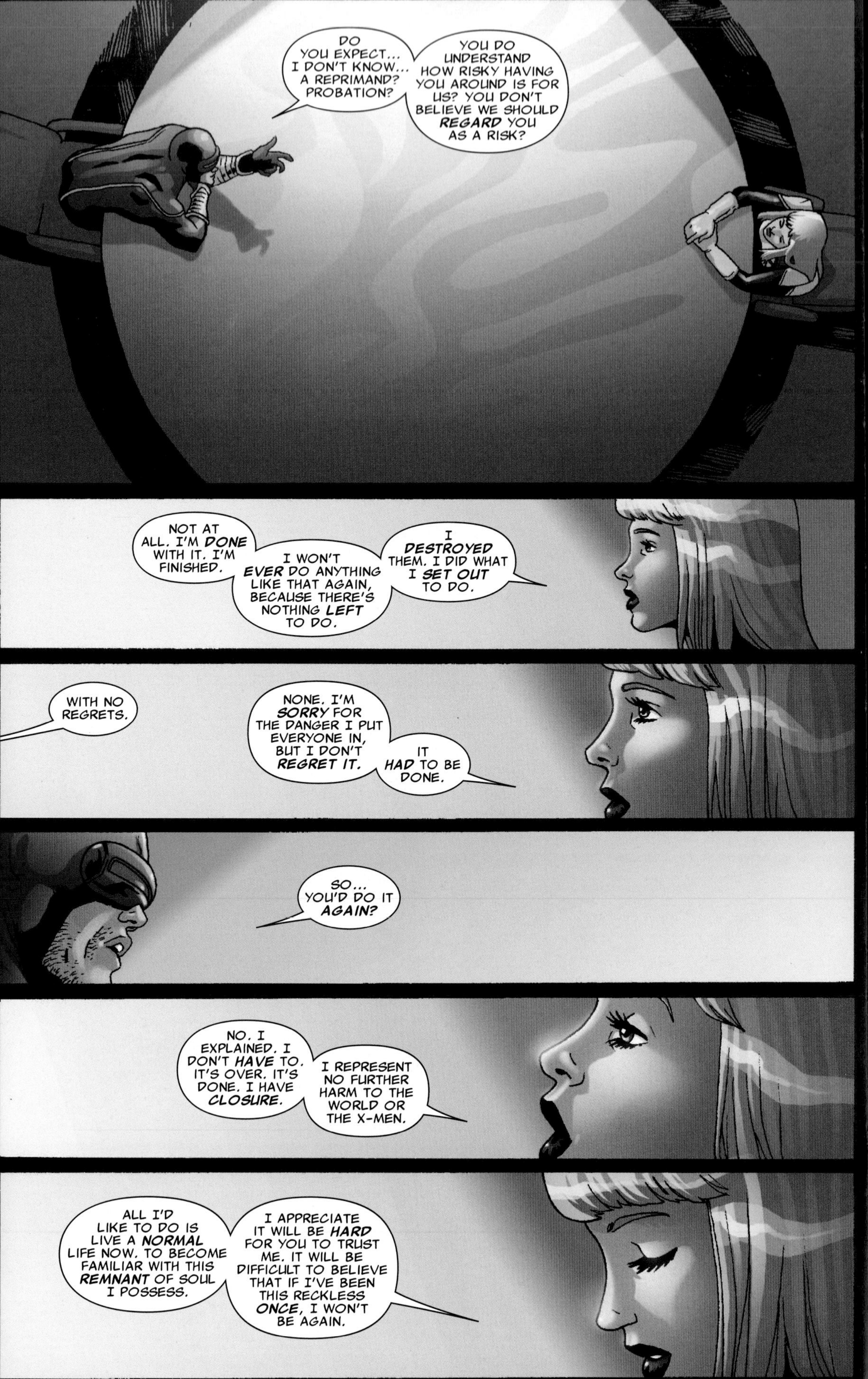
DO YOU EXPECT... I DON'T KNOW... A REPRIMAND? PROBATION?
YOU DO UNDERSTAND HOW RISKY HAVING YOU AROUND IS FOR US? YOU DON'T BELIEVE WE SHOULD REGARD YOU AS A RISK?
NOT AT ALL. I'M DONE WITH IT. I'M FINISHED.
I WON'T EVER DO ANYTHING LIKE THAT AGAIN, BECAUSE THERE'S NOTHING LEFT TO DO.
I DESTROYED THEM. I DID WHAT I SET OUT TO DO.
WITH NO REGRETS.
NONE. I'M SORRY FOR THE DANGER I PUT EVERYONE IN, BUT I DON'T REGRET IT.
IT HAD TO BE DONE.
SO... YOU'D DO IT AGAIN?
NO. I EXPLAINED. I DON'T HAVE TO. IT'S OVER. IT'S DONE. I HAVE CLOSURE.
I REPRESENT NO FURTHER HARM TO THE WORLD OR THE X-MEN.
ALL I'D LIKE TO DO IS LIVE A NORMAL LIFE NOW. TO BECOME FAMILIAR WITH THIS REMNANT OF SOUL I POSSESS.
I APPRECIATE IT WILL BE HARD FOR YOU TO TRUST ME. IT WILL BE DIFFICULT TO BELIEVE THAT IF I'VE BEEN THIS RECKLESS ONCE, I WON'T BE AGAIN.

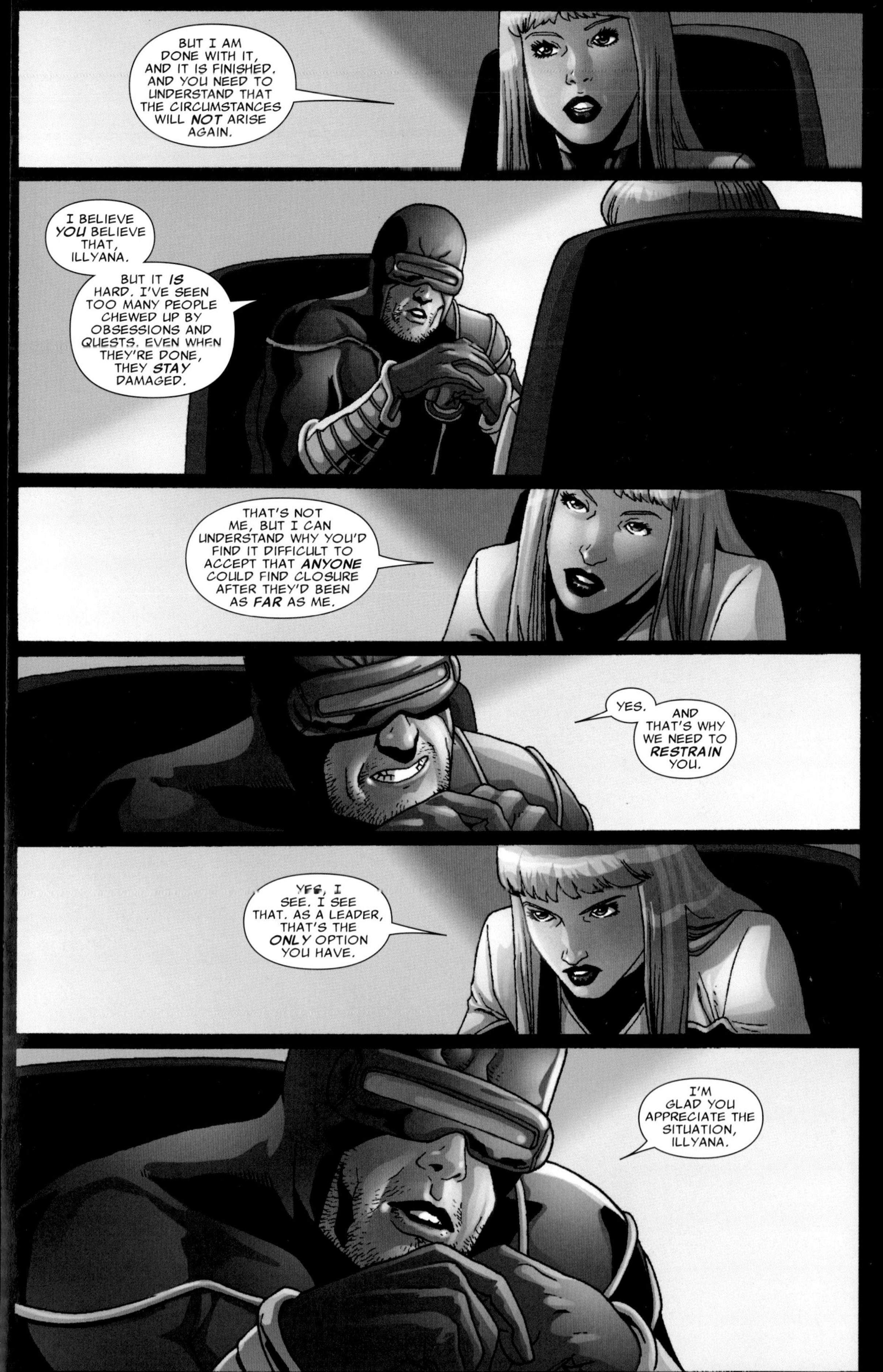

BUT I AM DONE WITH IT, AND IT IS FINISHED. AND YOU NEED TO UNDERSTAND THAT THE CIRCUMSTANCES WILL NOT ARISE AGAIN.
I BELIEVE YOU BELIEVE THAT, ILLYANA.
BUT IT IS HARD. I'VE SEEN TOO MANY PEOPLE CHEWED UP BY OBSESSIONS AND QUESTS. EVEN WHEN THEY'RE DONE, THEY STAY DAMAGED.
THAT'S NOT ME, BUT I CAN UNDERSTAND WHY YOU'D FIND IT DIFFICULT TO ACCEPT THAT ANYONE COULD FIND CLOSURE AFTER THEY'D BEEN AS FAR AS ME.
YES.
AND THAT'S WHY WE NEED TO RESTRAIN YOU.
YES, I SEE. I SEE THAT. AS A LEADER, THAT'S THE ONLY OPTION YOU HAVE.
I'M GLAD YOU APPRECIATE THE SITUATION, ILLYANA.

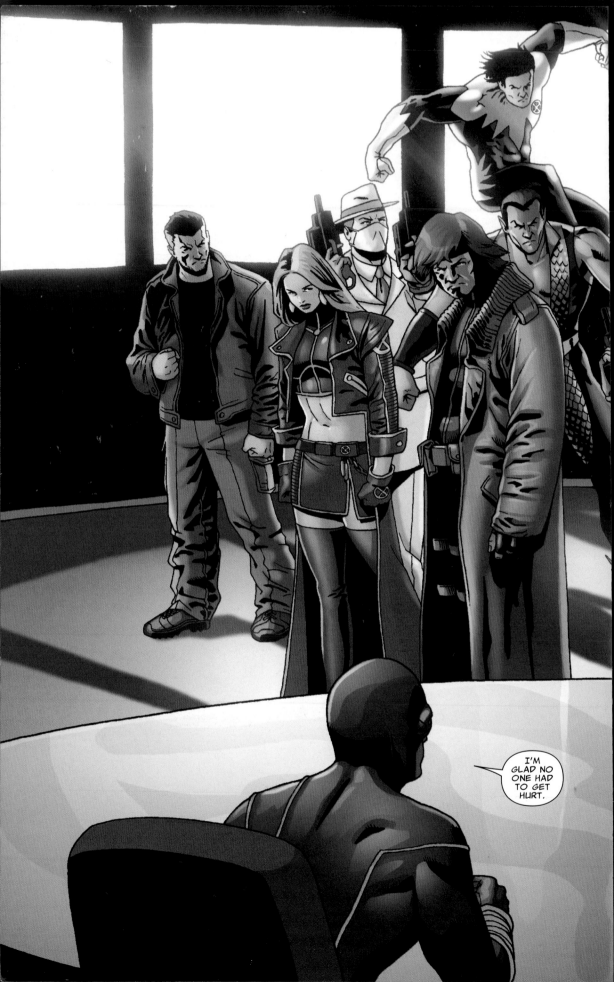

I'M GLAD NO ONE HAD TO GET HURT.

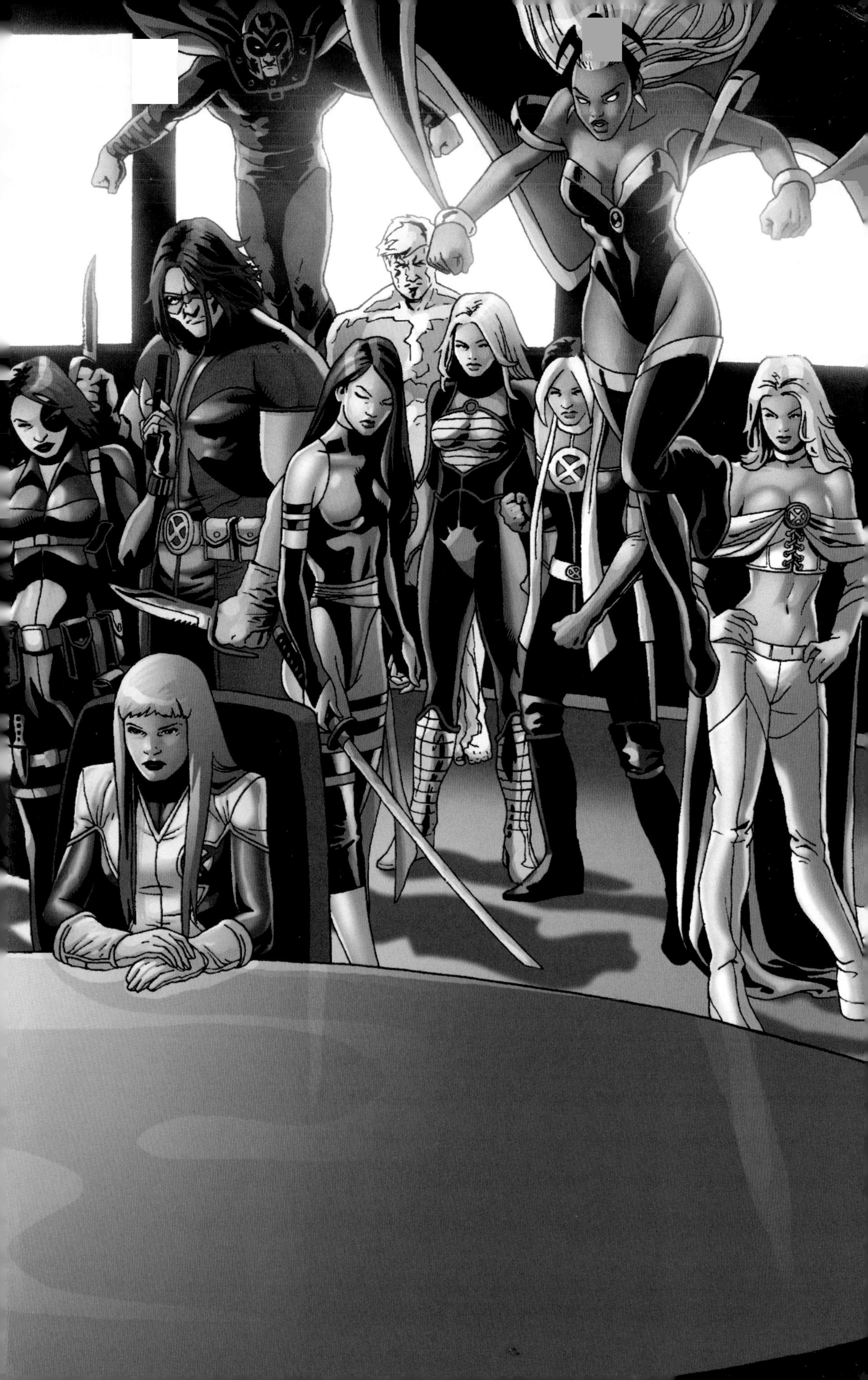

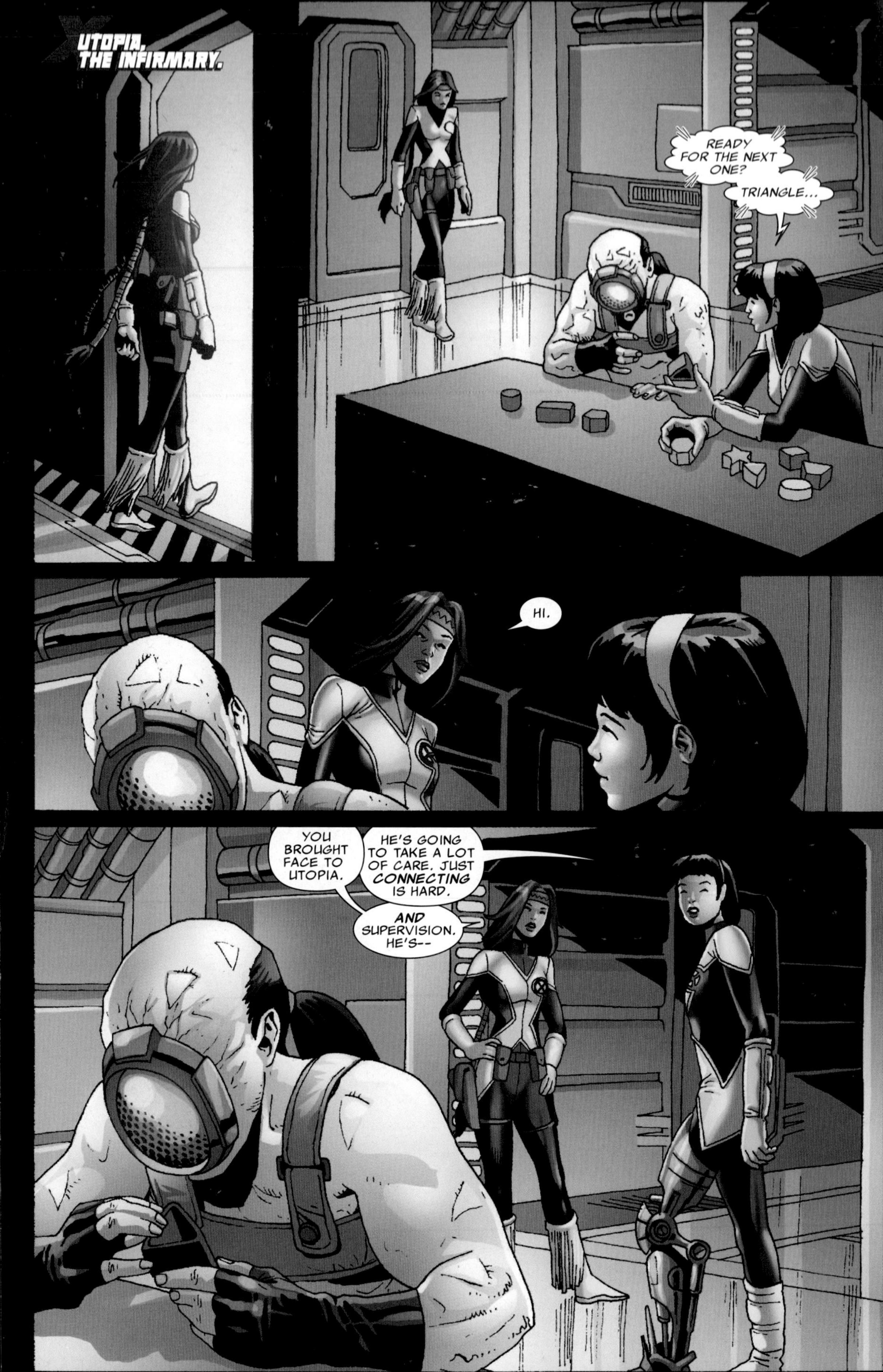
UTOPIA, THE INFIRMARY.
READY FOR THE NEXT ONE?
TRIANGLE...
HI.
YOU BROUGHT FACE TO UTOPIA.
HE'S GOING TO TAKE A LOT OF CARE. JUST CONNECTING IS HARD.
AND SUPERVISION. HE'S--

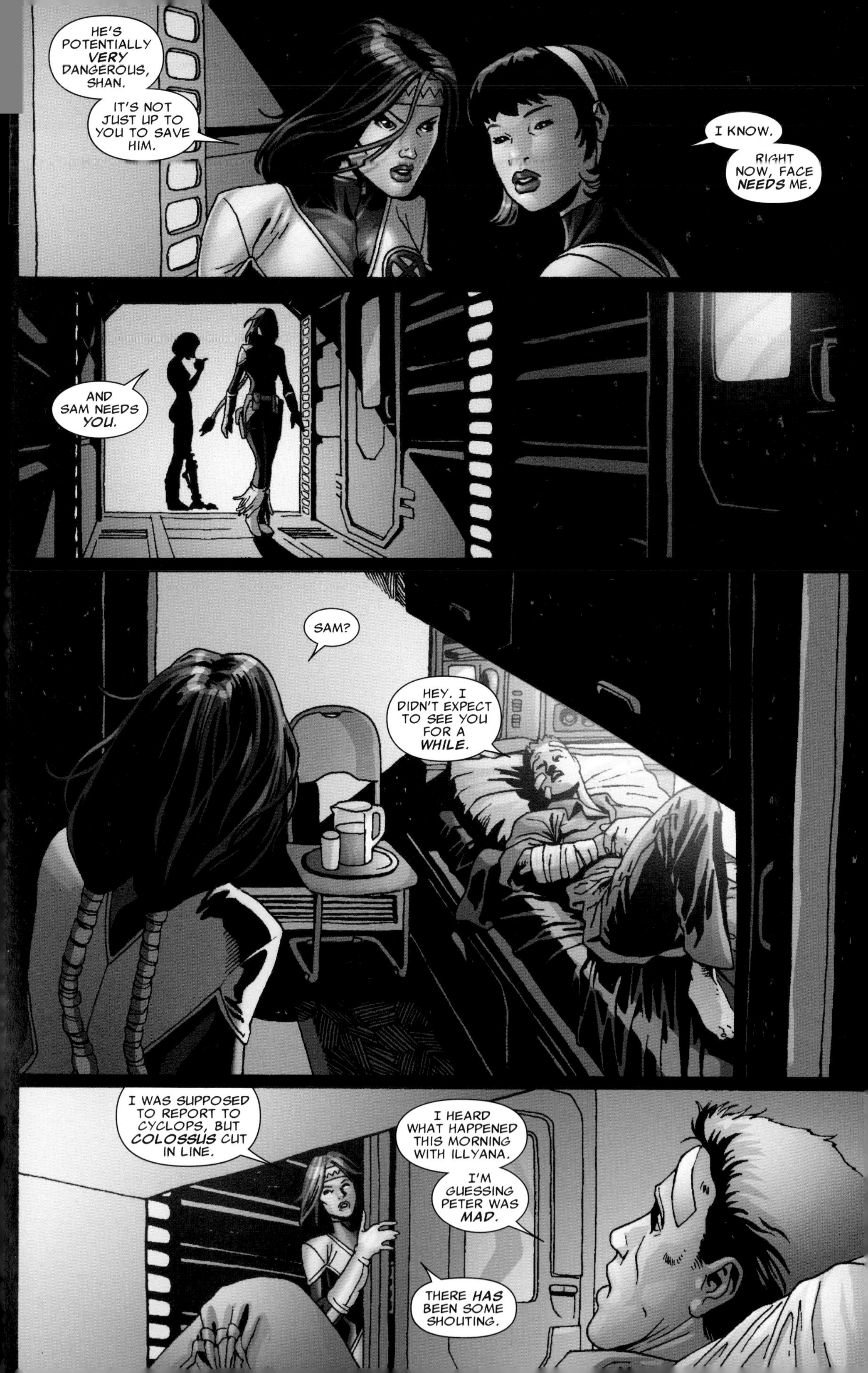

HE'S POTENTIALLY VERY DANGEROUS, SHAN.
IT'S NOT JUST UP TO YOU TO SAVE HIM.
I KNOW.
RIGHT NOW, FACE NEEDS ME.
AND SAM NEEDS YOU.
SAM?
HEY. I DIDN'T EXPECT TO SEE YOU FOR A WHILE.
I WAS SUPPOSED TO REPORT TO CYCLOPS, BUT COLOSSUS CUT IN LINE.
I HEARD WHAT HAPPENED THIS MORNING WITH ILLYANA.
I'M GUESSING PETER WAS MAD.
THERE HAS BEEN SOME SHOUTING.

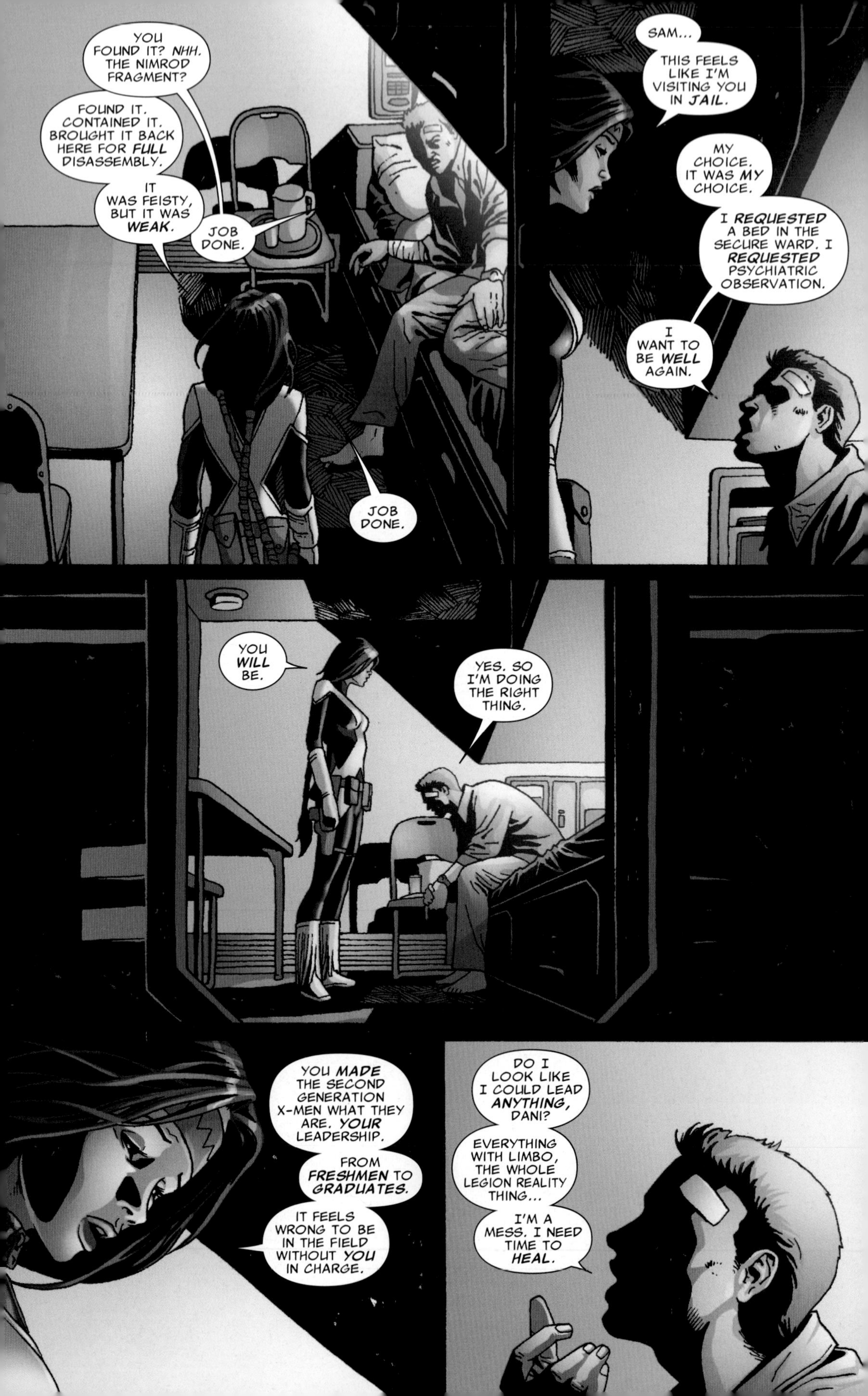
YOU FOUND IT? NHH. THE NIMROD FRAGMENT?
FOUND IT. CONTAINED IT. BROUGHT IT BACK HERE FOR FULL DISASSEMBLY.
IT WAS FEISTY, BUT IT WAS WEAK.
JOB DONE.
JOB DONE.
SAM...
THIS FEELS LIKE I'M VISITING YOU IN JAIL.
MY CHOICE. IT WAS MY CHOICE.
I REQUESTED A BED IN THE SECURE WARD. I REQUESTED PSYCHIATRIC OBSERVATION.
I WANT TO BE WELL AGAIN.
YOU WILL BE.
YES. SO I'M DOING THE RIGHT THING.
YOU MADE THE SECOND GENERATION X-MEN WHAT THEY ARE. YOUR LEADERSHIP.
FROM FRESHMEN TO GRADUATES.
IT FEELS WRONG TO BE IN THE FIELD WITHOUT YOU IN CHARGE.
DO I LOOK LIKE I COULD LEAD ANYTHING, DANI?
EVERYTHING WITH LIMBO, THE WHOLE LEGION REALITY THING...
I'M A MESS. I NEED TIME TO HEAL.

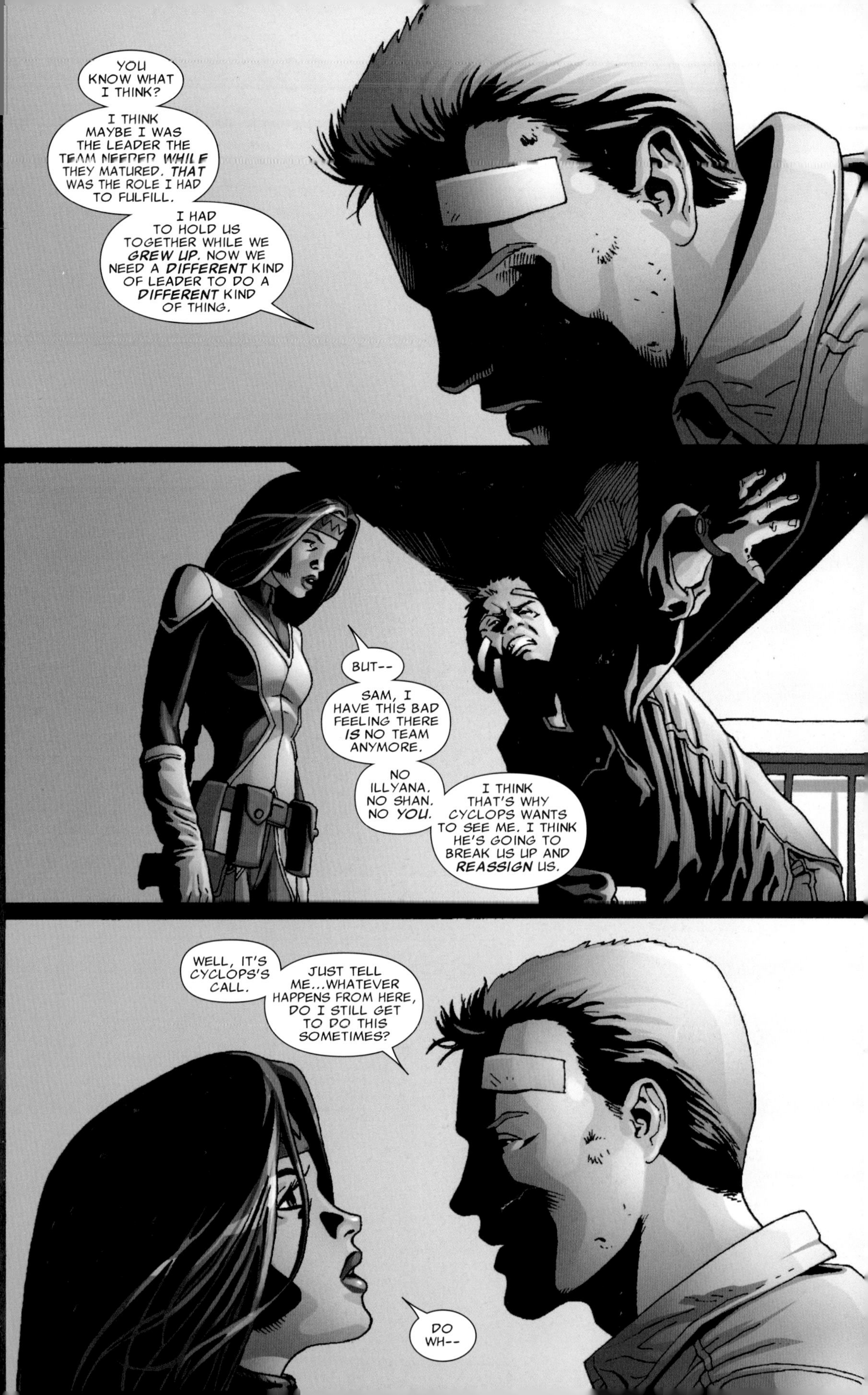
YOU KNOW WHAT I THINK?
I THINK MAYBE I WAS THE LEADER THE TEAM NEEDED WHILE THEY MATURED. THAT WAS THE ROLE I HAD TO FULFILL.
I HAD TO HOLD US TOGETHER WHILE WE GREW UP. NOW WE NEED A DIFFERENT KIND OF LEADER TO DO A DIFFERENT KIND OF THING.
BUT--
SAM, I HAVE THIS BAD FEELING THERE IS NO TEAM ANYMORE.
NO ILLYANA. NO SHAN. NO YOU.
I THINK THAT'S WHY CYCLOPS WANTS TO SEE ME. I THINK HE'S GOING TO BREAK US UP AND REASSIGN US.
WELL, IT'S CYCLOPS'S CALL.
JUST TELL ME...WHATEVER HAPPENS FROM HERE, DO I STILL GET TO DO THIS SOMETIMES?
DO WH--

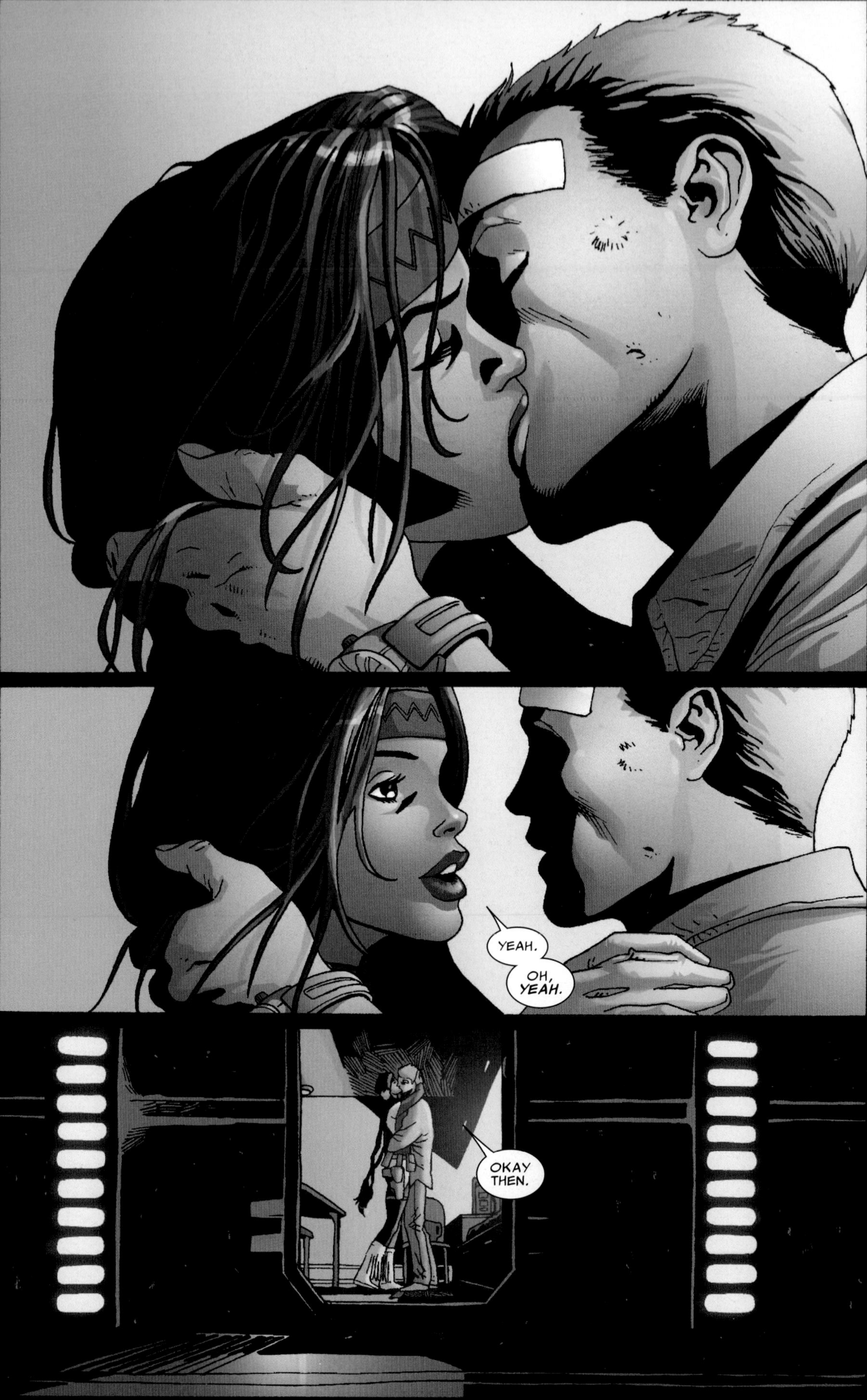
YEAH.
OH, YEAH.
OKAY THEN.

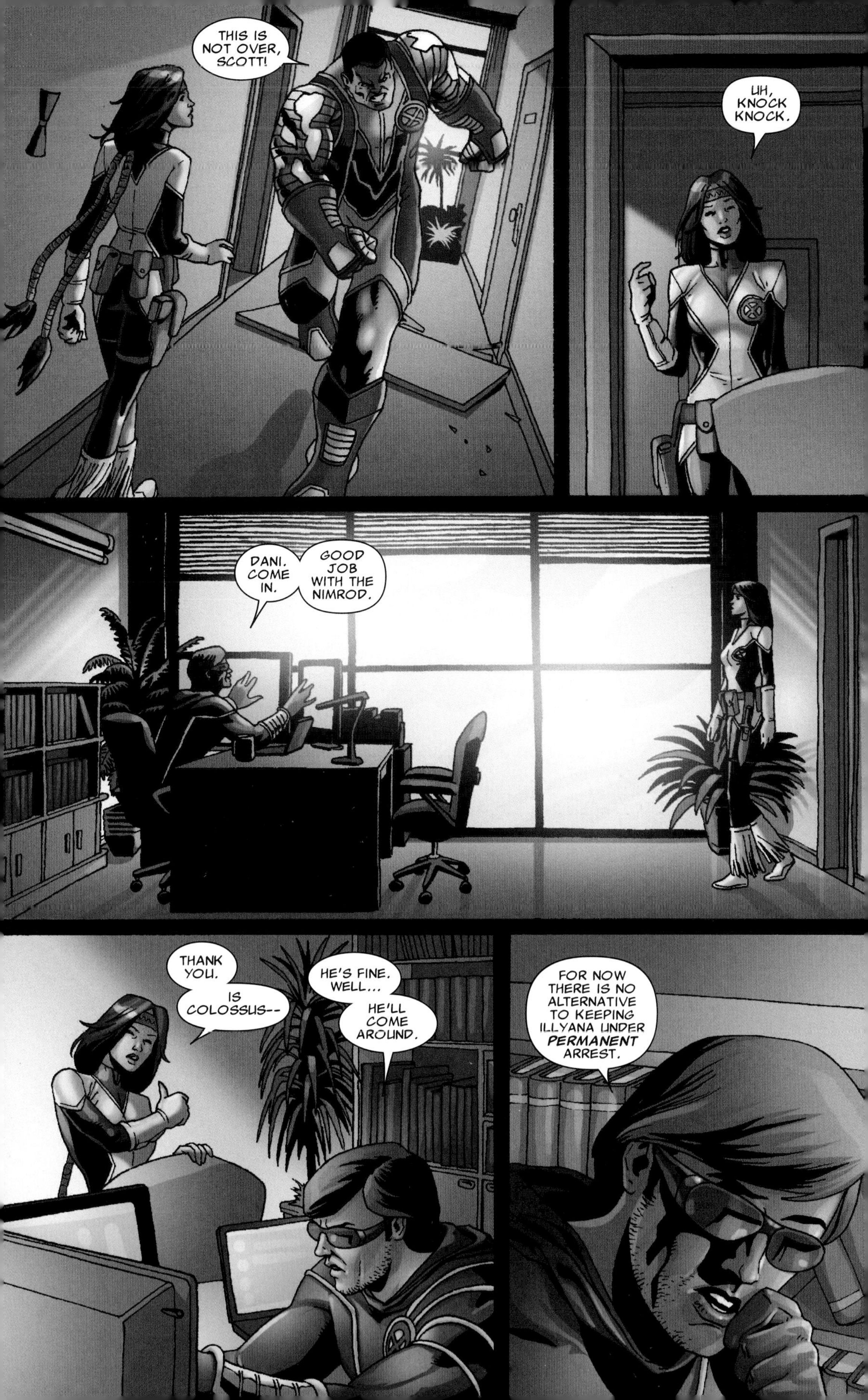
THIS IS NOT OVER, SCOTT!
UH, KNOCK KNOCK.
DANI. COME IN.
GOOD JOB WITH THE NIMROD.
THANK YOU.
IS COLOSSUS--
HE'S FINE. WELL...
HE'LL COME AROUND.
FOR NOW THERE IS NO ALTERNATIVE TO KEEPING ILLYANA UNDER *PERMANENT* ARREST.

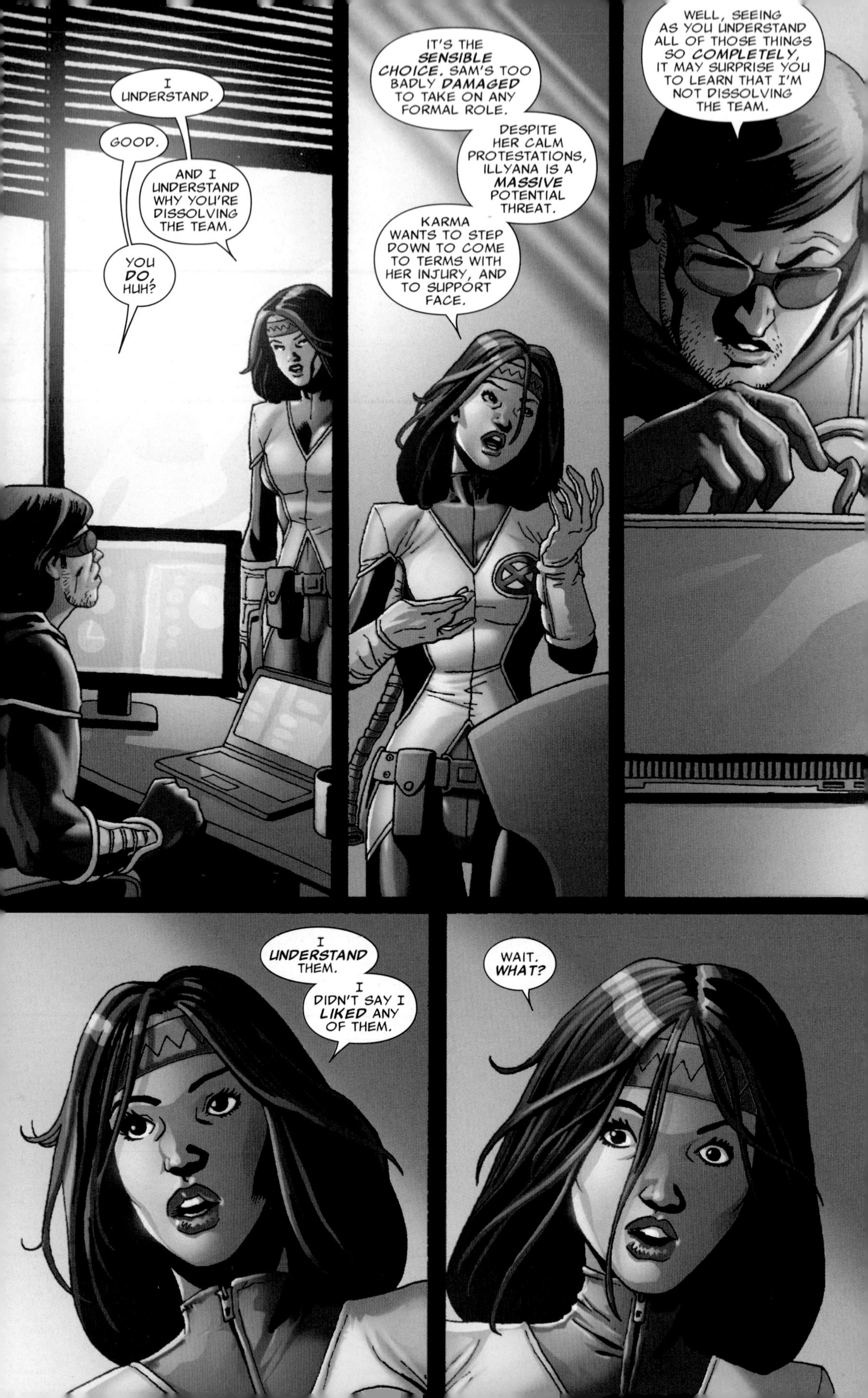
I UNDERSTAND.
GOOD.
AND I UNDERSTAND WHY YOU'RE DISSOLVING THE TEAM.
YOU DO, HUH?
IT'S THE SENSIBLE CHOICE. SAM'S TOO BADLY DAMAGED TO TAKE ON ANY FORMAL ROLE.
DESPITE HER CALM PROTESTATIONS, ILLYANA IS A MASSIVE POTENTIAL THREAT.
KARMA WANTS TO STEP DOWN TO COME TO TERMS WITH HER INJURY, AND TO SUPPORT FACE.
WELL, SEEING AS YOU UNDERSTAND ALL OF THOSE THINGS SO COMPLETELY, IT MAY SURPRISE YOU TO LEARN THAT I'M NOT DISSOLVING THE TEAM.
I UNDERSTAND THEM.
I DIDN'T SAY I LIKED ANY OF THEM.
WAIT. WHAT?

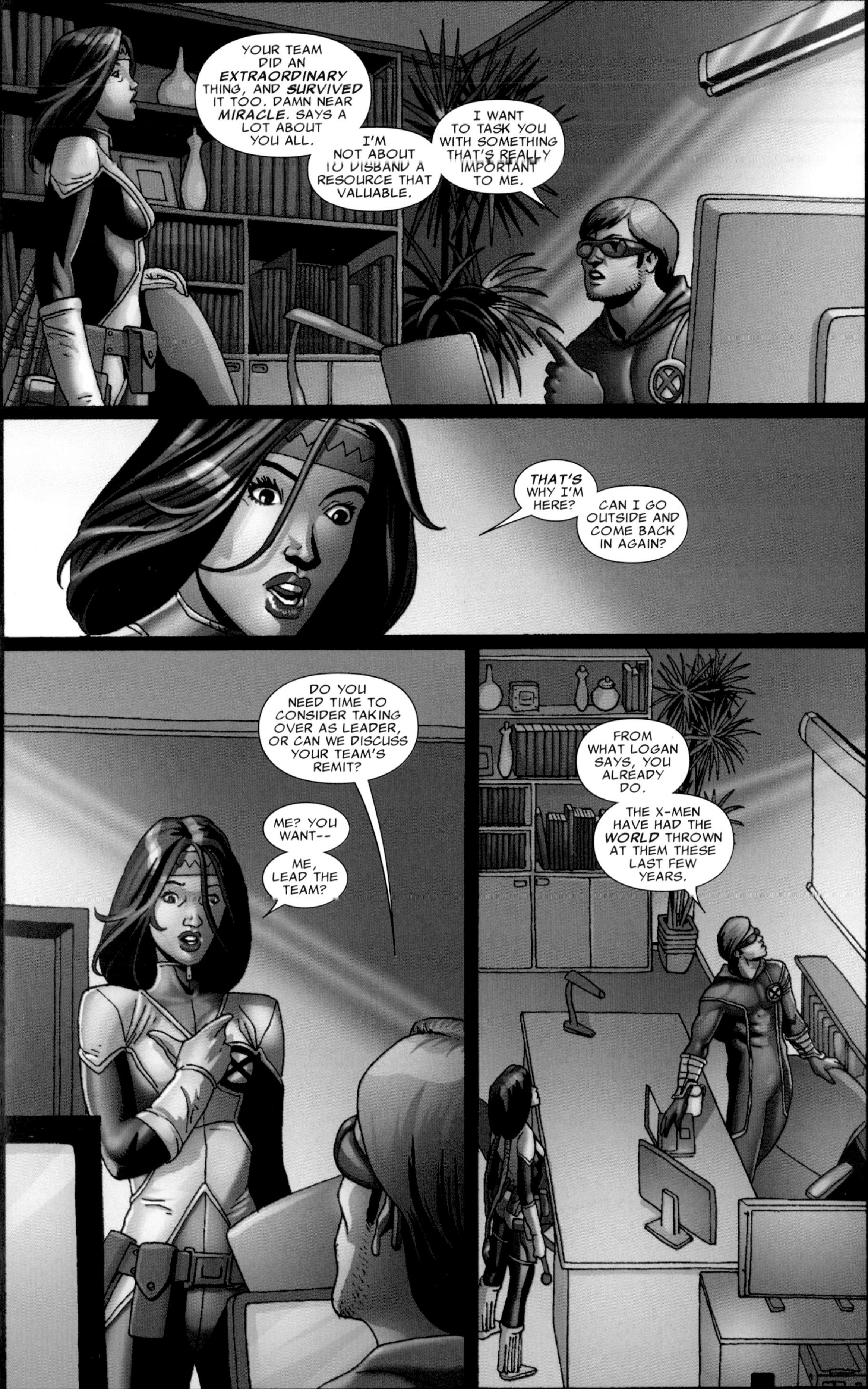

YOUR TEAM DID AN EXTRAORDINARY THING, AND SURVIVED IT TOO. DAMN NEAR MIRACLE. SAYS A LOT ABOUT YOU ALL.
I'M NOT ABOUT TO DISBAND A RESOURCE THAT VALUABLE.
I WANT TO TASK YOU WITH SOMETHING THAT'S REALLY IMPORTANT TO ME.
THAT'S WHY I'M HERE?
CAN I GO OUTSIDE AND COME BACK IN AGAIN?
DO YOU NEED TIME TO CONSIDER TAKING OVER AS LEADER, OR CAN WE DISCUSS YOUR TEAM'S REMIT?
ME? YOU WANT--
ME, LEAD THE TEAM?
FROM WHAT LOGAN SAYS, YOU ALREADY DO.
THE X-MEN HAVE HAD THE WORLD THROWN AT THEM THESE LAST FEW YEARS.

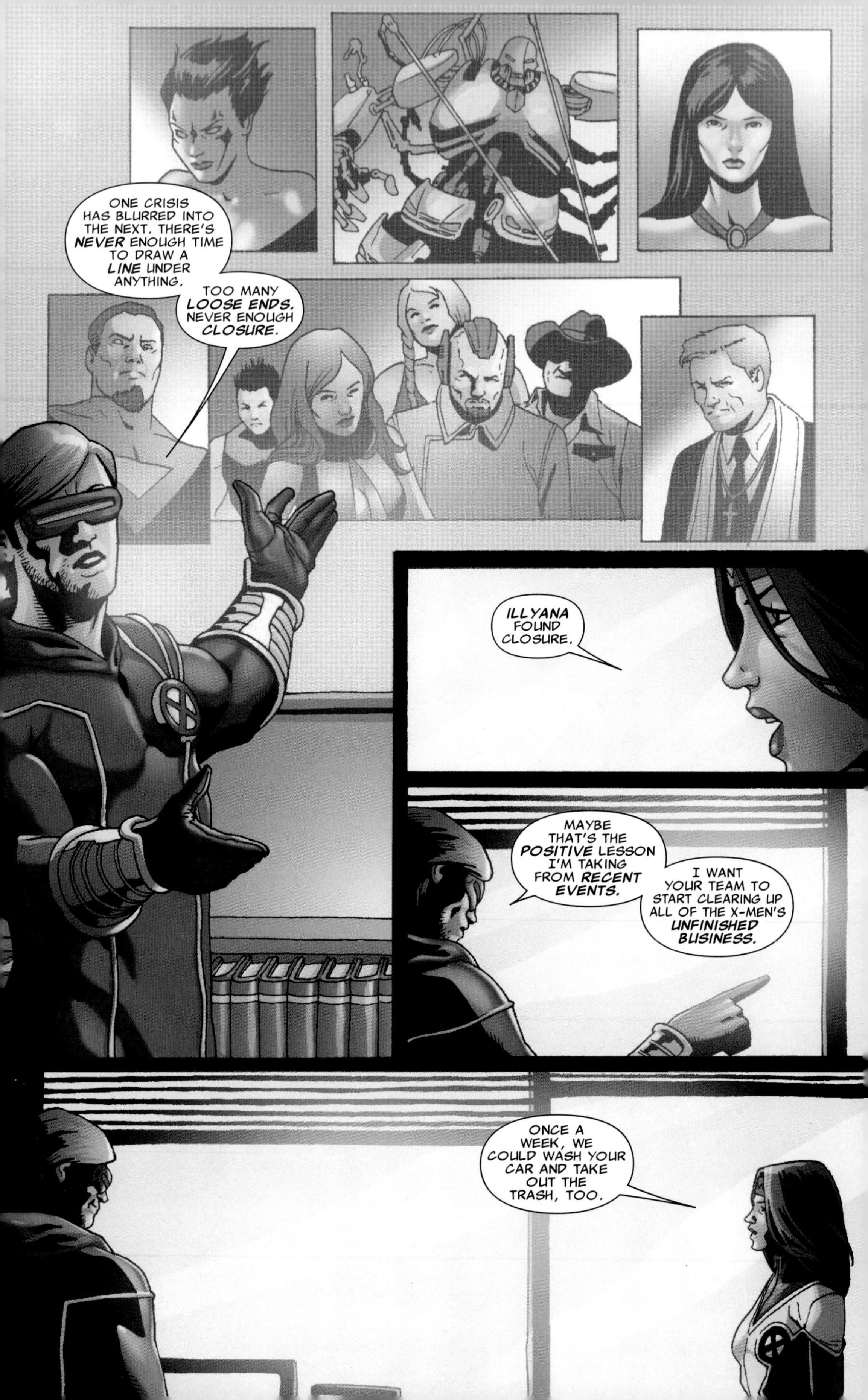
ONE CRISIS HAS BLURRED INTO THE NEXT. THERE'S NEVER ENOUGH TIME TO DRAW A LINE UNDER ANYTHING.
TOO MANY LOOSE ENDS. NEVER ENOUGH CLOSURE.
ILLYANA FOUND CLOSURE.
MAYBE THAT'S THE POSITIVE LESSON I'M TAKING FROM RECENT EVENTS.
I WANT YOUR TEAM TO START CLEARING UP ALL OF THE X-MEN'S UNFINISHED BUSINESS.
ONCE A WEEK, WE COULD WASH YOUR CAR AND TAKE OUT THE TRASH, TOO.

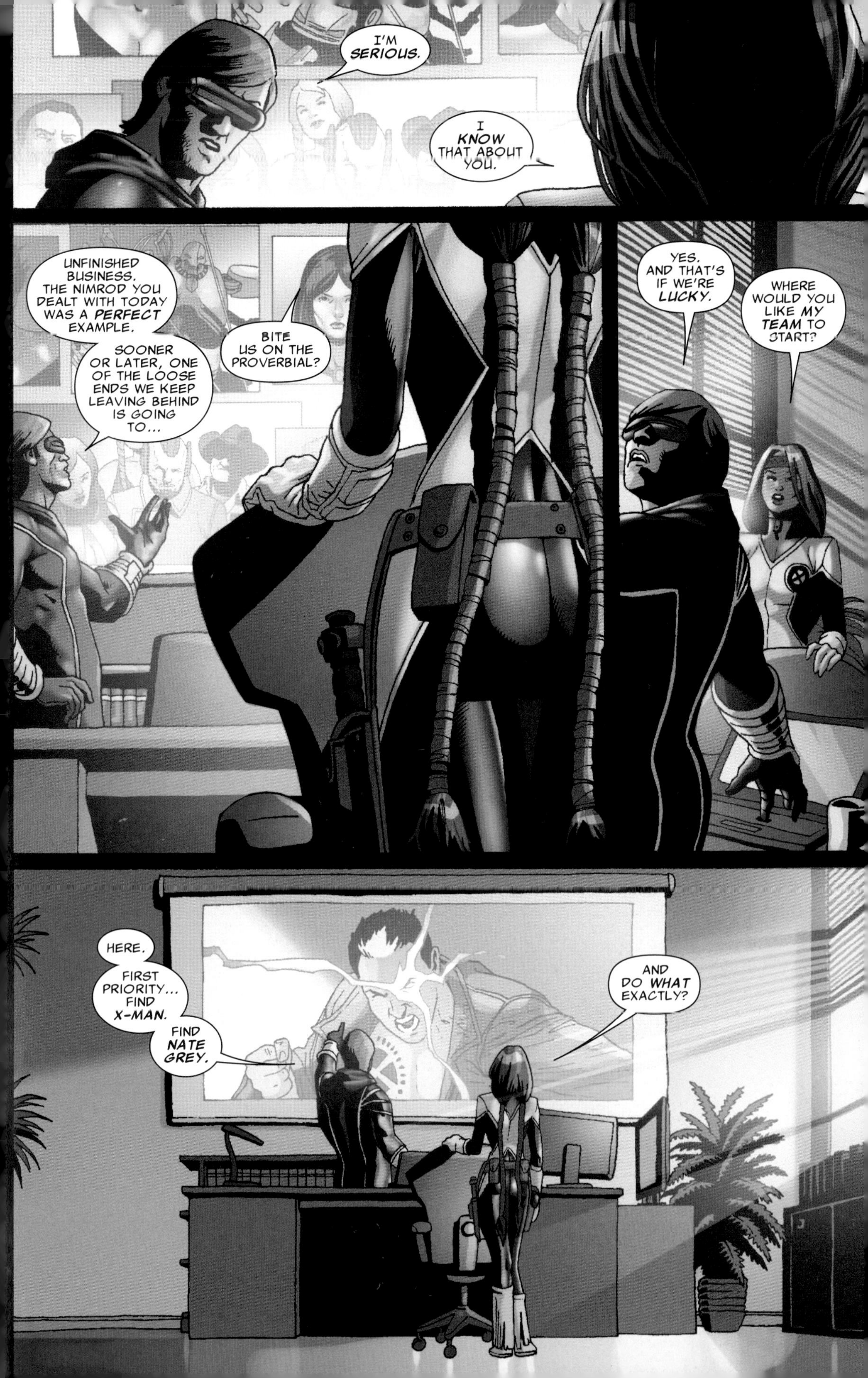
I'M SERIOUS.
I KNOW THAT ABOUT YOU.
UNFINISHED BUSINESS. THE NIMROD YOU DEALT WITH TODAY WAS A PERFECT EXAMPLE.
SOONER OR LATER, ONE OF THE LOOSE ENDS WE KEEP LEAVING BEHIND IS GOING TO...
BITE US ON THE PROVERBIAL?
YES. AND THAT'S IF WE'RE LUCKY.
WHERE WOULD YOU LIKE MY TEAM TO START?
HERE.
FIRST PRIORITY... FIND X-MAN.
FIND NATE GREY.
AND DO WHAT EXACTLY?

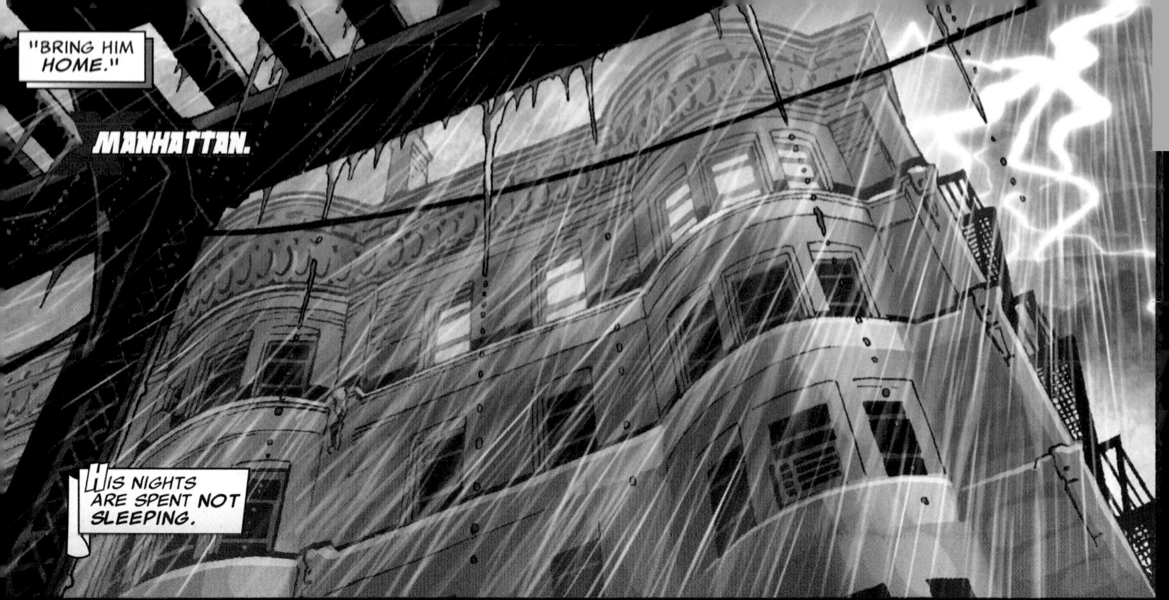
"BRING HIM HOME."
MANHATTAN.
HIS NIGHTS ARE SPENT NOT SLEEPING.

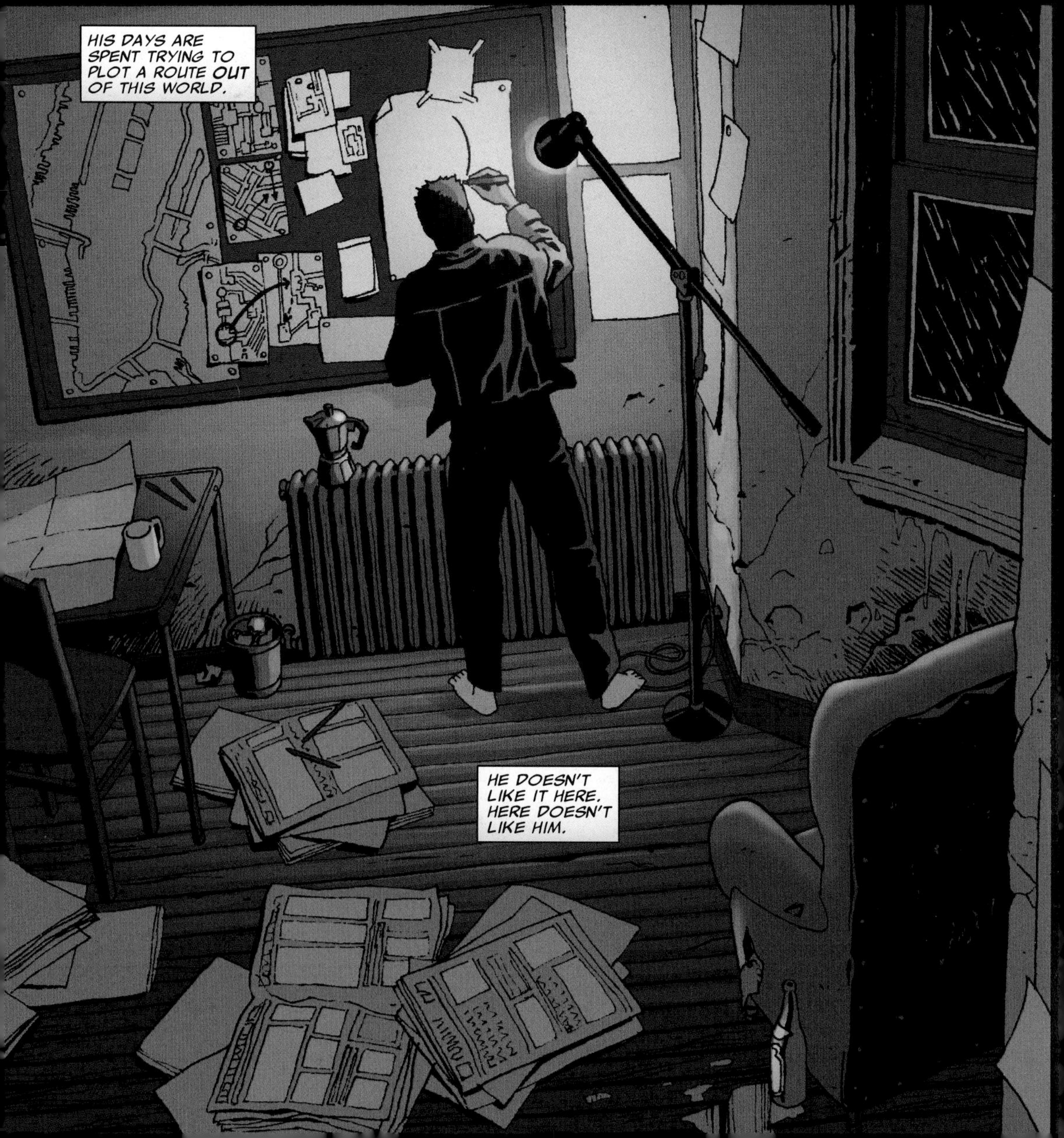
HIS DAYS ARE SPENT TRYING TO PLOT A ROUTE OUT OF THIS WORLD.
HE DOESN'T LIKE IT HERE. HERE DOESN'T LIKE HIM.

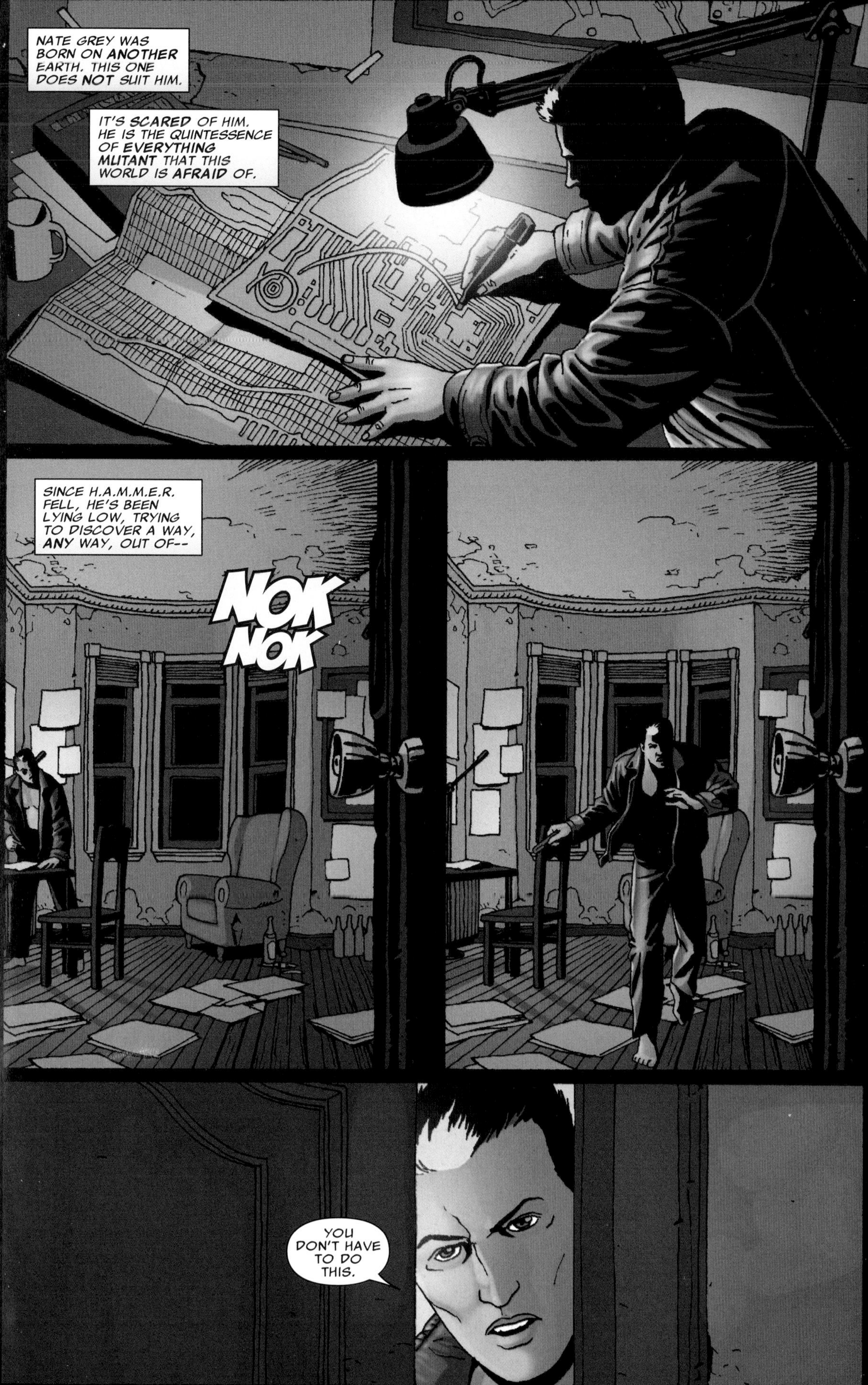
NATE GREY WAS BORN ON ANOTHER EARTH. THIS ONE DOES NOT SUIT HIM.
IT'S SCARED OF HIM. HE IS THE QUINTESSENCE OF EVERYTHING MUTANT THAT THIS WORLD IS AFRAID OF.
SINCE H.A.M.M.E.R. FELL, HE'S BEEN LYING LOW, TRYING TO DISCOVER A WAY, ANY WAY, OUT OF--
NOK NOK
YOU DON'T HAVE TO DO THIS.

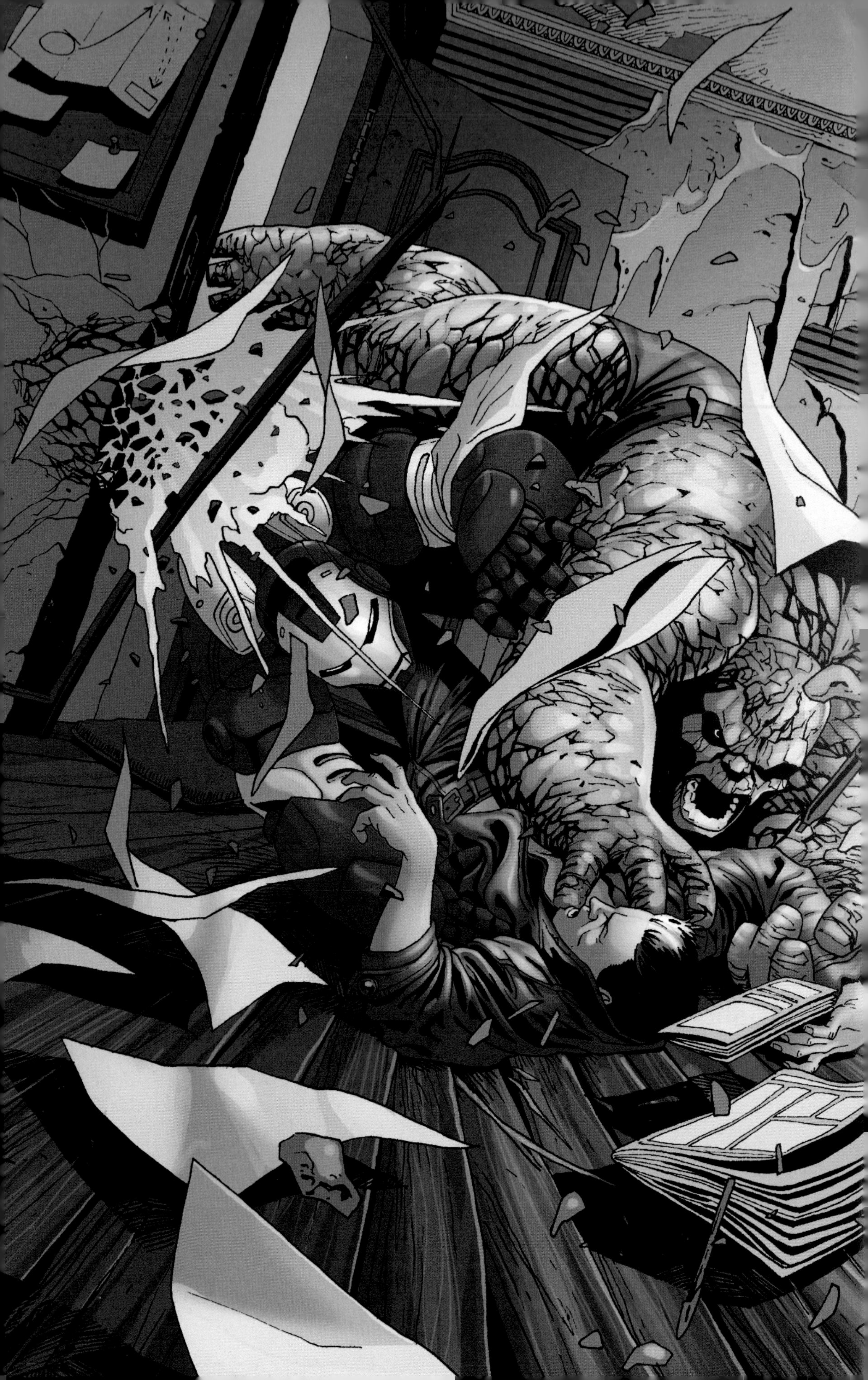

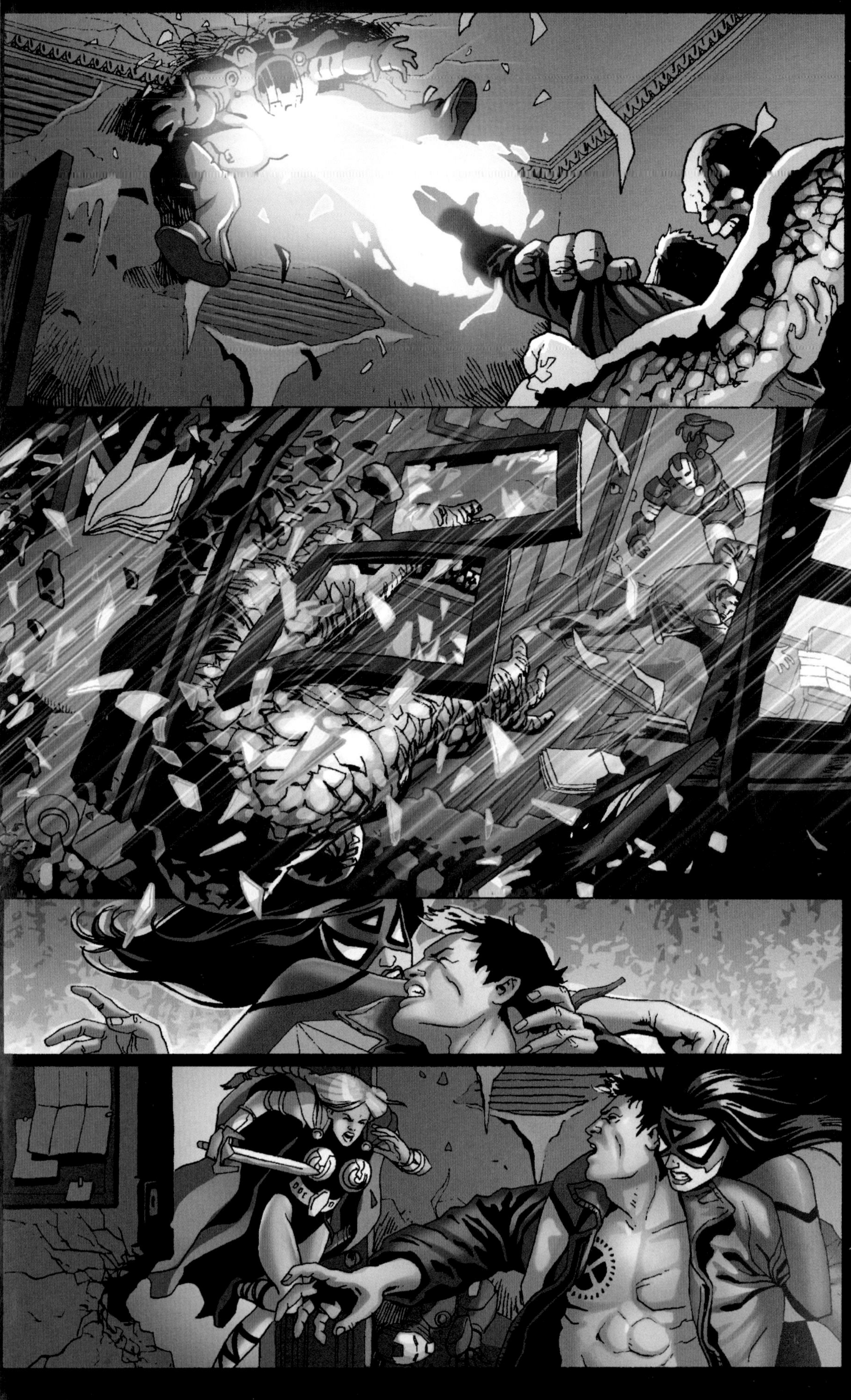

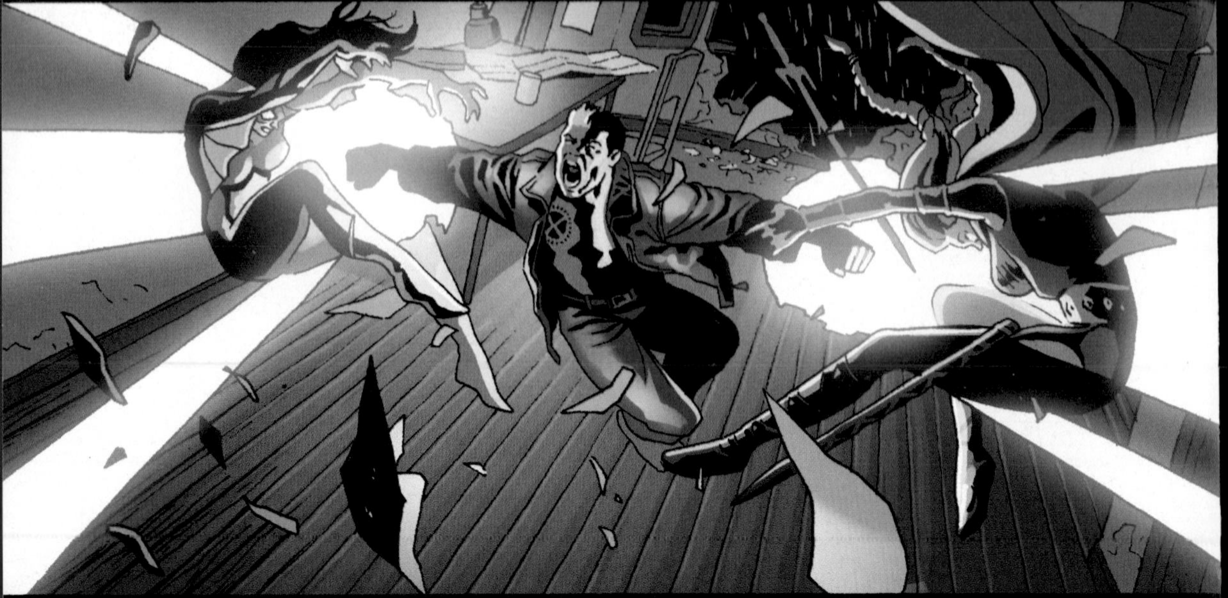

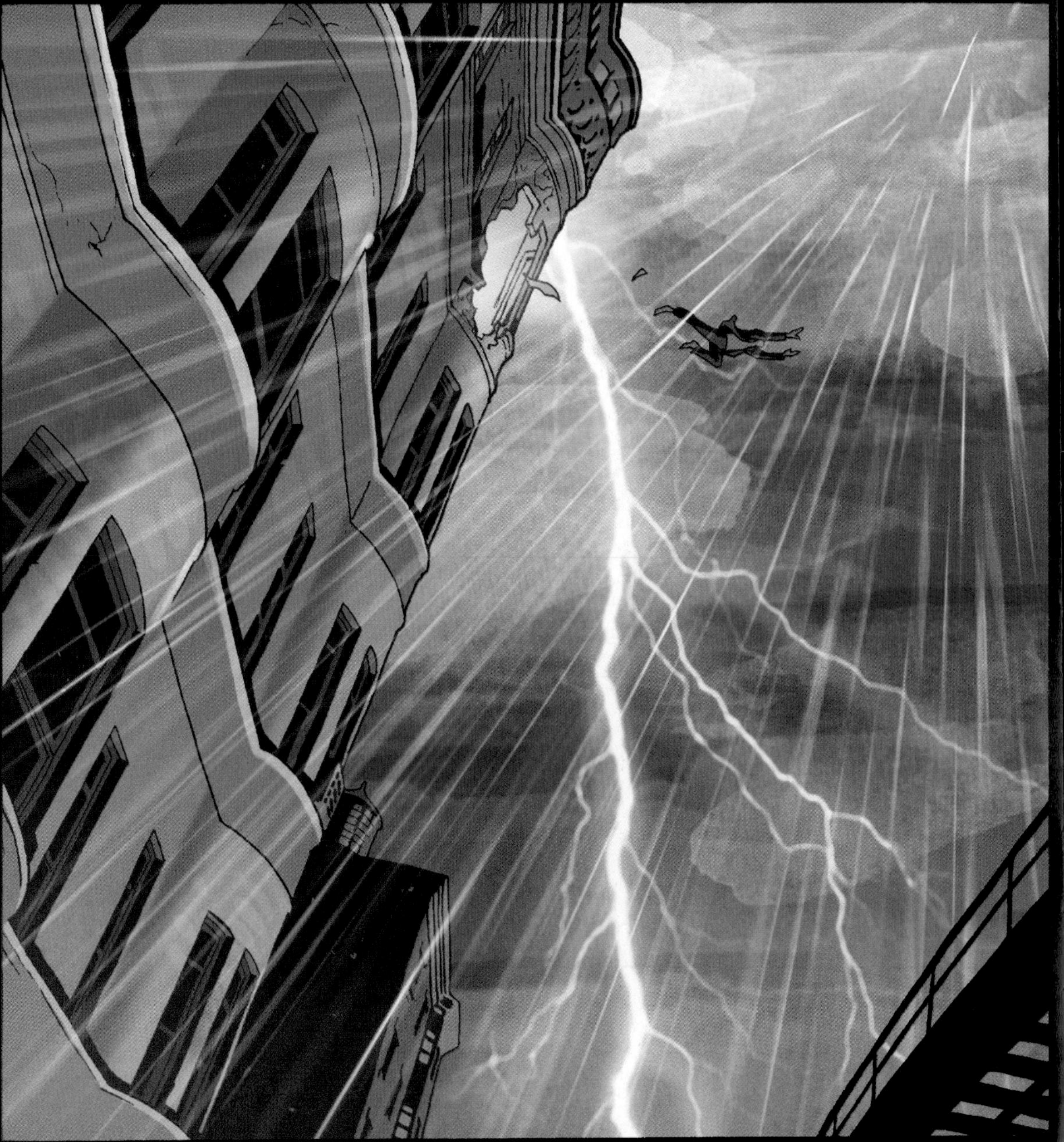

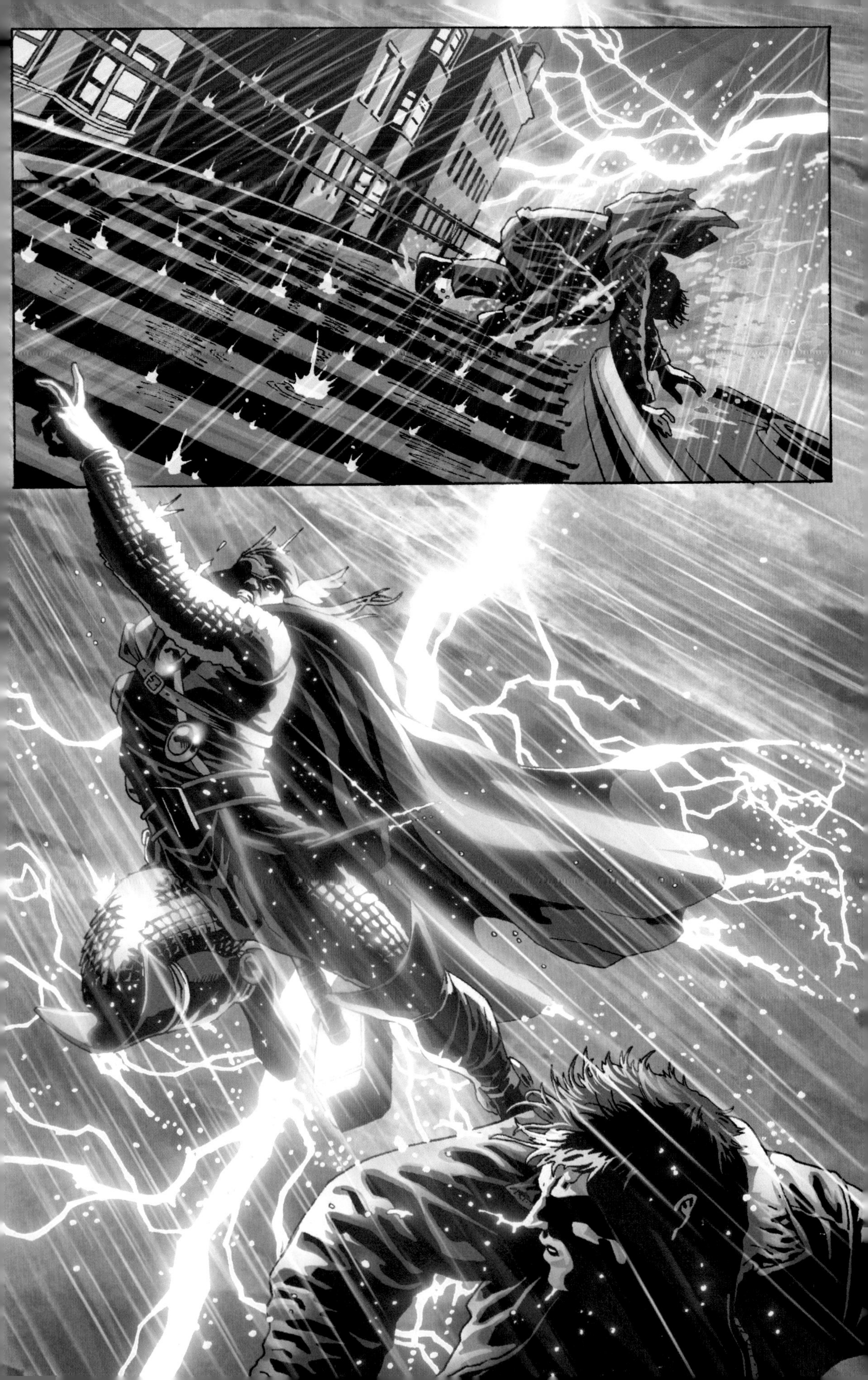

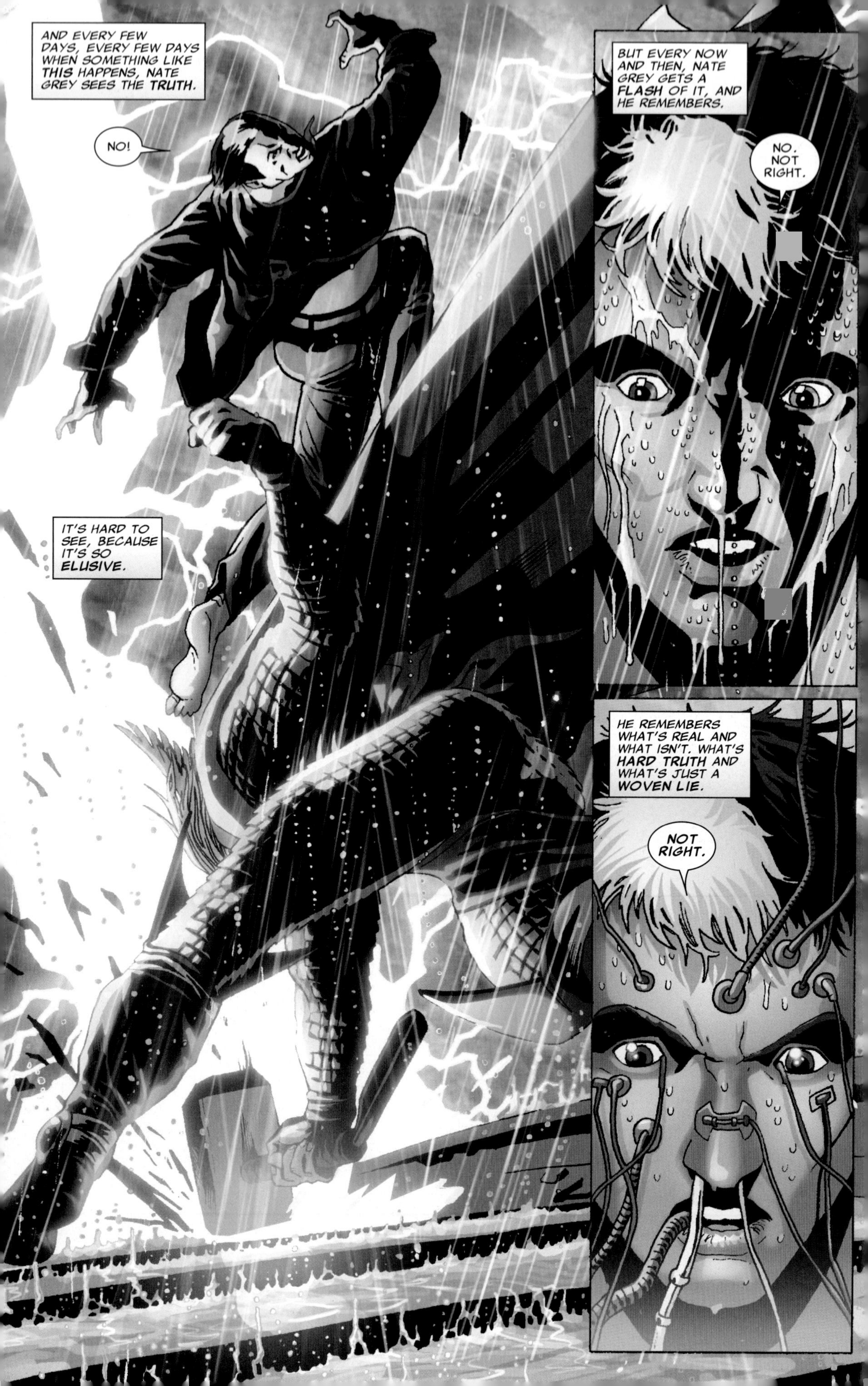
AND EVERY FEW DAYS, EVERY FEW DAYS WHEN SOMETHING LIKE THIS HAPPENS, NATE GREY SEES THE TRUTH.
NO!
IT'S HARD TO SEE, BECAUSE IT'S SO ELUSIVE.
BUT EVERY NOW AND THEN, NATE GREY GETS A FLASH OF IT, AND HE REMEMBERS.
NO. NOT RIGHT.
HE REMEMBERS WHAT'S REAL AND WHAT ISN'T. WHAT'S HARD TRUTH AND WHAT'S JUST A WOVEN LIE.
NOT RIGHT.

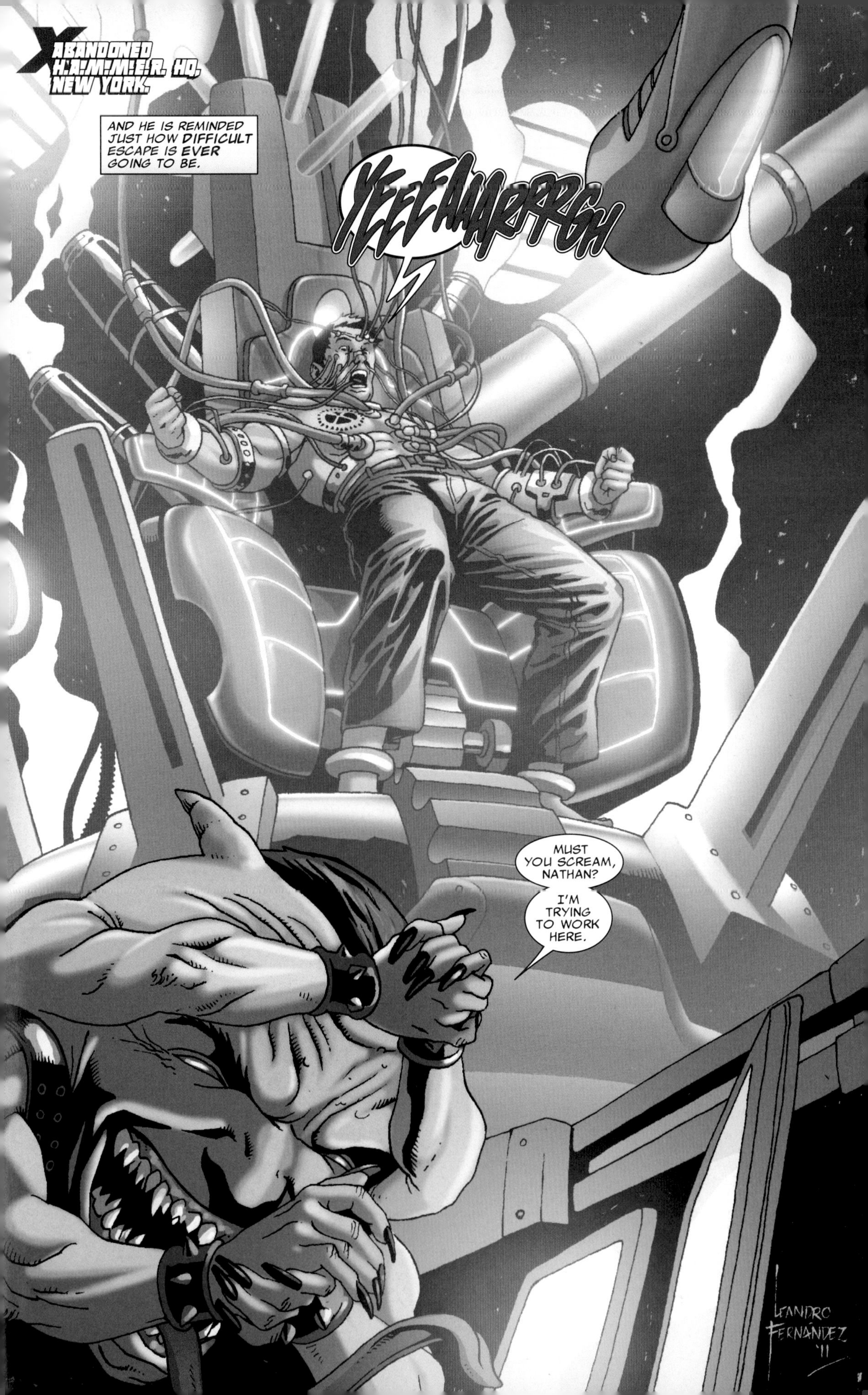
ABANDONED H.A.M.M.E.R. HQ, NEW YORK.
AND HE IS REMINDED JUST HOW DIFFICULT ESCAPE IS EVER GOING TO BE.
YEEEAAARRRGH
MUST YOU SCREAM, NATHAN?
I'M TRYING TO WORK HERE.
LEANDRO FERNÁNDEZ '11

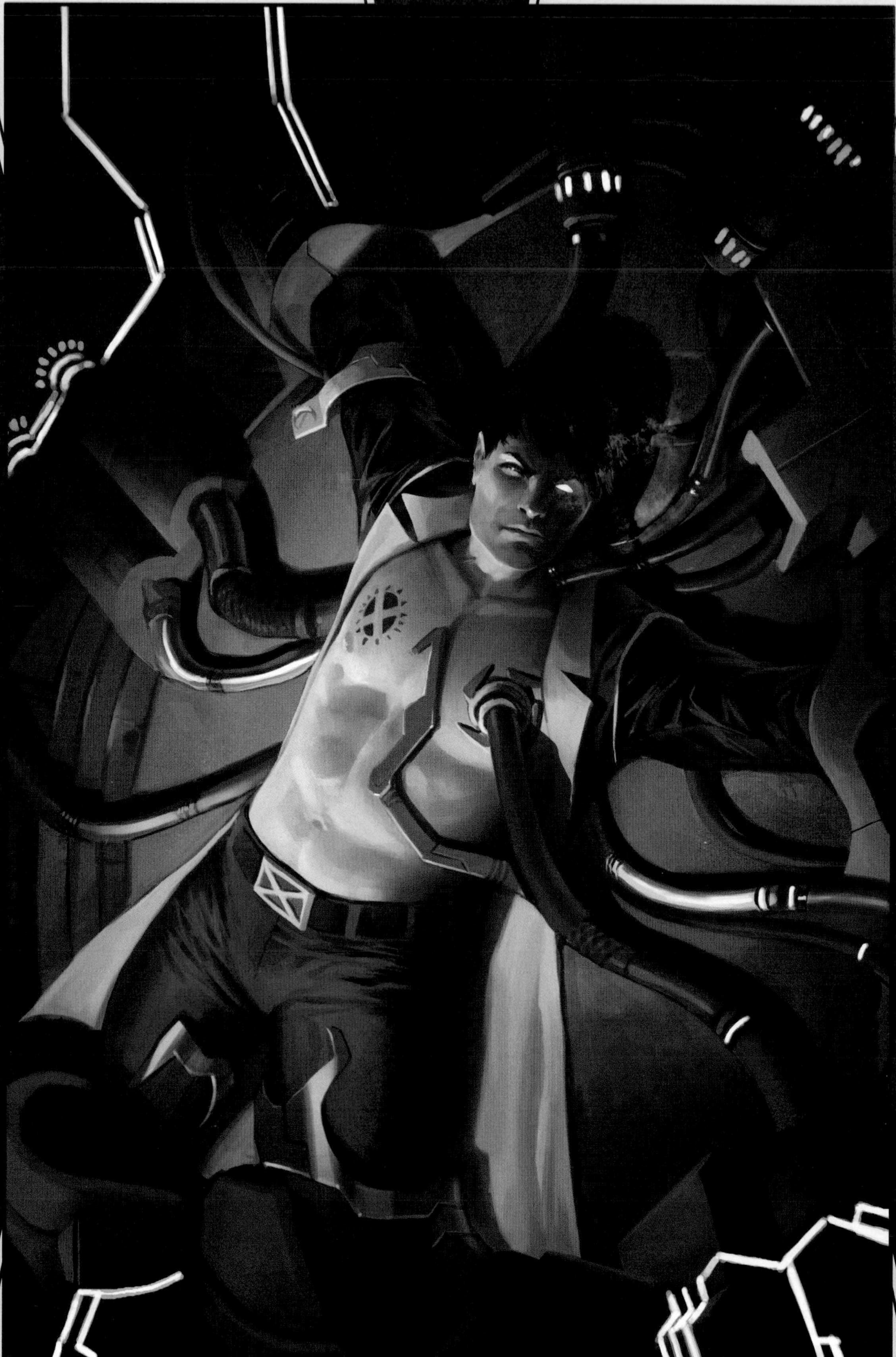

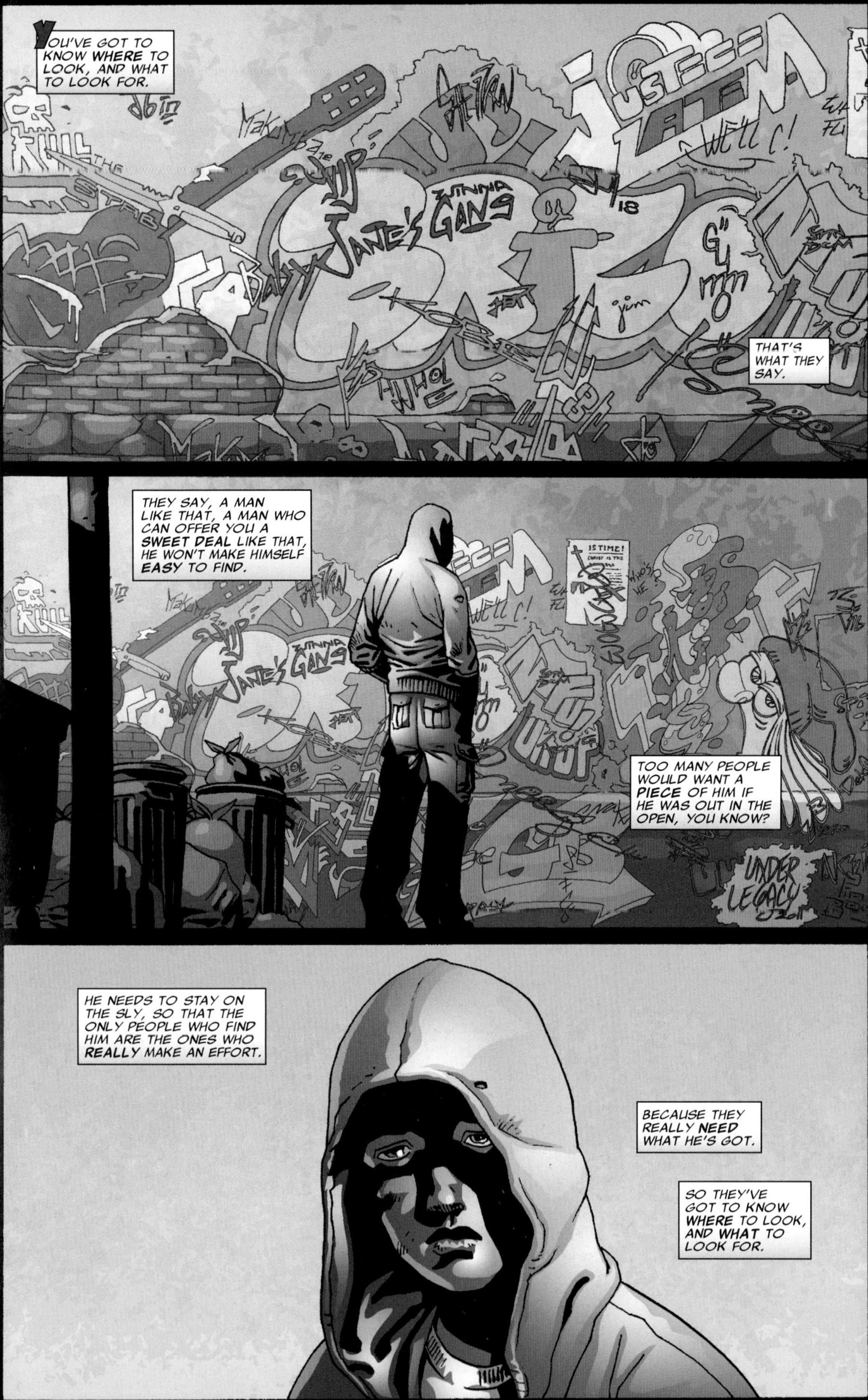
YOU'VE GOT TO KNOW WHERE TO LOOK, AND WHAT TO LOOK FOR.
THAT'S WHAT THEY SAY.
THEY SAY, A MAN LIKE THAT, A MAN WHO CAN OFFER YOU A SWEET DEAL LIKE THAT, HE WON'T MAKE HIMSELF EASY TO FIND.
TOO MANY PEOPLE WOULD WANT A PIECE OF HIM IF HE WAS OUT IN THE OPEN, YOU KNOW?
HE NEEDS TO STAY ON THE SLY, SO THAT THE ONLY PEOPLE WHO FIND HIM ARE THE ONES WHO REALLY MAKE AN EFFORT.
BECAUSE THEY REALLY NEED WHAT HE'S GOT.
SO THEY'VE GOT TO KNOW WHERE TO LOOK, AND WHAT TO LOOK FOR.

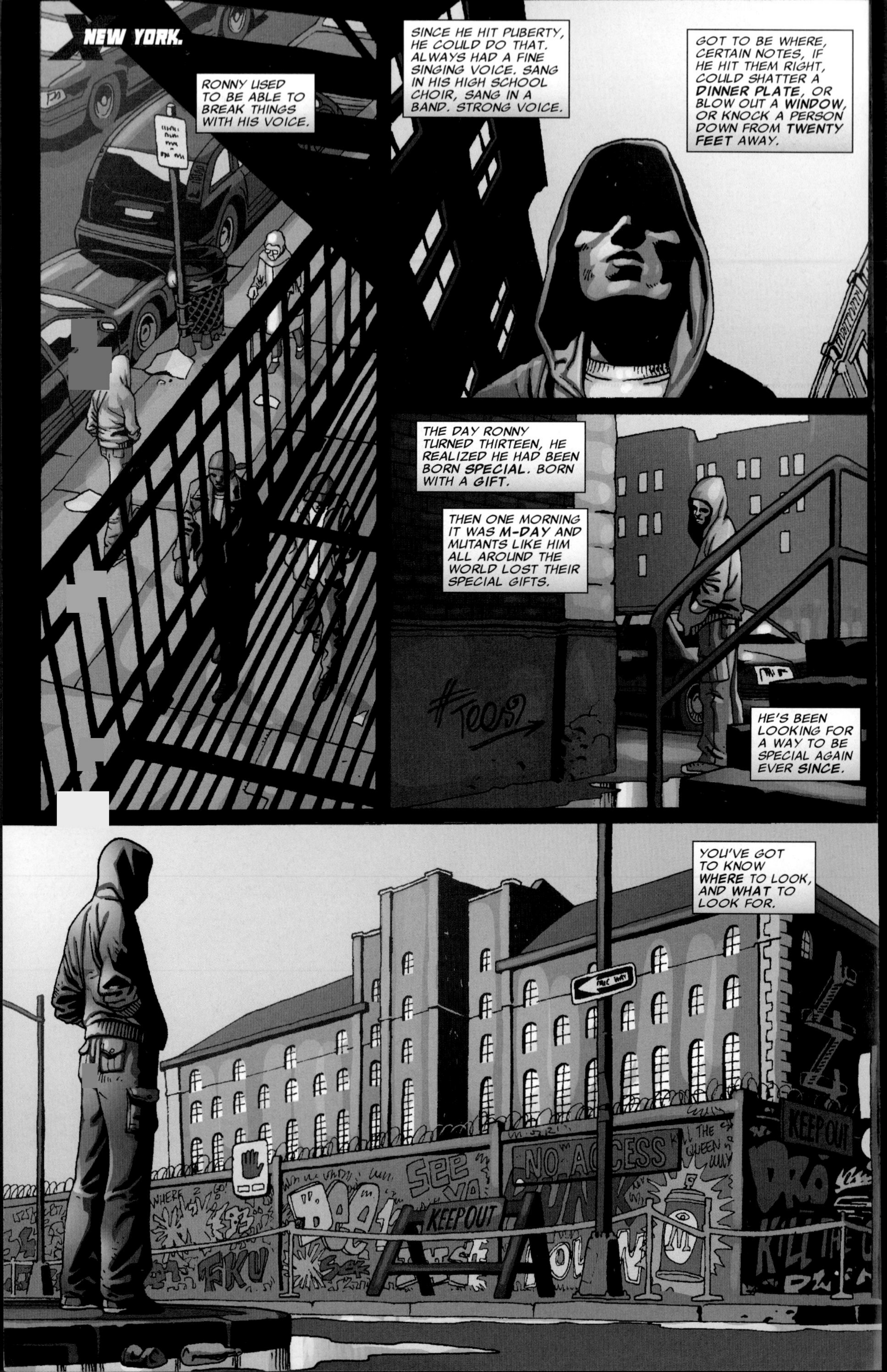
NEW YORK.
RONNY USED TO BE ABLE TO BREAK THINGS WITH HIS VOICE.
SINCE HE HIT PUBERTY, HE COULD DO THAT. ALWAYS HAD A FINE SINGING VOICE. SANG IN HIS HIGH SCHOOL CHOIR, SANG IN A BAND. STRONG VOICE.
GOT TO BE WHERE, CERTAIN NOTES, IF HE HIT THEM RIGHT, COULD SHATTER A DINNER PLATE, OR BLOW OUT A WINDOW, OR KNOCK A PERSON DOWN FROM TWENTY FEET AWAY.
THE DAY RONNY TURNED THIRTEEN, HE REALIZED HE HAD BEEN BORN SPECIAL. BORN WITH A GIFT.
THEN ONE MORNING IT WAS M-DAY AND MUTANTS LIKE HIM ALL AROUND THE WORLD LOST THEIR SPECIAL GIFTS.
HE'S BEEN LOOKING FOR A WAY TO BE SPECIAL AGAIN EVER SINCE.
YOU'VE GOT TO KNOW WHERE TO LOOK, AND WHAT TO LOOK FOR.
NO ACCESS
KEEP OUT
KEEP OUT

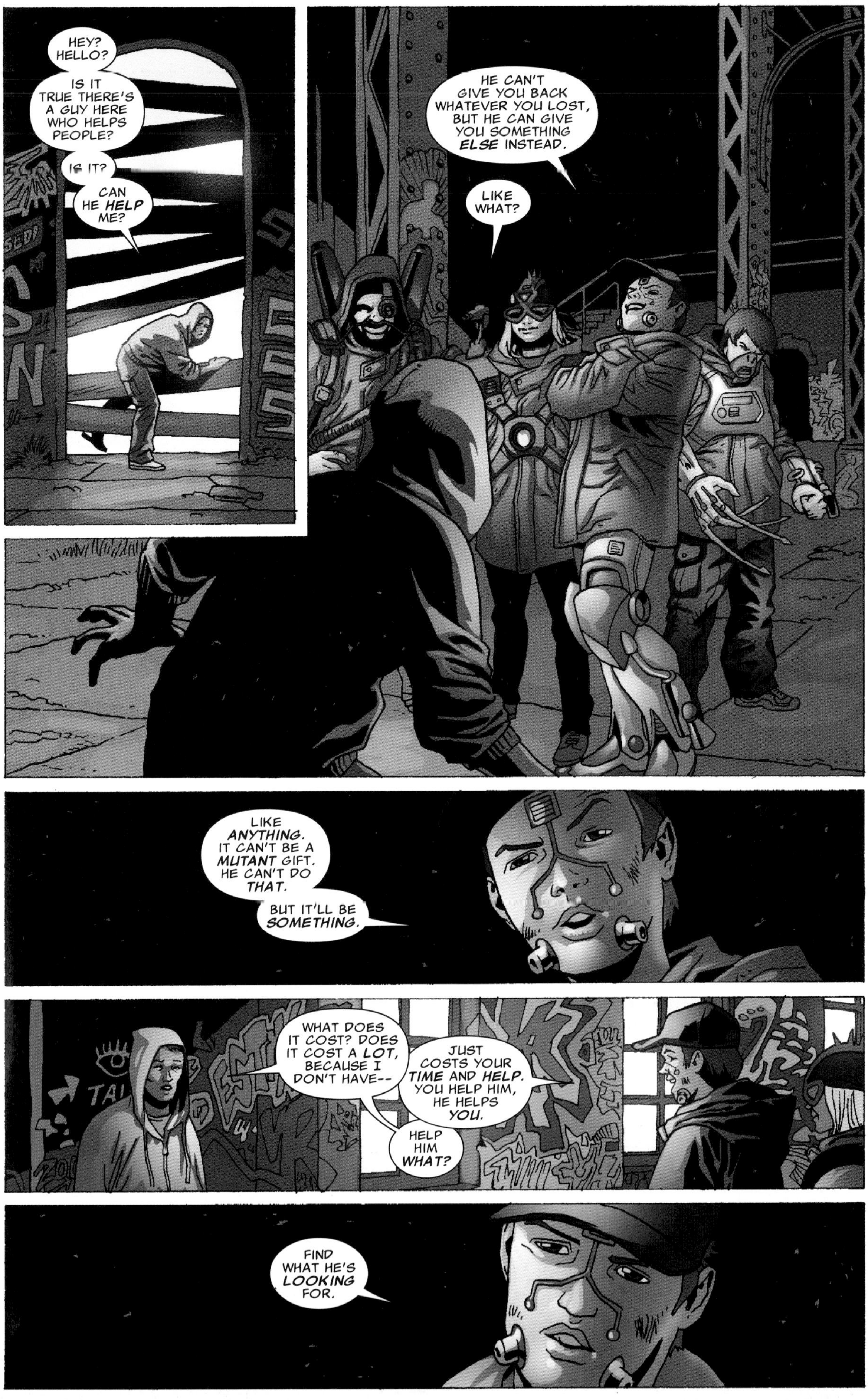
HEY? HELLO?
IS IT TRUE THERE'S A GUY HERE WHO HELPS PEOPLE?
IS IT?
CAN HE *HELP* ME?
HE CAN'T GIVE YOU BACK WHATEVER YOU LOST, BUT HE CAN GIVE YOU SOMETHING *ELSE* INSTEAD.
LIKE WHAT?
LIKE *ANYTHING*. IT CAN'T BE A *MUTANT* GIFT. HE CAN'T DO *THAT*.
BUT IT'LL BE *SOMETHING*.
WHAT DOES IT COST? DOES IT COST A *LOT*, BECAUSE I DON'T HAVE--
JUST COSTS YOUR *TIME* AND *HELP*. YOU HELP HIM, HE HELPS *YOU*.
HELP HIM *WHAT?*
FIND WHAT HE'S *LOOKING* FOR.

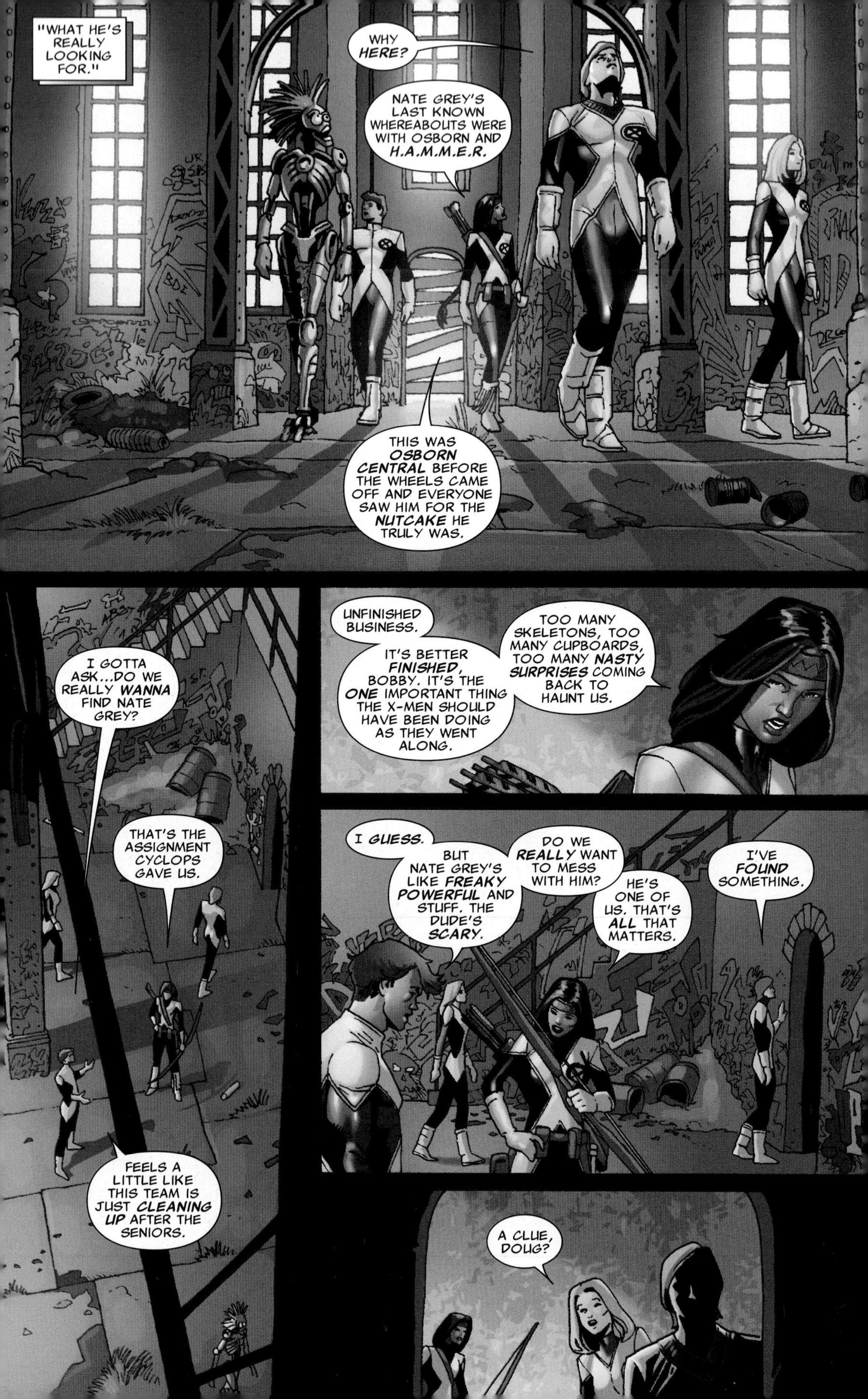
"WHAT HE'S REALLY LOOKING FOR."
WHY HERE?
NATE GREY'S LAST KNOWN WHEREABOUTS WERE WITH OSBORN AND H.A.M.M.E.R.
THIS WAS OSBORN CENTRAL BEFORE THE WHEELS CAME OFF AND EVERYONE SAW HIM FOR THE NUTCAKE HE TRULY WAS.
I GOTTA ASK...DO WE REALLY WANNA FIND NATE GREY?
THAT'S THE ASSIGNMENT CYCLOPS GAVE US.
FEELS A LITTLE LIKE THIS TEAM IS JUST CLEANING UP AFTER THE SENIORS.
UNFINISHED BUSINESS.
IT'S BETTER FINISHED, BOBBY. IT'S THE ONE IMPORTANT THING THE X-MEN SHOULD HAVE BEEN DOING AS THEY WENT ALONG.
TOO MANY SKELETONS, TOO MANY CUPBOARDS, TOO MANY NASTY SURPRISES COMING BACK TO HAUNT US.
I GUESS.
BUT NATE GREY'S LIKE FREAKY POWERFUL AND STUFF. THE DUDE'S SCARY.
DO WE REALLY WANT TO MESS WITH HIM?
HE'S ONE OF US. THAT'S ALL THAT MATTERS.
I'VE FOUND SOMETHING.
A CLUE, DOUG?

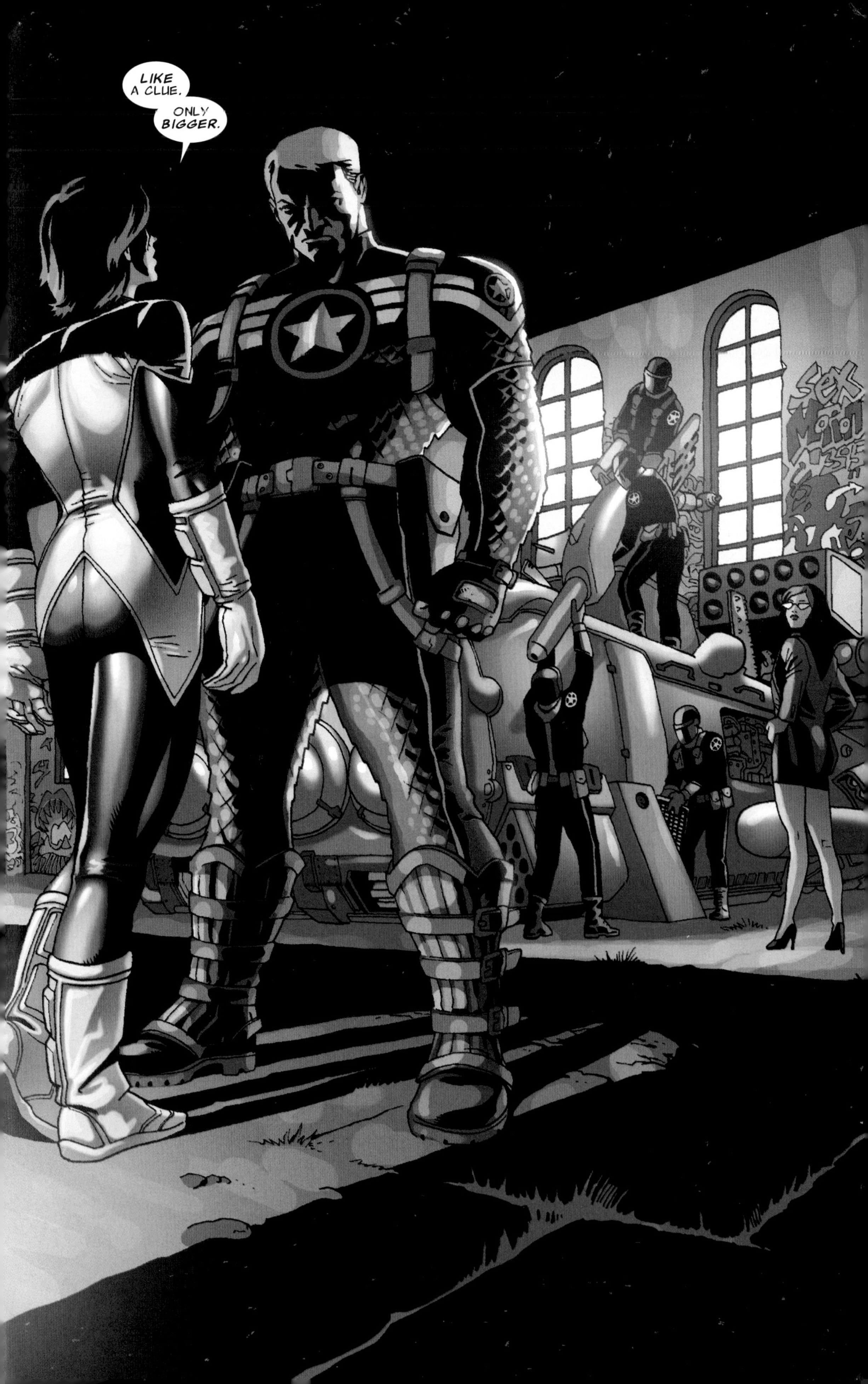
LIKE A CLUE.
ONLY BIGGER.

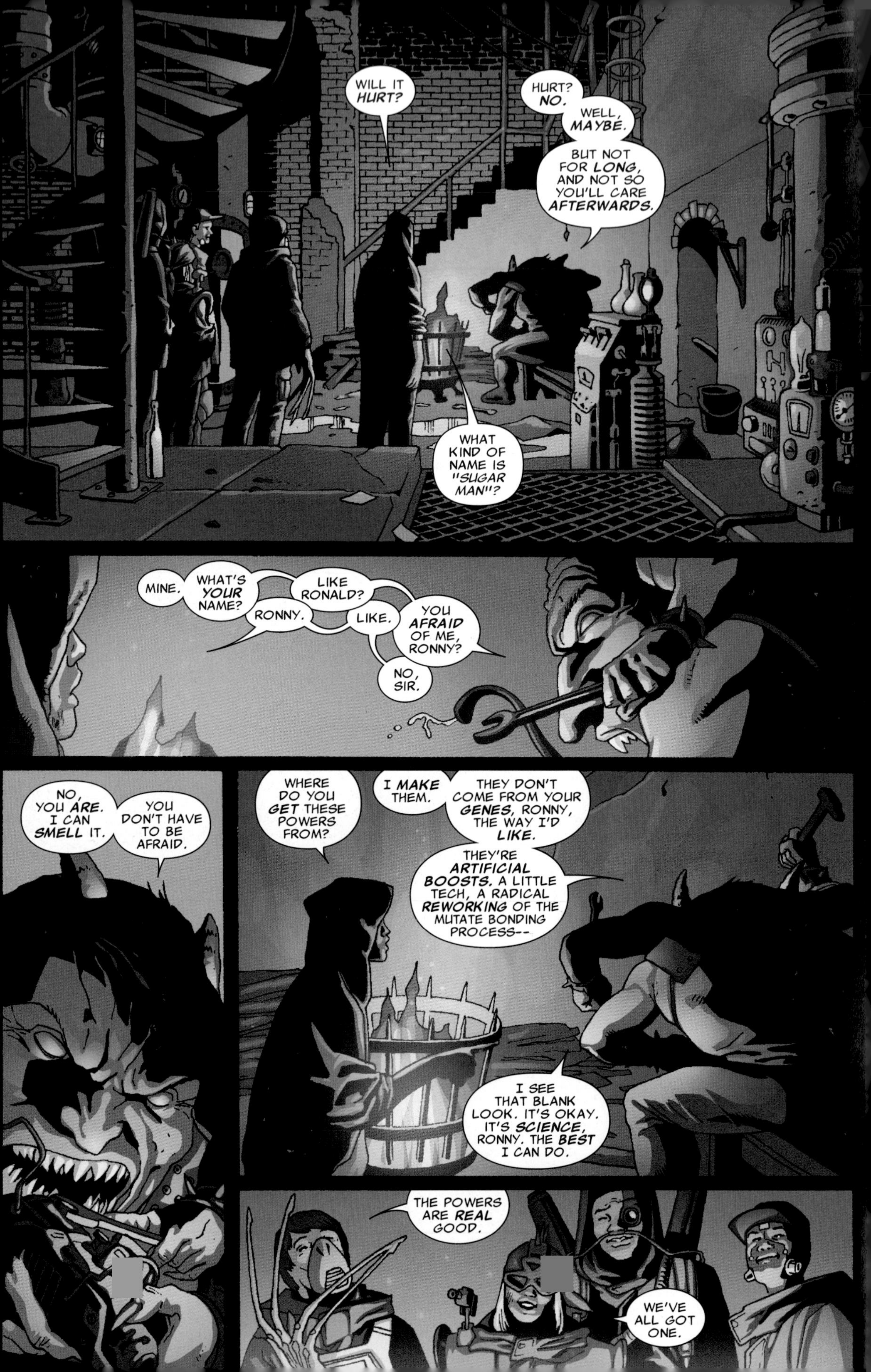

WILL IT HURT?
HURT? NO.
WELL, MAYBE.
BUT NOT FOR LONG, AND NOT SO YOU'LL CARE AFTERWARDS.
WHAT KIND OF NAME IS "SUGAR MAN"?
MINE.
WHAT'S YOUR NAME?
RONNY.
LIKE RONALD?
LIKE.
YOU AFRAID OF ME, RONNY?
NO, SIR.
NO, YOU ARE. I CAN SMELL IT.
YOU DON'T HAVE TO BE AFRAID.
WHERE DO YOU GET THESE POWERS FROM?
I MAKE THEM.
THEY DON'T COME FROM YOUR GENES, RONNY, THE WAY I'D LIKE.
THEY'RE ARTIFICIAL BOOSTS. A LITTLE TECH, A RADICAL REWORKING OF THE MUTATE BONDING PROCESS--
I SEE THAT BLANK LOOK. IT'S OKAY. IT'S SCIENCE, RONNY. THE BEST I CAN DO.
THE POWERS ARE REAL GOOD.
WE'VE ALL GOT ONE.

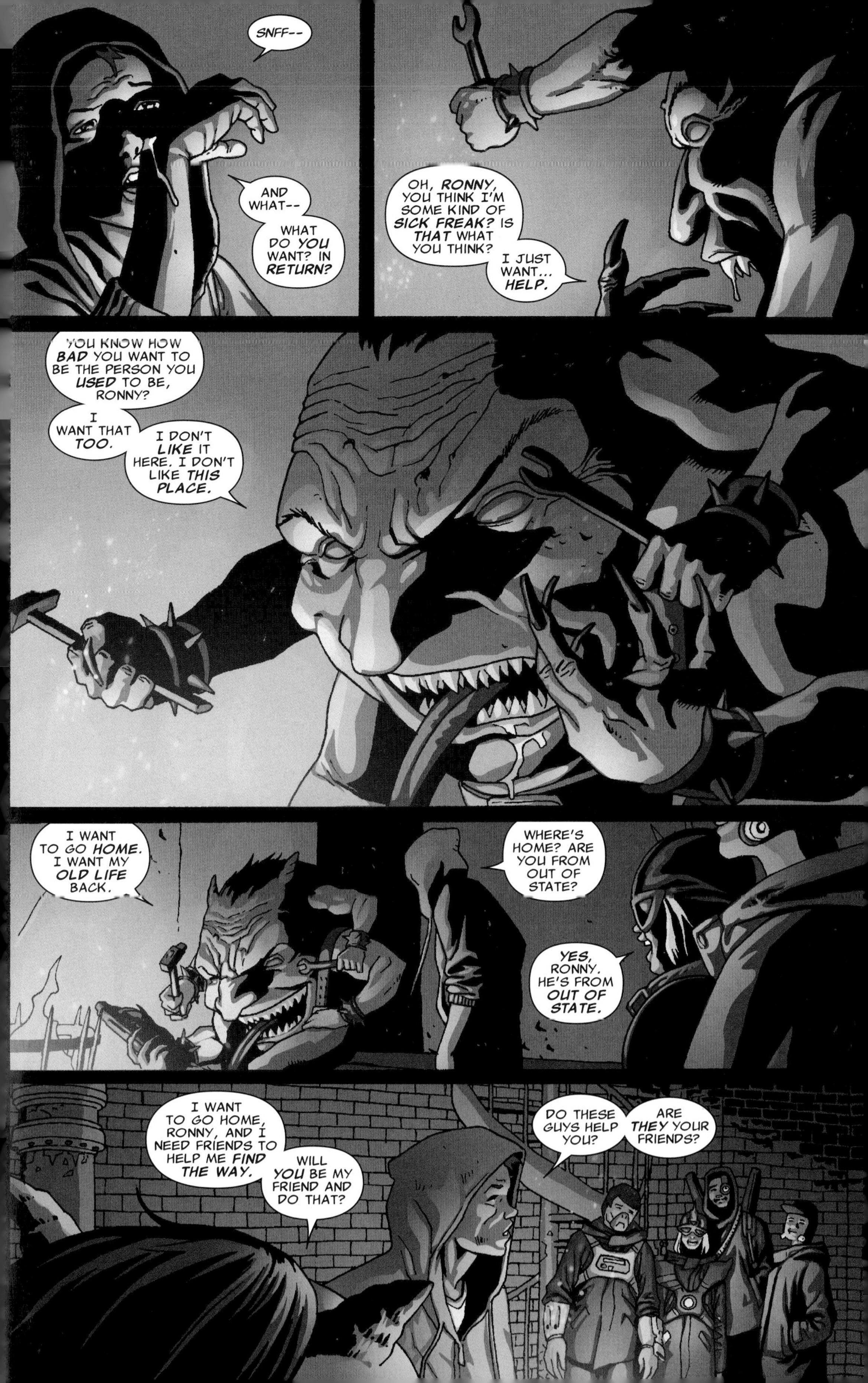
SNFF--
AND WHAT--
WHAT DO YOU WANT? IN RETURN?
OH, RONNY, YOU THINK I'M SOME KIND OF SICK FREAK? IS THAT WHAT YOU THINK?
I JUST WANT... HELP.
YOU KNOW HOW BAD YOU WANT TO BE THE PERSON YOU USED TO BE, RONNY?
I WANT THAT TOO.
I DON'T LIKE IT HERE. I DON'T LIKE THIS PLACE.
I WANT TO GO HOME. I WANT MY OLD LIFE BACK.
WHERE'S HOME? ARE YOU FROM OUT OF STATE?
YES, RONNY. HE'S FROM OUT OF STATE.
I WANT TO GO HOME, RONNY, AND I NEED FRIENDS TO HELP ME FIND THE WAY.
WILL YOU BE MY FRIEND AND DO THAT?
DO THESE GUYS HELP YOU?
ARE THEY YOUR FRIENDS?

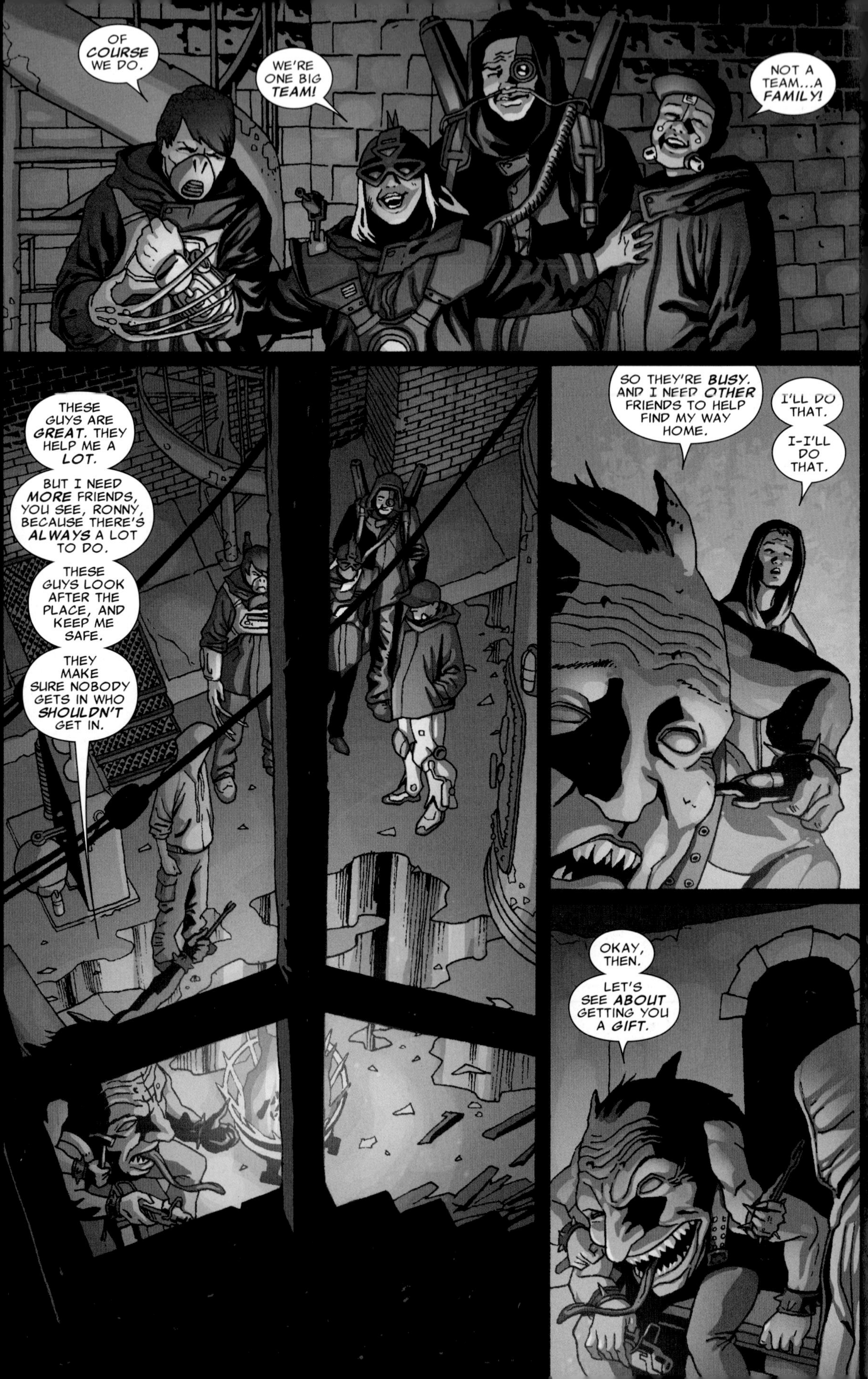
OF COURSE WE DO.
WE'RE ONE BIG TEAM!
NOT A TEAM...A FAMILY!
THESE GUYS ARE GREAT. THEY HELP ME A LOT.
BUT I NEED MORE FRIENDS, YOU SEE, RONNY, BECAUSE THERE'S ALWAYS A LOT TO DO.
THESE GUYS LOOK AFTER THE PLACE, AND KEEP ME SAFE.
THEY MAKE SURE NOBODY GETS IN WHO SHOULDN'T GET IN.
SO THEY'RE BUSY. AND I NEED OTHER FRIENDS TO HELP FIND MY WAY HOME.
I'LL DO THAT.
I-I'LL DO THAT.
OKAY, THEN.
LET'S SEE ABOUT GETTING YOU A GIFT.

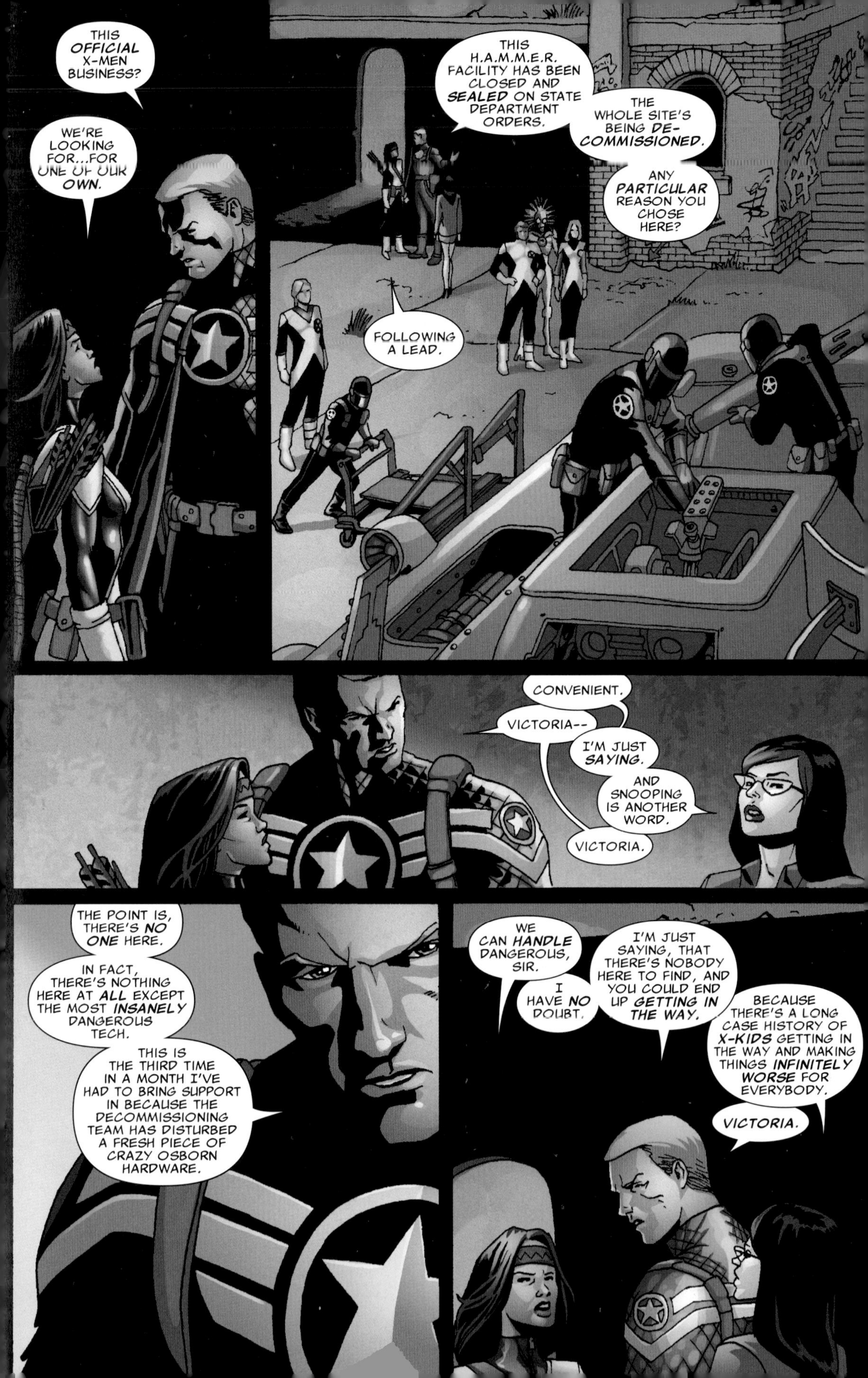
THIS OFFICIAL X-MEN BUSINESS?
WE'RE LOOKING FOR...FOR ONE OF OUR OWN.
THIS H.A.M.M.E.R. FACILITY HAS BEEN CLOSED AND SEALED ON STATE DEPARTMENT ORDERS.
THE WHOLE SITE'S BEING DE-COMMISSIONED.
ANY PARTICULAR REASON YOU CHOSE HERE?
FOLLOWING A LEAD.
CONVENIENT.
VICTORIA--
I'M JUST SAYING.
AND SNOOPING IS ANOTHER WORD.
VICTORIA.
THE POINT IS, THERE'S NO ONE HERE.
IN FACT, THERE'S NOTHING HERE AT ALL EXCEPT THE MOST INSANELY DANGEROUS TECH.
THIS IS THE THIRD TIME IN A MONTH I'VE HAD TO BRING SUPPORT IN BECAUSE THE DECOMMISSIONING TEAM HAS DISTURBED A FRESH PIECE OF CRAZY OSBORN HARDWARE.
WE CAN HANDLE DANGEROUS, SIR.
I HAVE NO DOUBT.
I'M JUST SAYING, THAT THERE'S NOBODY HERE TO FIND, AND YOU COULD END UP GETTING IN THE WAY.
BECAUSE THERE'S A LONG CASE HISTORY OF X-KIDS GETTING IN THE WAY AND MAKING THINGS INFINITELY WORSE FOR EVERYBODY.
VICTORIA.

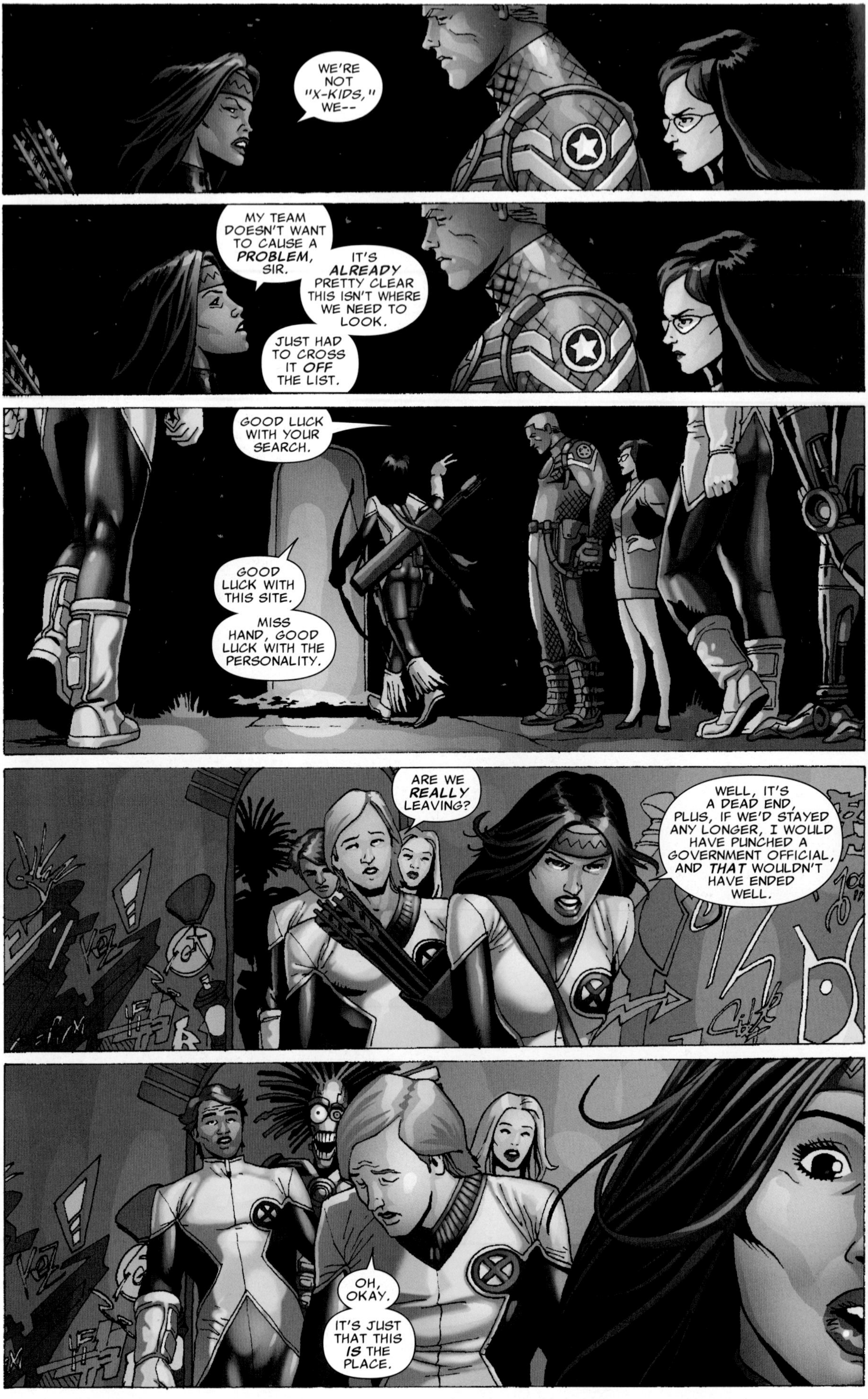
WE'RE NOT "X-KIDS," WE--
MY TEAM DOESN'T WANT TO CAUSE A PROBLEM, SIR.
IT'S ALREADY PRETTY CLEAR THIS ISN'T WHERE WE NEED TO LOOK.
JUST HAD TO CROSS IT OFF THE LIST.
GOOD LUCK WITH YOUR SEARCH.
GOOD LUCK WITH THIS SITE.
MISS HAND, GOOD LUCK WITH THE PERSONALITY.
ARE WE REALLY LEAVING?
WELL, IT'S A DEAD END, PLUS, IF WE'D STAYED ANY LONGER, I WOULD HAVE PUNCHED A GOVERNMENT OFFICIAL, AND THAT WOULDN'T HAVE ENDED WELL.
OH, OKAY.
IT'S JUST THAT THIS IS THE PLACE.

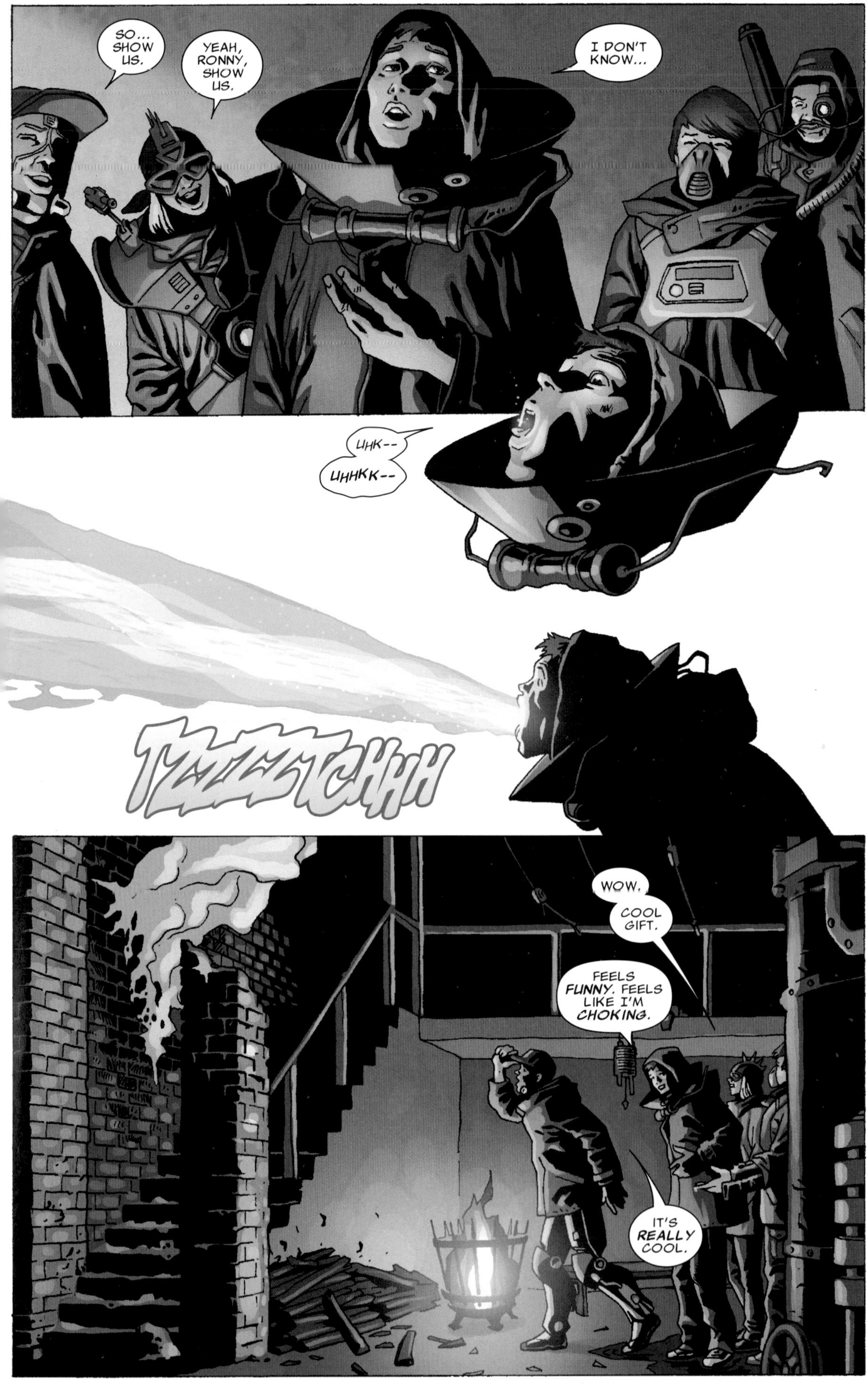
SO... SHOW US.
YEAH, RONNY, SHOW US.
I DON'T KNOW...
UHK--
UHHKK--
TZZZZTCHHH
WOW.
COOL GIFT.
FEELS FUNNY. FEELS LIKE I'M CHOKING.
IT'S REALLY COOL.

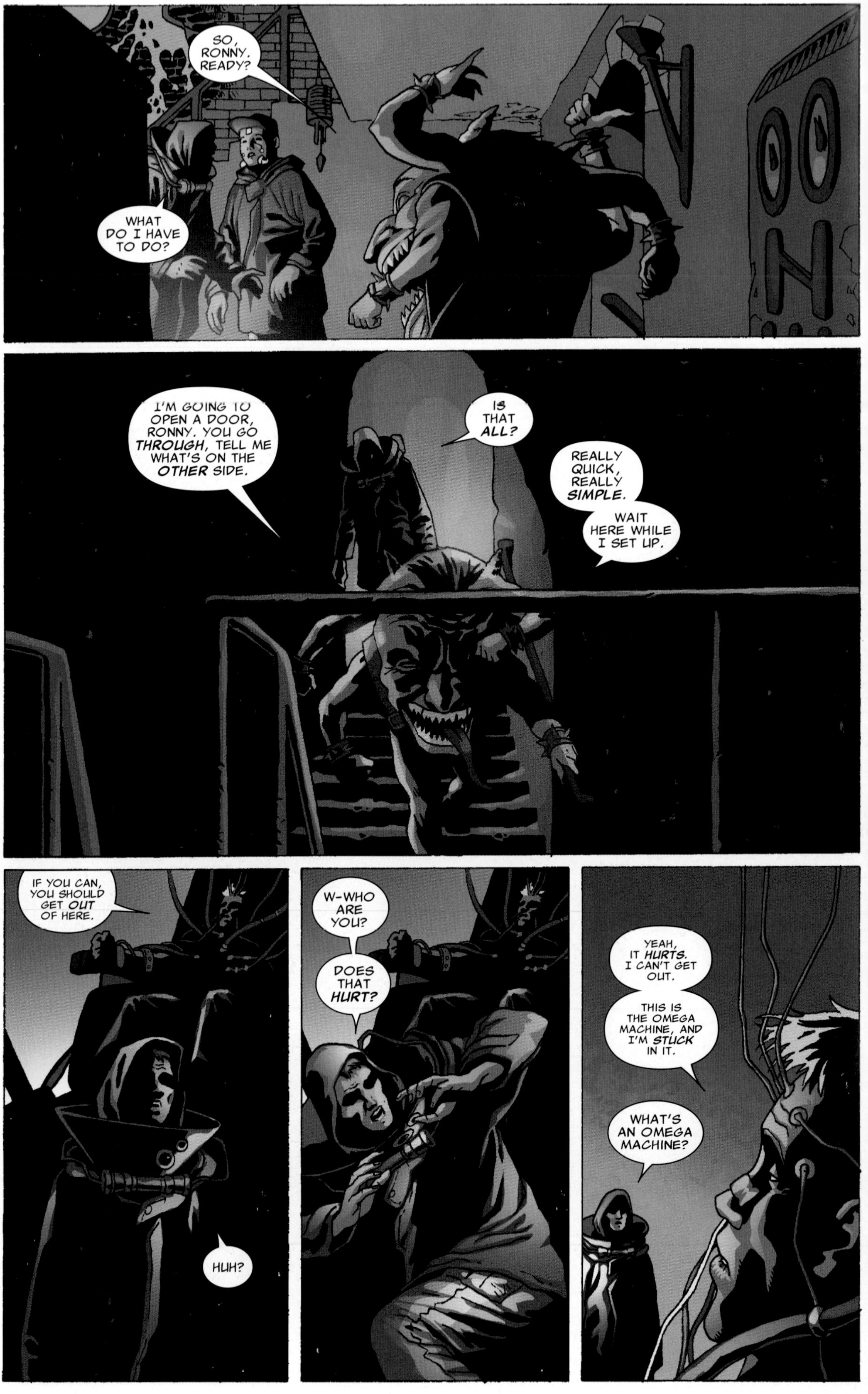
SO, RONNY. READY?
WHAT DO I HAVE TO DO?
I'M GOING TO OPEN A DOOR, RONNY. YOU GO THROUGH, TELL ME WHAT'S ON THE OTHER SIDE.
IS THAT ALL?
REALLY QUICK, REALLY SIMPLE.
WAIT HERE WHILE I SET UP.
IF YOU CAN, YOU SHOULD GET OUT OF HERE.
HUH?
W-WHO ARE YOU?
DOES THAT HURT?
YEAH, IT HURTS. I CAN'T GET OUT.
THIS IS THE OMEGA MACHINE, AND I'M STUCK IN IT.
WHAT'S AN OMEGA MACHINE?

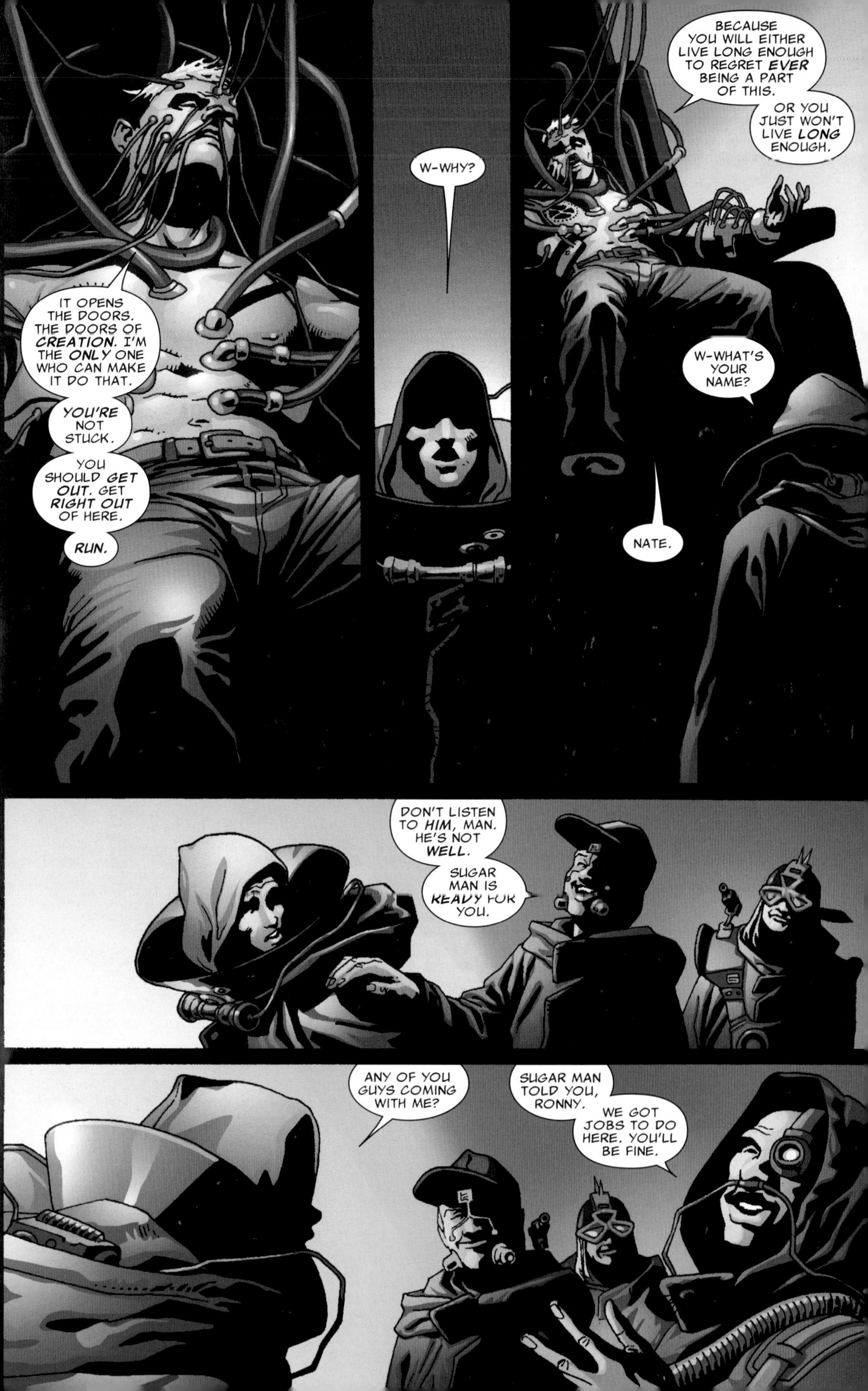
IT OPENS THE DOORS. THE DOORS OF CREATION. I'M THE ONLY ONE WHO CAN MAKE IT DO THAT.
YOU'RE NOT STUCK.
YOU SHOULD GET OUT. GET RIGHT OUT OF HERE.
RUN.
W-WHY?
BECAUSE YOU WILL EITHER LIVE LONG ENOUGH TO REGRET EVER BEING A PART OF THIS.
OR YOU JUST WON'T LIVE LONG ENOUGH.
W-WHAT'S YOUR NAME?
NATE.
DON'T LISTEN TO HIM, MAN. HE'S NOT WELL.
SUGAR MAN IS READY FOR YOU.
ANY OF YOU GUYS COMING WITH ME?
SUGAR MAN TOLD YOU, RONNY.
WE GOT JOBS TO DO HERE. YOU'LL BE FINE.

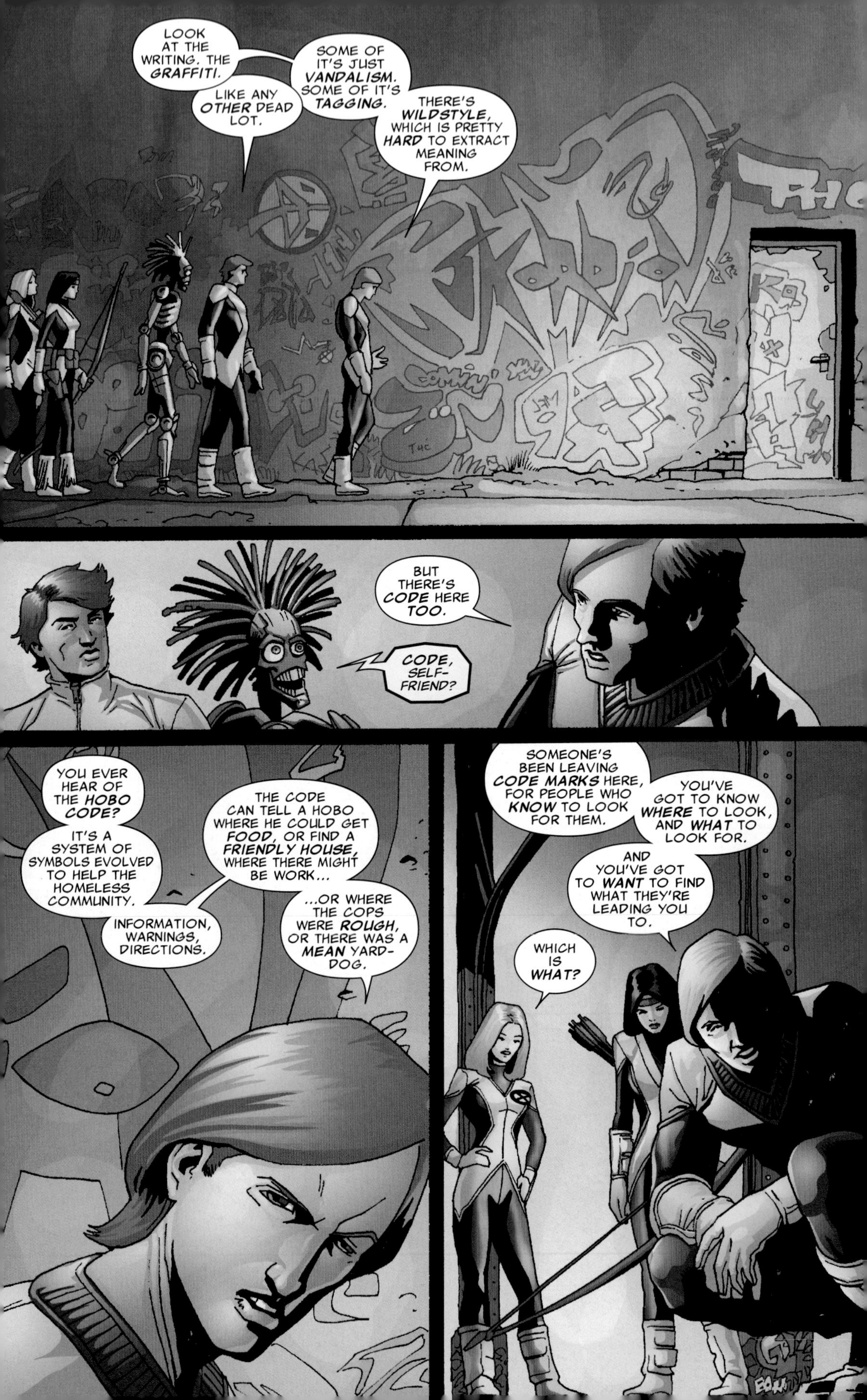
LOOK AT THE WRITING. THE GRAFFITI.
SOME OF IT'S JUST VANDALISM. SOME OF IT'S TAGGING.
LIKE ANY OTHER DEAD LOT.
THERE'S WILDSTYLE, WHICH IS PRETTY HARD TO EXTRACT MEANING FROM.
BUT THERE'S CODE HERE TOO.
CODE, SELF-FRIEND?
YOU EVER HEAR OF THE HOBO CODE?
IT'S A SYSTEM OF SYMBOLS EVOLVED TO HELP THE HOMELESS COMMUNITY.
INFORMATION, WARNINGS, DIRECTIONS.
THE CODE CAN TELL A HOBO WHERE HE COULD GET FOOD, OR FIND A FRIENDLY HOUSE, WHERE THERE MIGHT BE WORK...
...OR WHERE THE COPS WERE ROUGH, OR THERE WAS A MEAN YARD-DOG.
SOMEONE'S BEEN LEAVING CODE MARKS HERE, FOR PEOPLE WHO KNOW TO LOOK FOR THEM.
YOU'VE GOT TO KNOW WHERE TO LOOK, AND WHAT TO LOOK FOR.
AND YOU'VE GOT TO WANT TO FIND WHAT THEY'RE LEADING YOU TO.
WHICH IS WHAT?

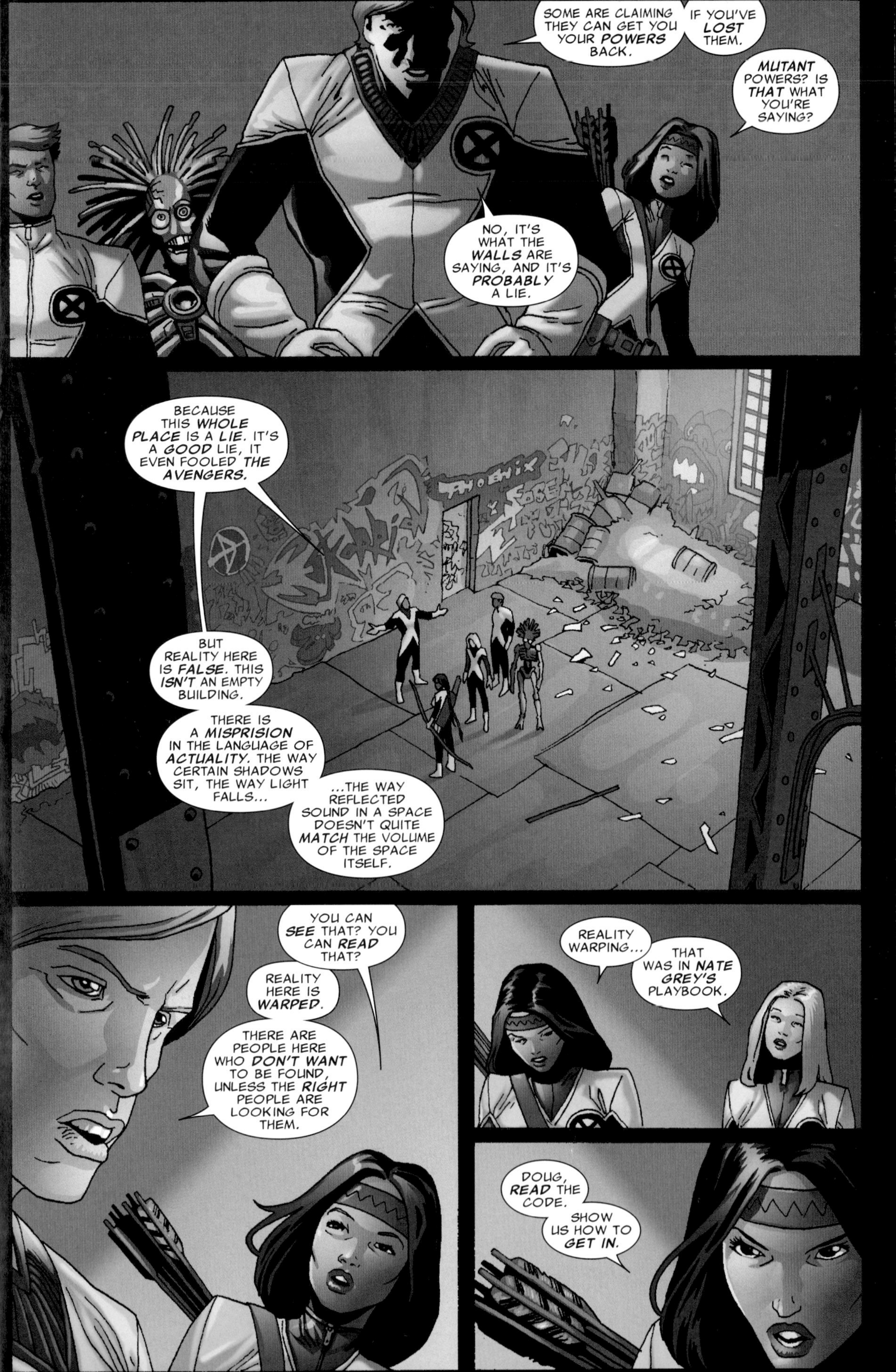
SOME ARE CLAIMING THEY CAN GET YOU YOUR POWERS BACK.
IF YOU'VE LOST THEM.
MUTANT POWERS? IS THAT WHAT YOU'RE SAYING?
NO, IT'S WHAT THE WALLS ARE SAYING, AND IT'S PROBABLY A LIE.
BECAUSE THIS WHOLE PLACE IS A LIE. IT'S A GOOD LIE, IT EVEN FOOLED THE AVENGERS.
BUT REALITY HERE IS FALSE. THIS ISN'T AN EMPTY BUILDING.
THERE IS A MISPRISION IN THE LANGUAGE OF ACTUALITY. THE WAY CERTAIN SHADOWS SIT, THE WAY LIGHT FALLS...
...THE WAY REFLECTED SOUND IN A SPACE DOESN'T QUITE MATCH THE VOLUME OF THE SPACE ITSELF.
YOU CAN SEE THAT? YOU CAN READ THAT?
REALITY HERE IS WARPED.
THERE ARE PEOPLE HERE WHO DON'T WANT TO BE FOUND, UNLESS THE RIGHT PEOPLE ARE LOOKING FOR THEM.
REALITY WARPING...
THAT WAS IN NATE GREY'S PLAYBOOK.
DOUG, READ THE CODE.
SHOW US HOW TO GET IN.

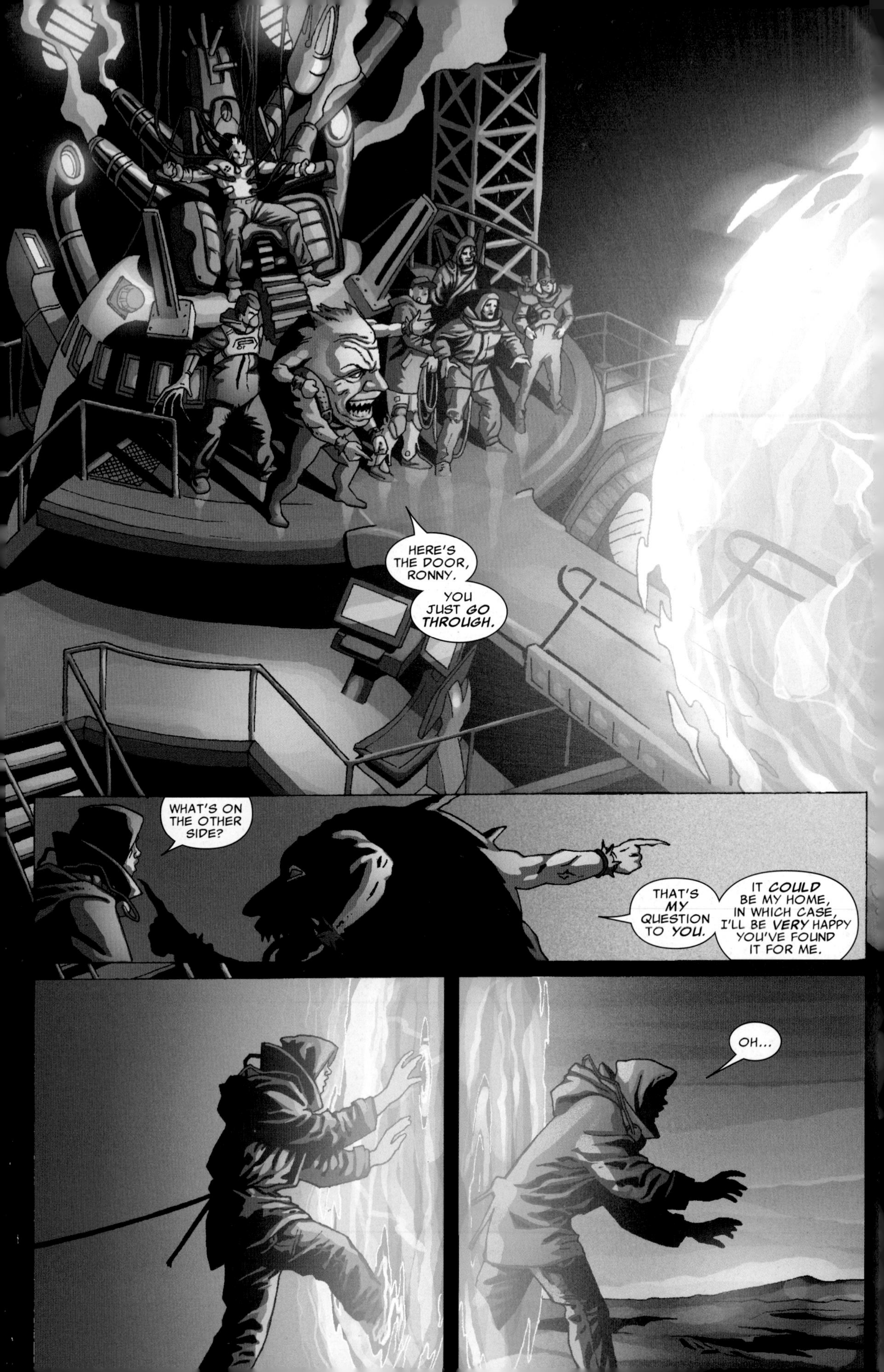
HERE'S THE DOOR, RONNY.
YOU JUST GO THROUGH.
WHAT'S ON THE OTHER SIDE?
THAT'S MY QUESTION TO YOU.
IT COULD BE MY HOME, IN WHICH CASE, I'LL BE VERY HAPPY YOU'VE FOUND IT FOR ME.
OH...

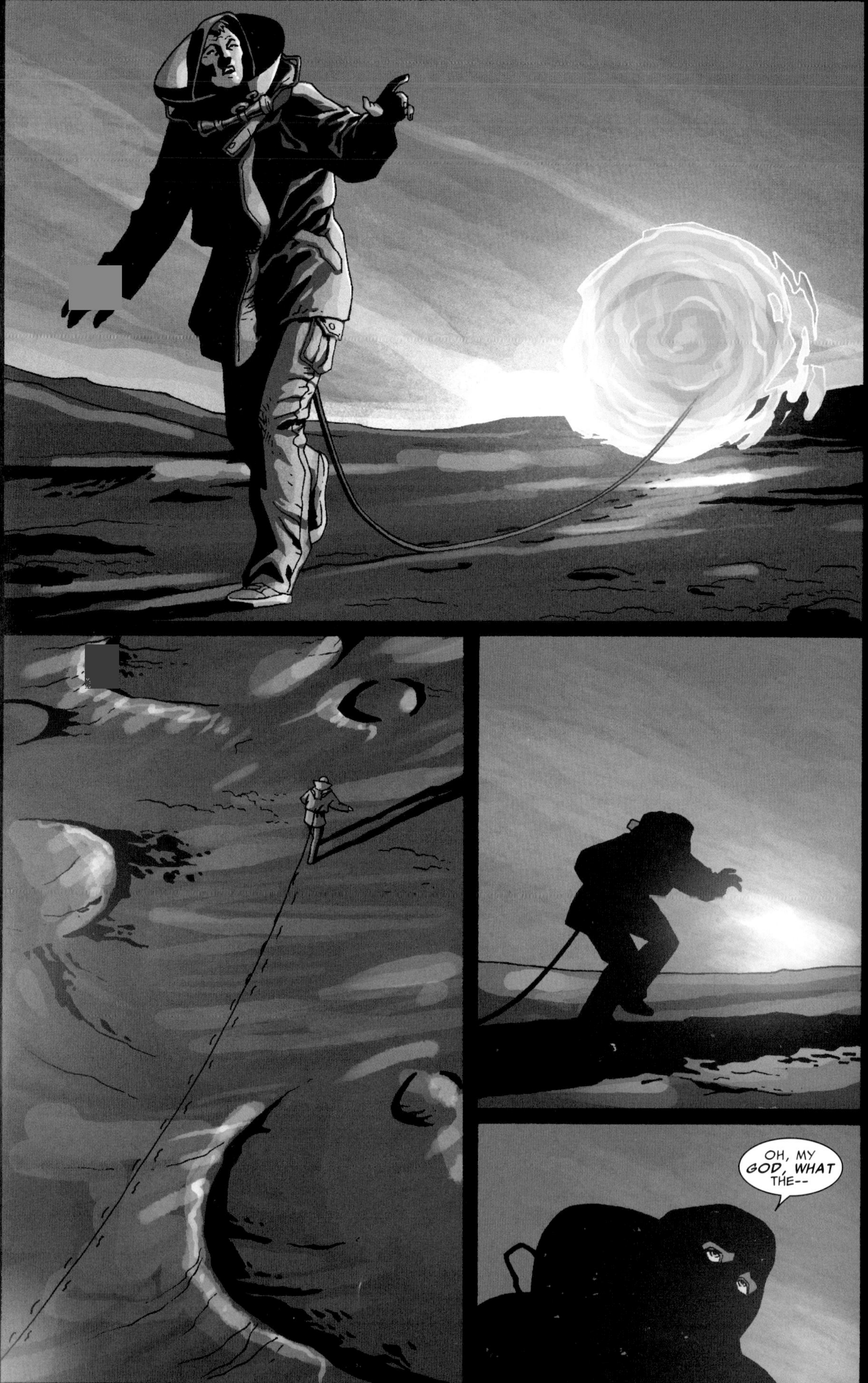
OH, MY GOD, WHAT THE--

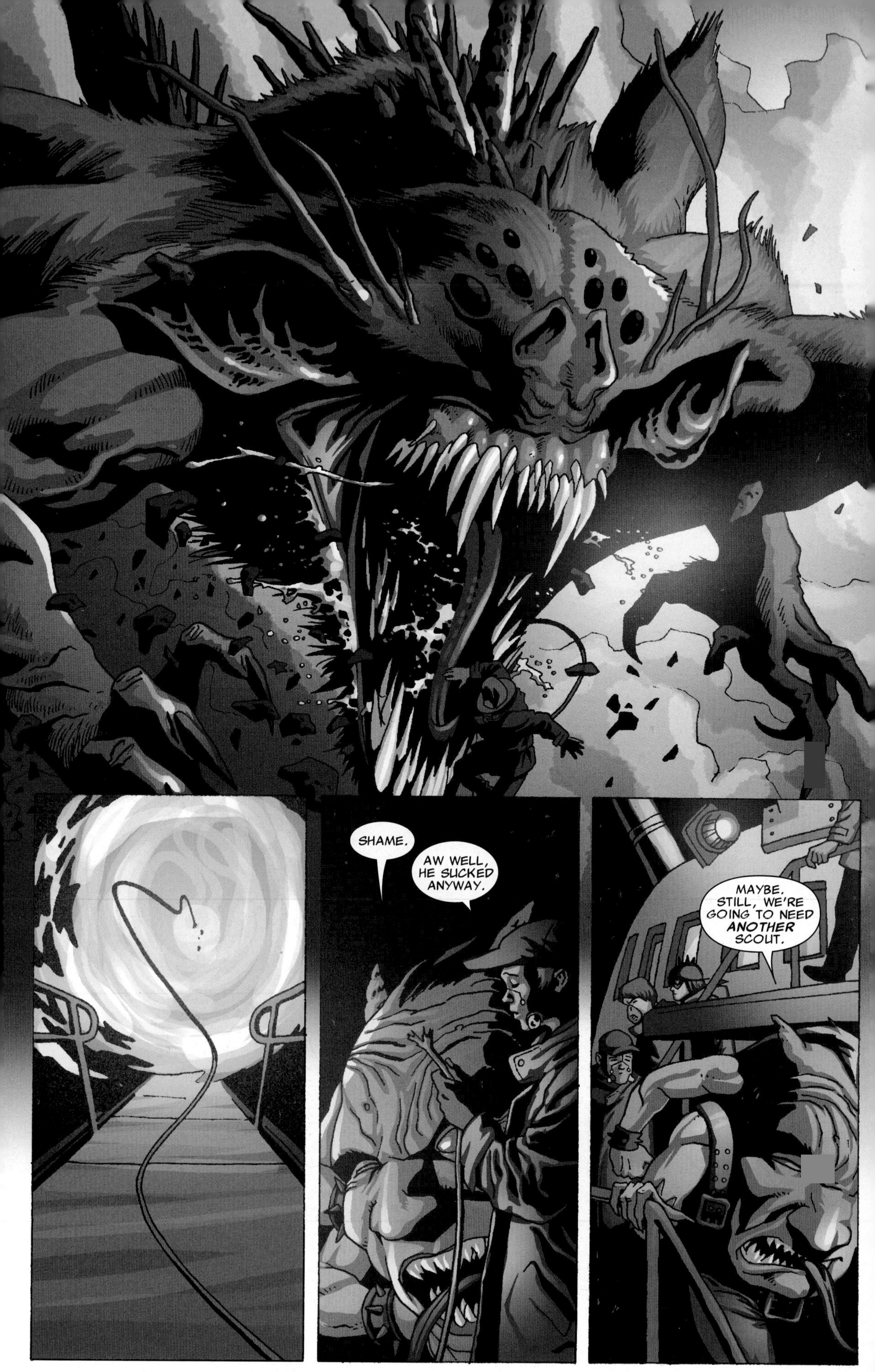
SHAME.
AW WELL, HE SUCKED ANYWAY.
MAYBE. STILL, WE'RE GOING TO NEED ANOTHER SCOUT.

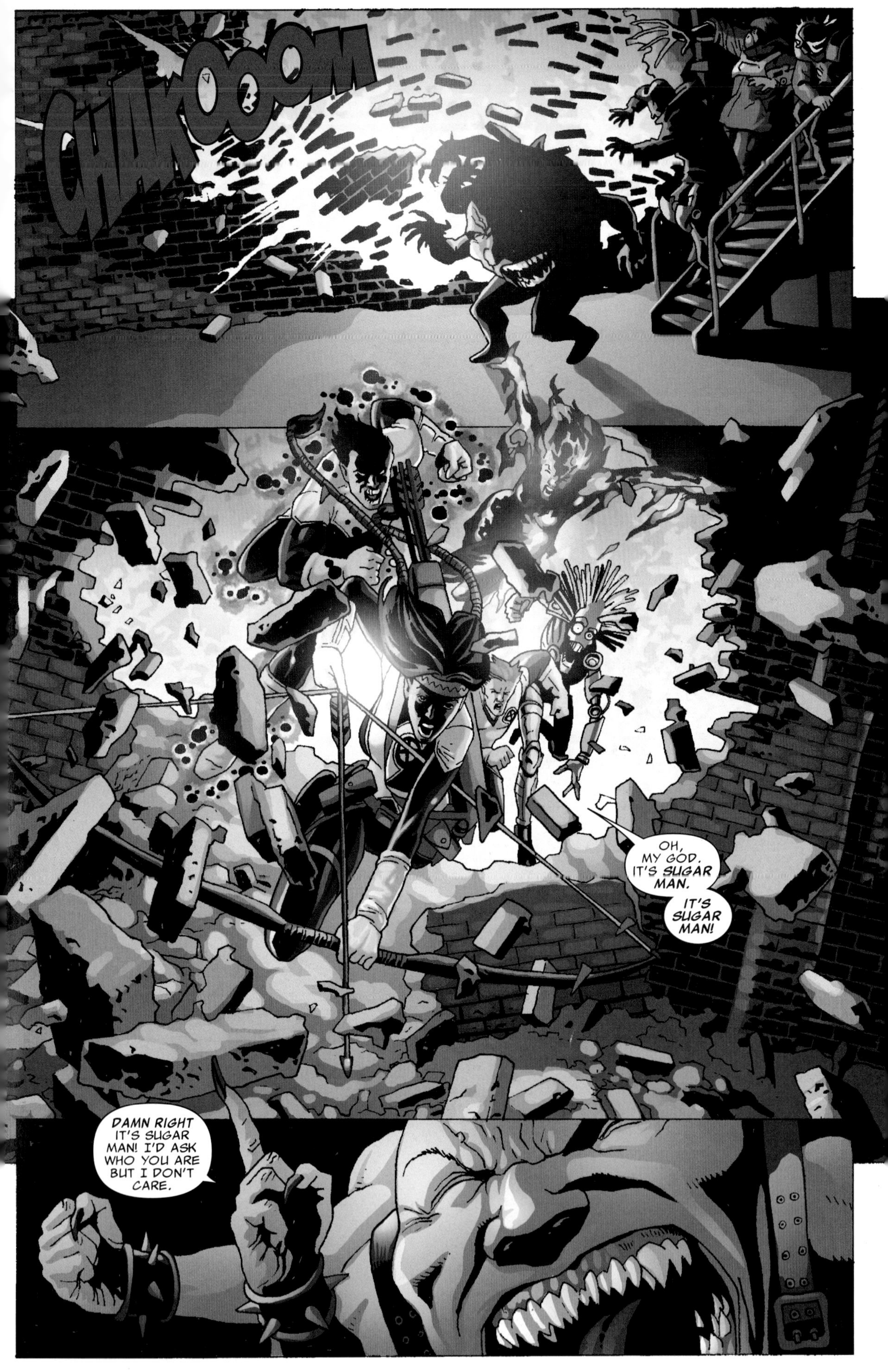
CHAKOOOM
OH, MY GOD. IT'S SUGAR MAN.
IT'S SUGAR MAN!
DAMN RIGHT IT'S SUGAR MAN! I'D ASK WHO YOU ARE BUT I DON'T CARE.

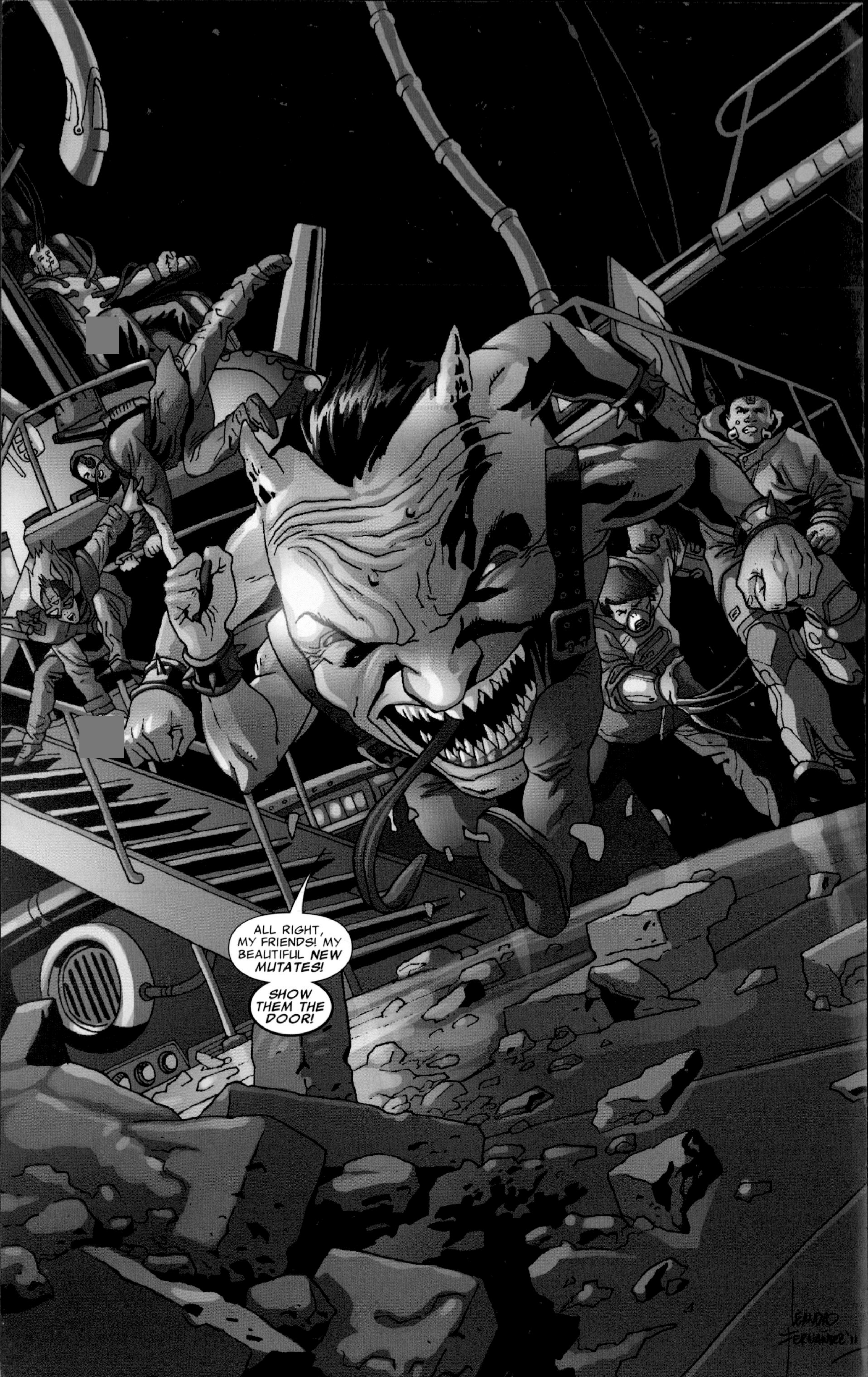
ALL RIGHT, MY FRIENDS! MY BEAUTIFUL NEW MUTATES!
SHOW THEM THE DOOR!

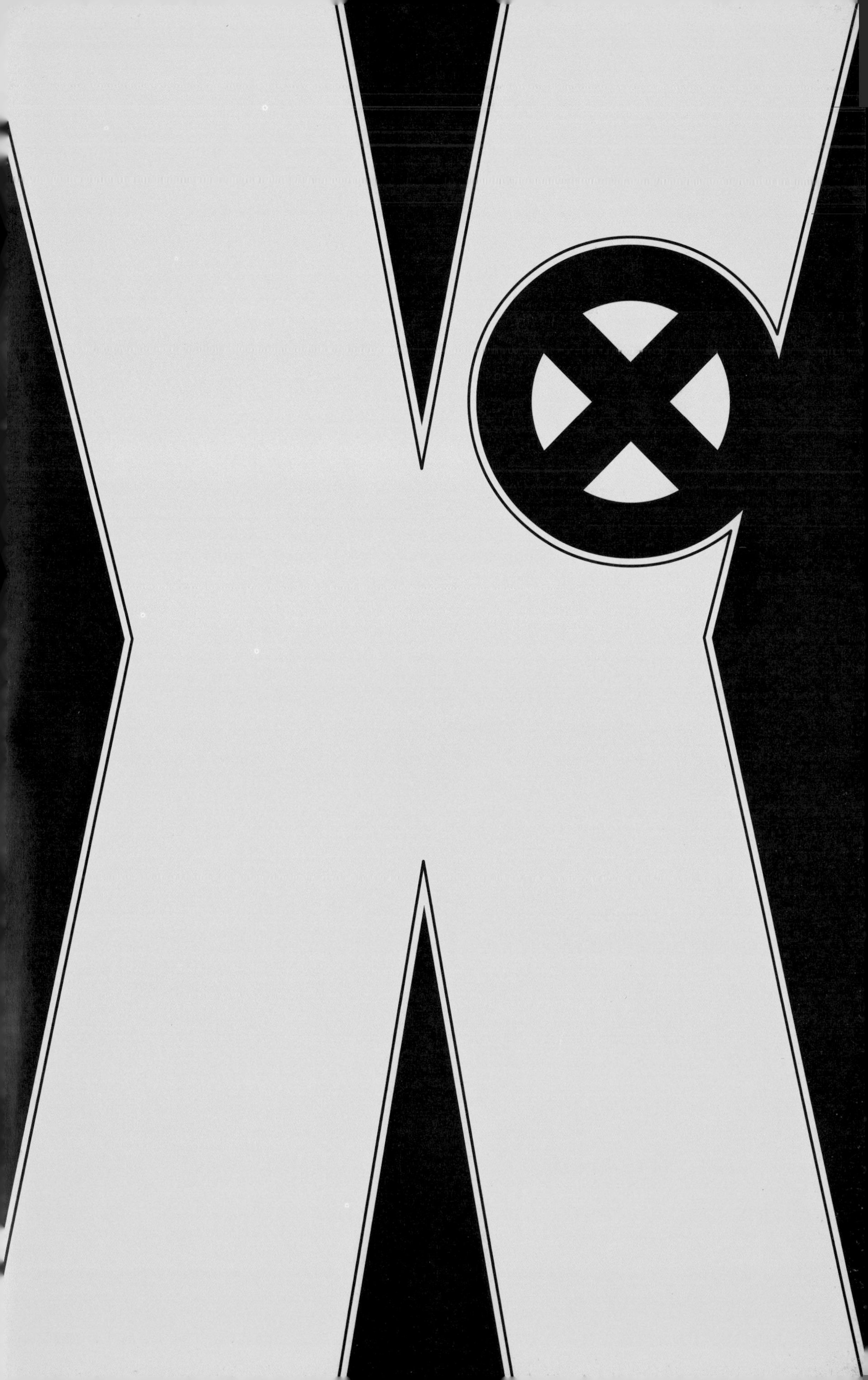

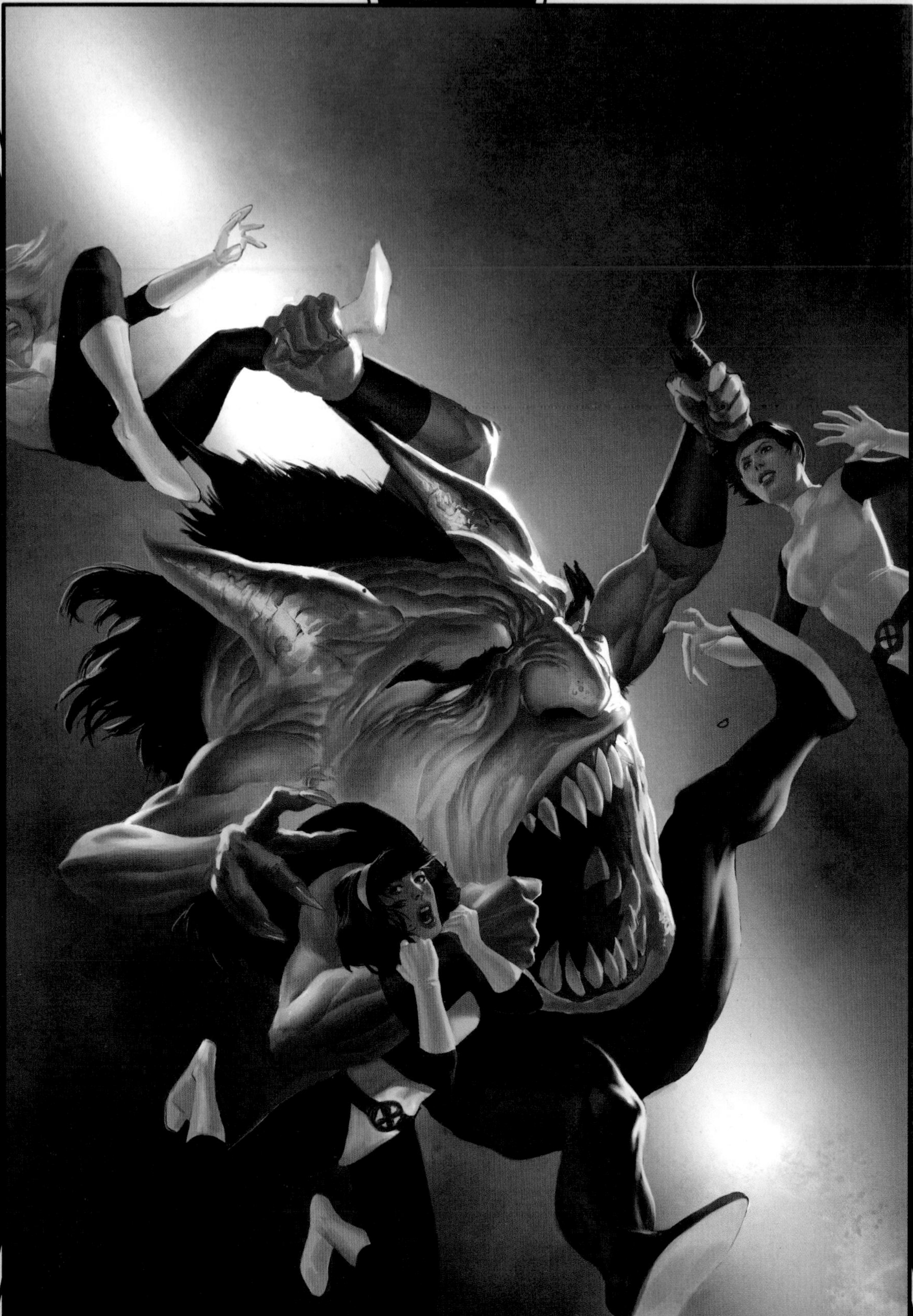

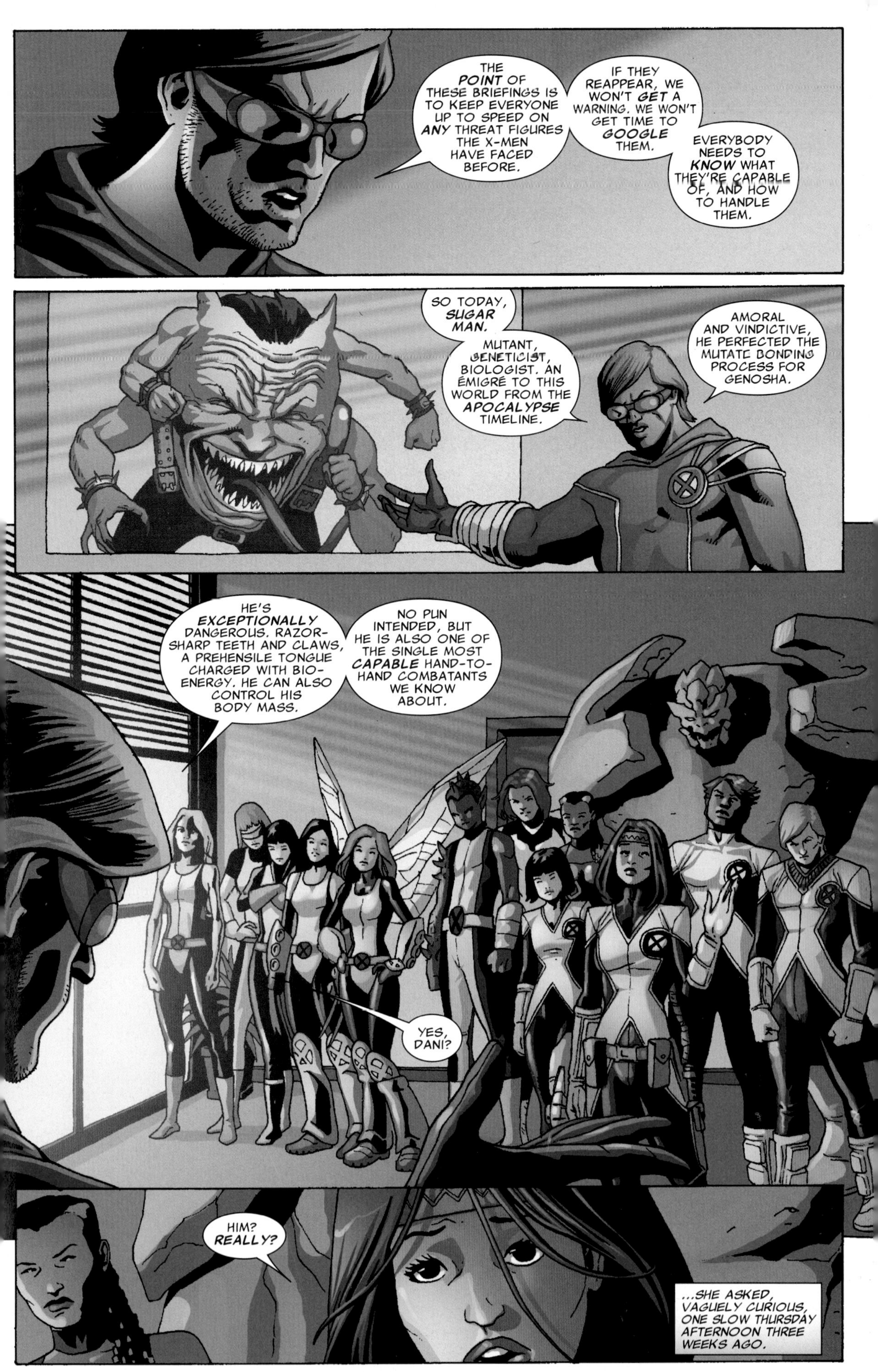
THE POINT OF THESE BRIEFINGS IS TO KEEP EVERYONE UP TO SPEED ON ANY THREAT FIGURES THE X-MEN HAVE FACED BEFORE.
IF THEY REAPPEAR, WE WON'T GET A WARNING. WE WON'T GET TIME TO GOOGLE THEM.
EVERYBODY NEEDS TO KNOW WHAT THEY'RE CAPABLE OF, AND HOW TO HANDLE THEM.
SO TODAY, SUGAR MAN.
MUTANT, GENETICIST, BIOLOGIST. AN ÉMIGRÉ TO THIS WORLD FROM THE APOCALYPSE TIMELINE.
AMORAL AND VINDICTIVE, HE PERFECTED THE MUTATE BONDING PROCESS FOR GENOSHA.
HE'S EXCEPTIONALLY DANGEROUS. RAZOR-SHARP TEETH AND CLAWS, A PREHENSILE TONGUE CHARGED WITH BIO-ENERGY. HE CAN ALSO CONTROL HIS BODY MASS.
NO PUN INTENDED, BUT HE IS ALSO ONE OF THE SINGLE MOST CAPABLE HAND-TO-HAND COMBATANTS WE KNOW ABOUT.
YES, DANI?
HIM? REALLY?
...SHE ASKED, VAGUELY CURIOUS, ONE SLOW THURSDAY AFTERNOON THREE WEEKS AGO.

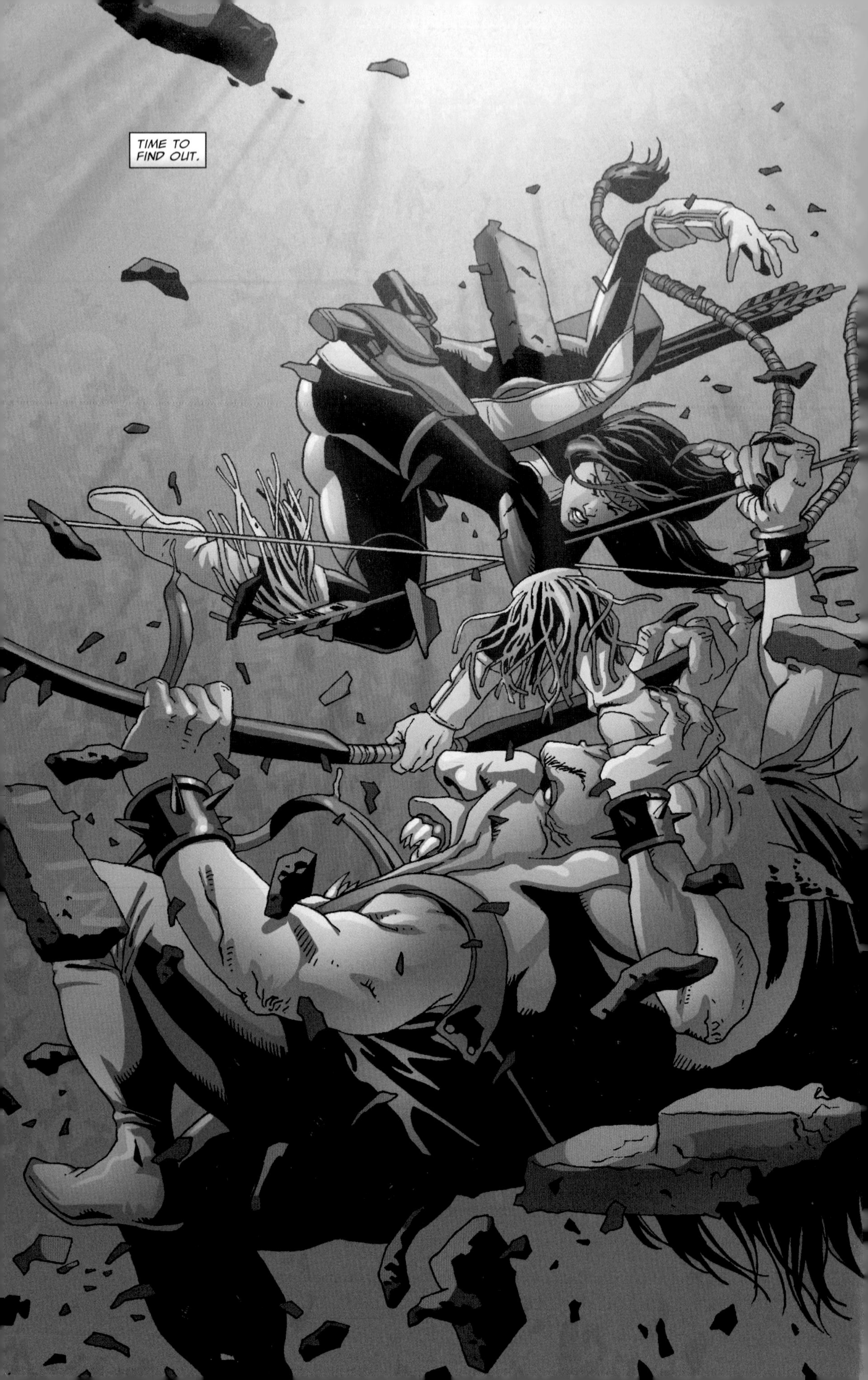
TIME TO FIND OUT.

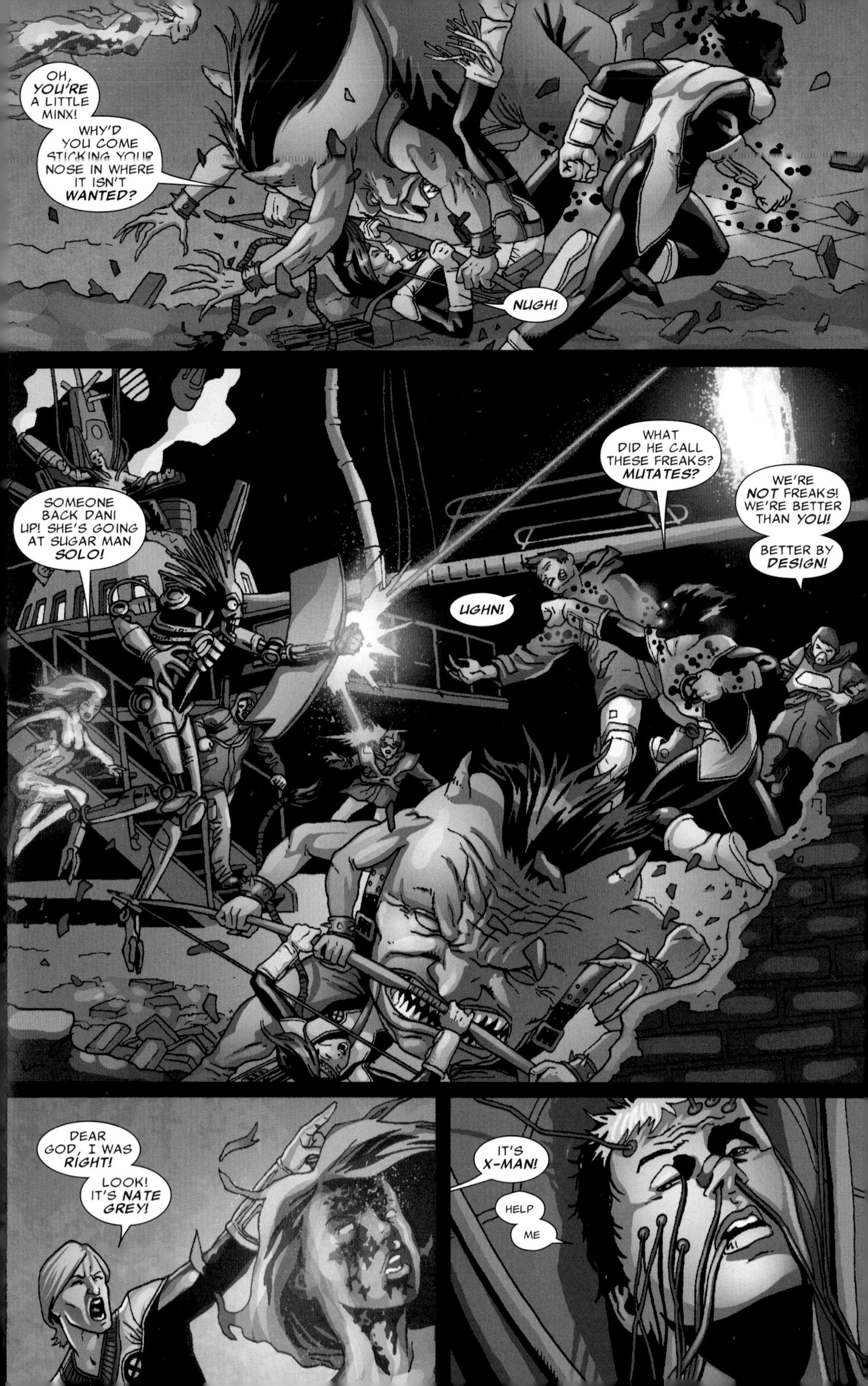
OH, YOU'RE A LITTLE MINX!
WHY'D YOU COME STICKING YOUR NOSE IN WHERE IT ISN'T WANTED?
NUGH!
SOMEONE BACK DANI UP! SHE'S GOING AT SUGAR MAN SOLO!
WHAT DID HE CALL THESE FREAKS? MUTATES?
WE'RE NOT FREAKS! WE'RE BETTER THAN YOU!
BETTER BY DESIGN!
UGHN!
DEAR GOD, I WAS RIGHT!
LOOK! IT'S NATE GREY!
IT'S X-MAN!
HELP
ME

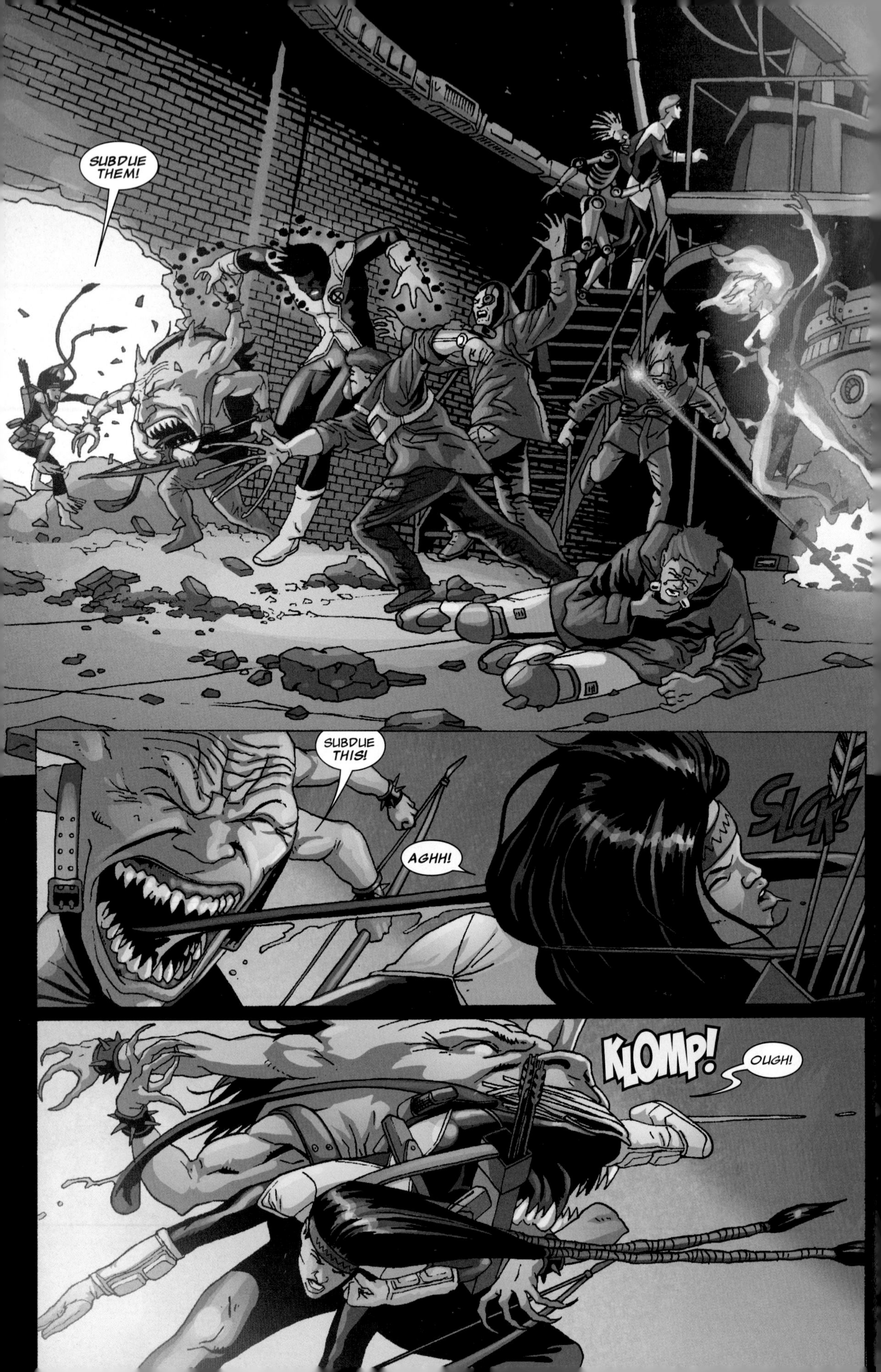
SUBDUE THEM!
SUBDUE THIS!
AGHH!
SLCK!
KLOMP!
OUGH!

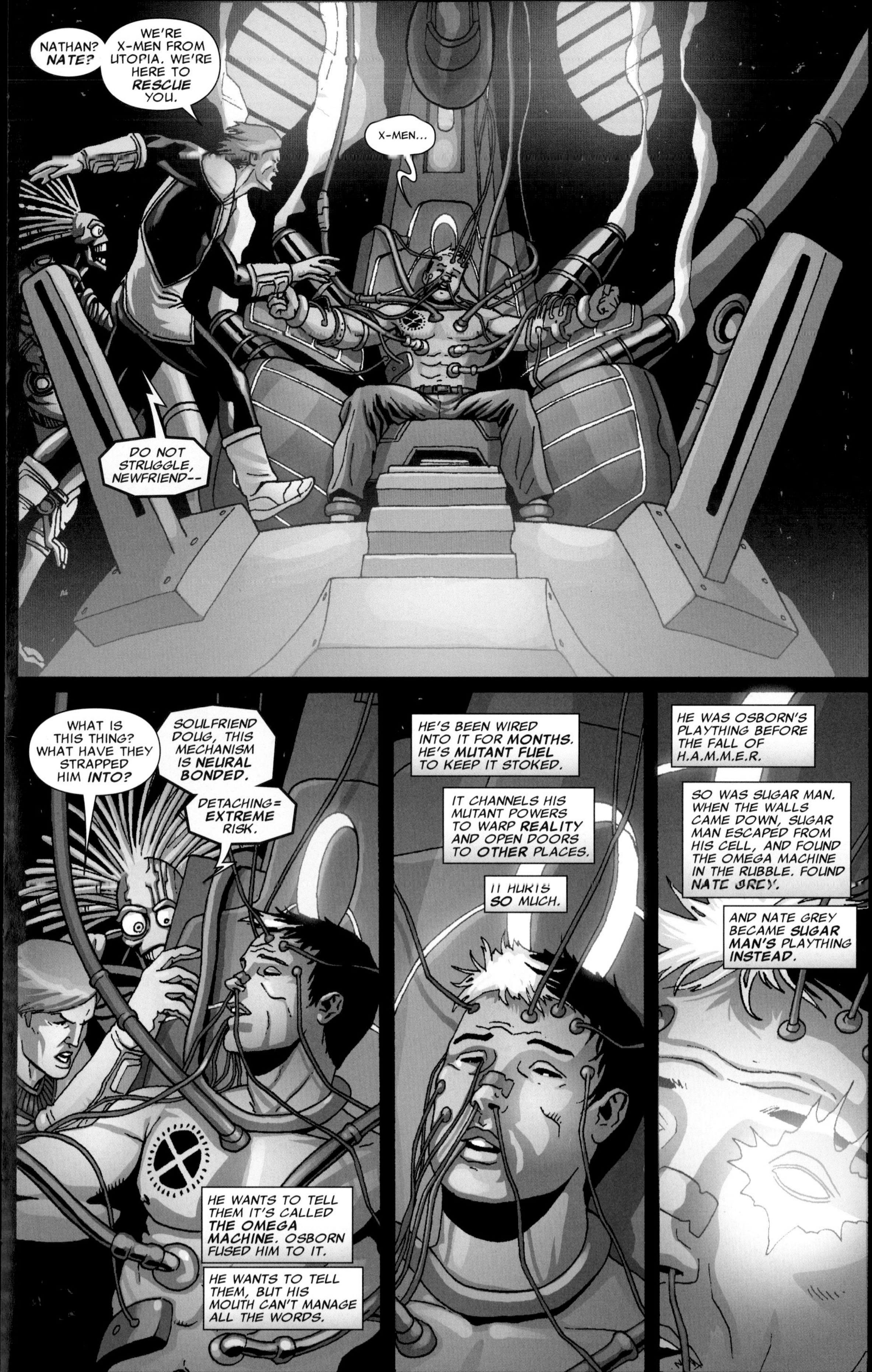
NATHAN? NATE?
WE'RE X-MEN FROM UTOPIA. WE'RE HERE TO RESCUE YOU.
X-MEN...
DO NOT STRUGGLE, NEWFRIEND--
WHAT IS THIS THING? WHAT HAVE THEY STRAPPED HIM INTO?
SOULFRIEND DOUG, THIS MECHANISM IS NEURAL BONDED.
DETACHING= EXTREME RISK.
HE WANTS TO TELL THEM IT'S CALLED THE OMEGA MACHINE. OSBORN FUSED HIM TO IT.
HE WANTS TO TELL THEM, BUT HIS MOUTH CAN'T MANAGE ALL THE WORDS.
HE'S BEEN WIRED INTO IT FOR MONTHS. HE'S MUTANT FUEL TO KEEP IT STOKED.
IT CHANNELS HIS MUTANT POWERS TO WARP REALITY AND OPEN DOORS TO OTHER PLACES.
IT HURTS SO MUCH.
HE WAS OSBORN'S PLAYTHING BEFORE THE FALL OF H.A.M.M.E.R.
SO WAS SUGAR MAN. WHEN THE WALLS CAME DOWN, SUGAR MAN ESCAPED FROM HIS CELL, AND FOUND THE OMEGA MACHINE IN THE RUBBLE. FOUND NATE GREY.
AND NATE GREY BECAME SUGAR MAN'S PLAYTHING INSTEAD.

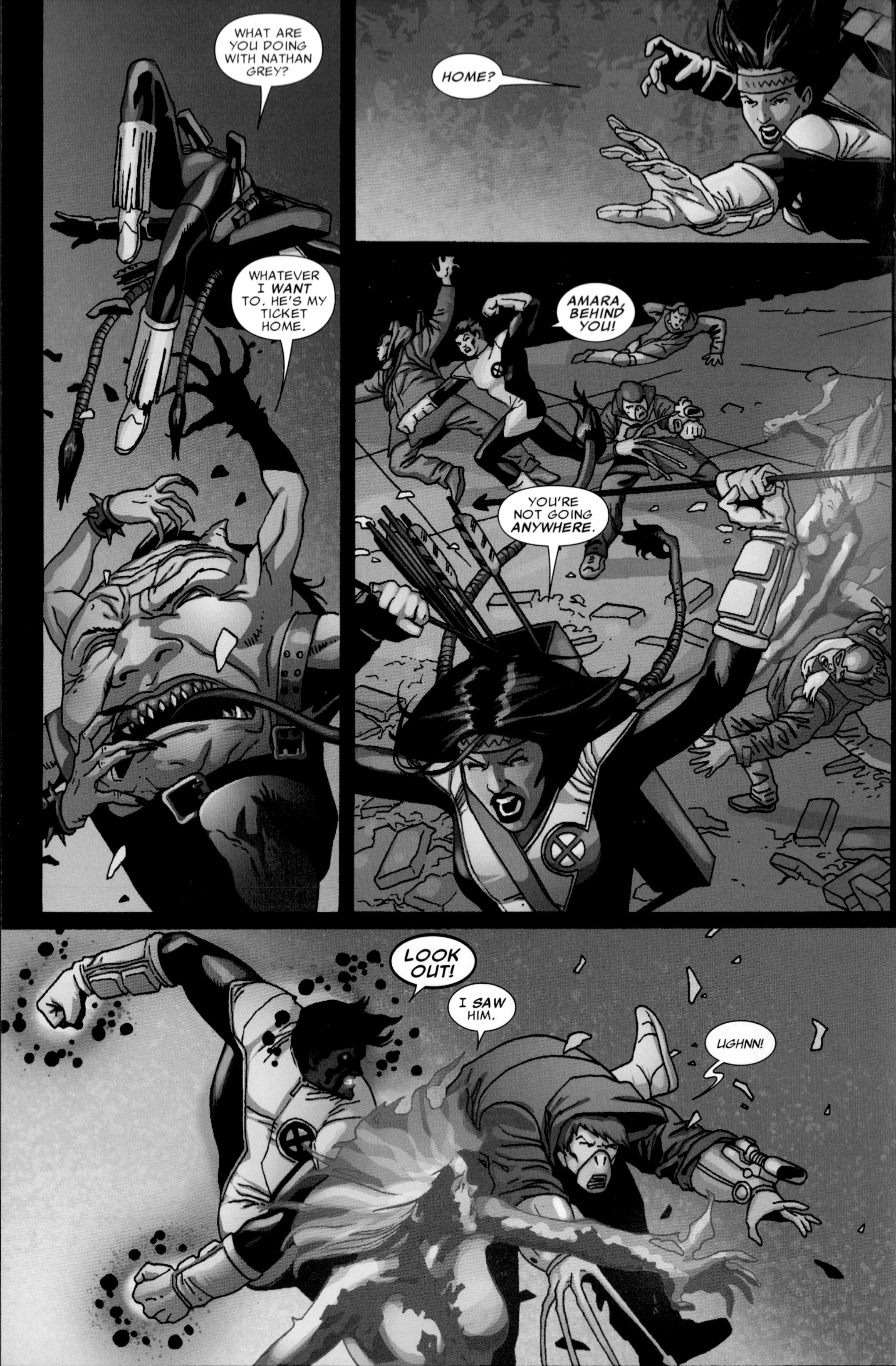
WHAT ARE YOU DOING WITH NATHAN GREY?
WHATEVER I WANT TO. HE'S MY TICKET HOME.
HOME?
AMARA, BEHIND YOU!
YOU'RE NOT GOING ANYWHERE.
LOOK OUT!
I SAW HIM.
UGHNN!

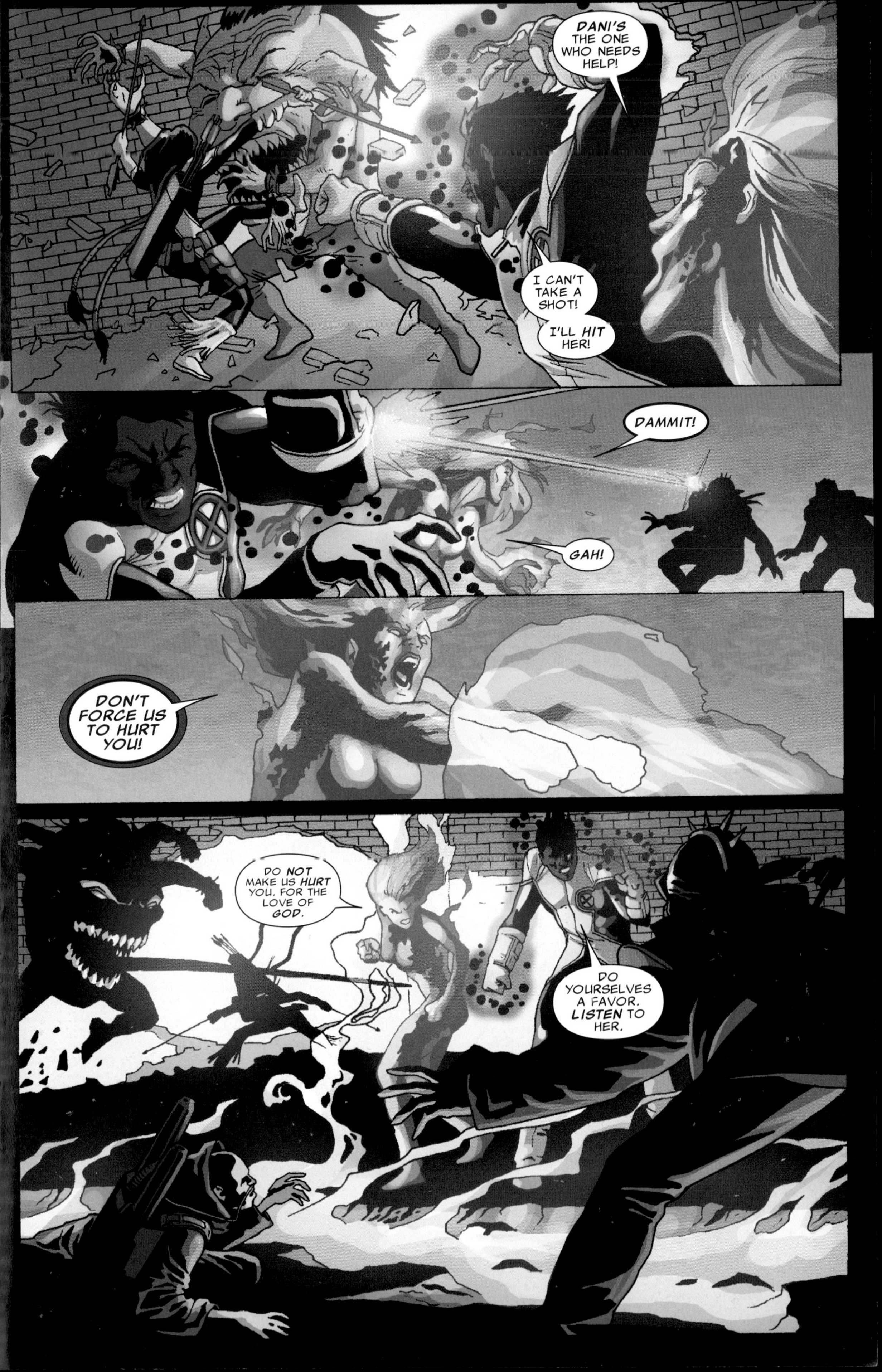
DANI'S THE ONE WHO NEEDS HELP!
I CAN'T TAKE A SHOT!
I'LL HIT HER!
DAMMIT!
GAH!
DON'T FORCE US TO HURT YOU!
DO NOT MAKE US HURT YOU. FOR THE LOVE OF GOD.
DO YOURSELVES A FAVOR. LISTEN TO HER.

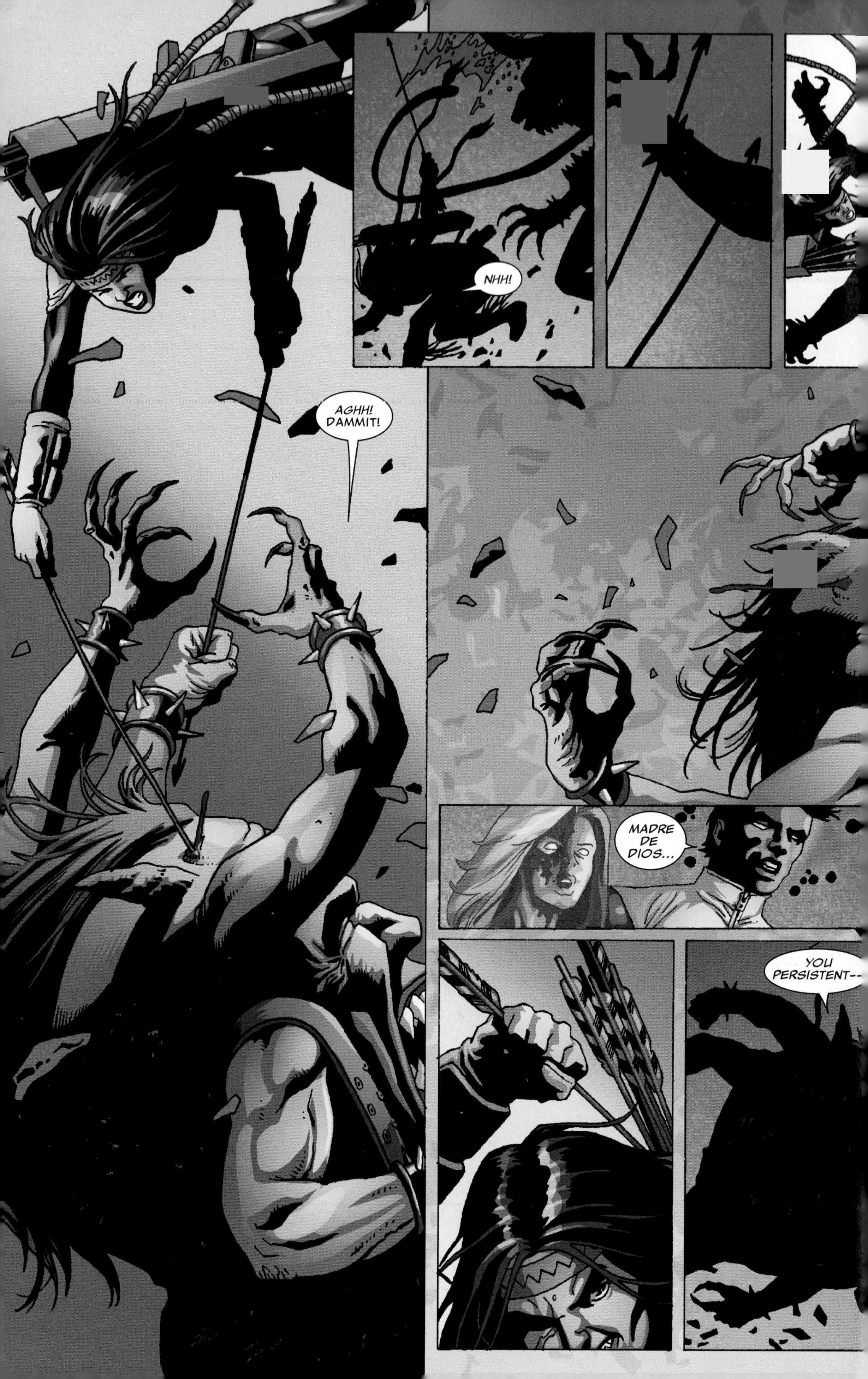

NHH!
AGHH! DAMMIT!
MADRE DE DIOS...
YOU PERSISTENT--

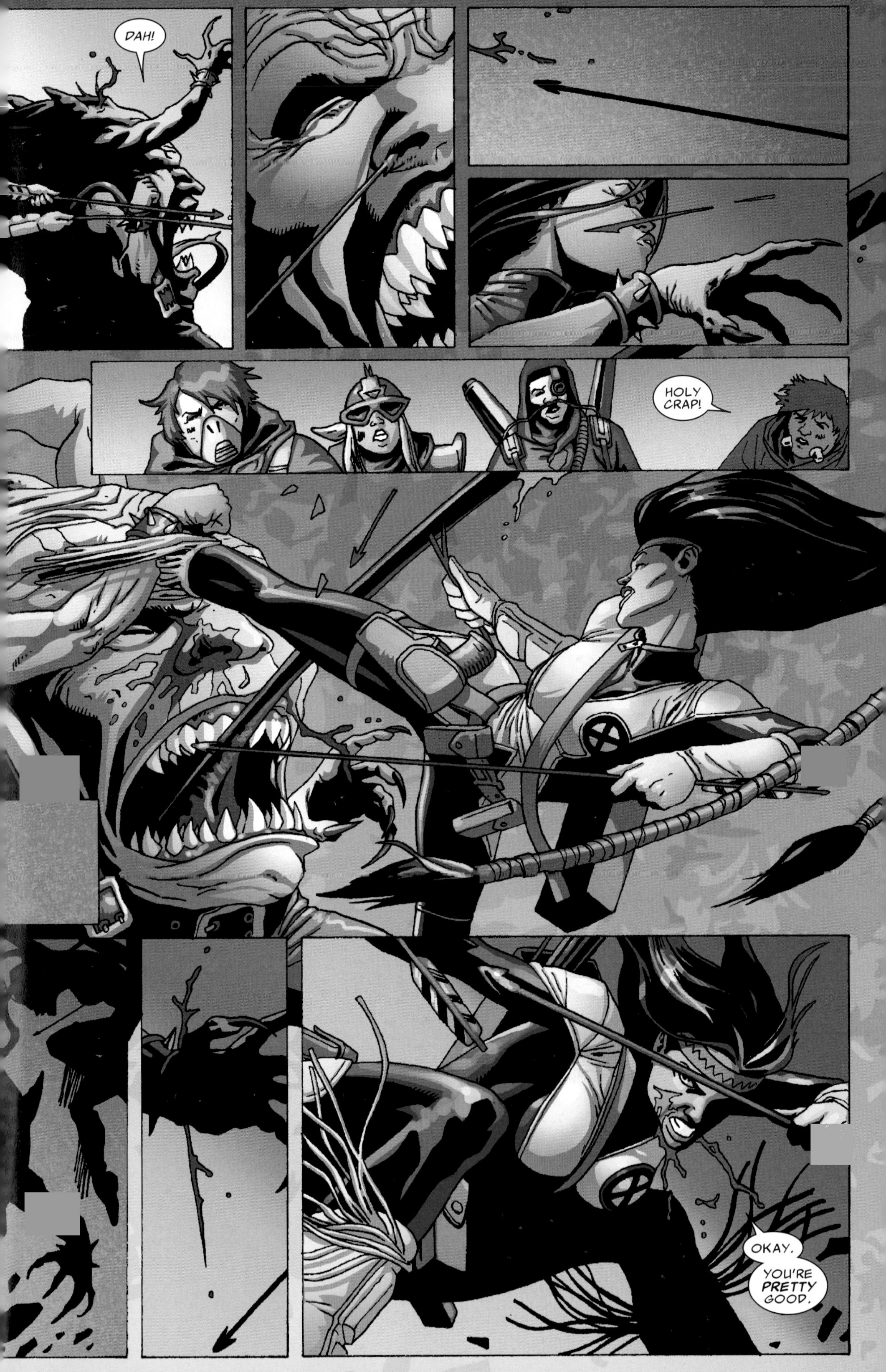
DAH!
HOLY CRAP!
OKAY. YOU'RE PRETTY GOOD.

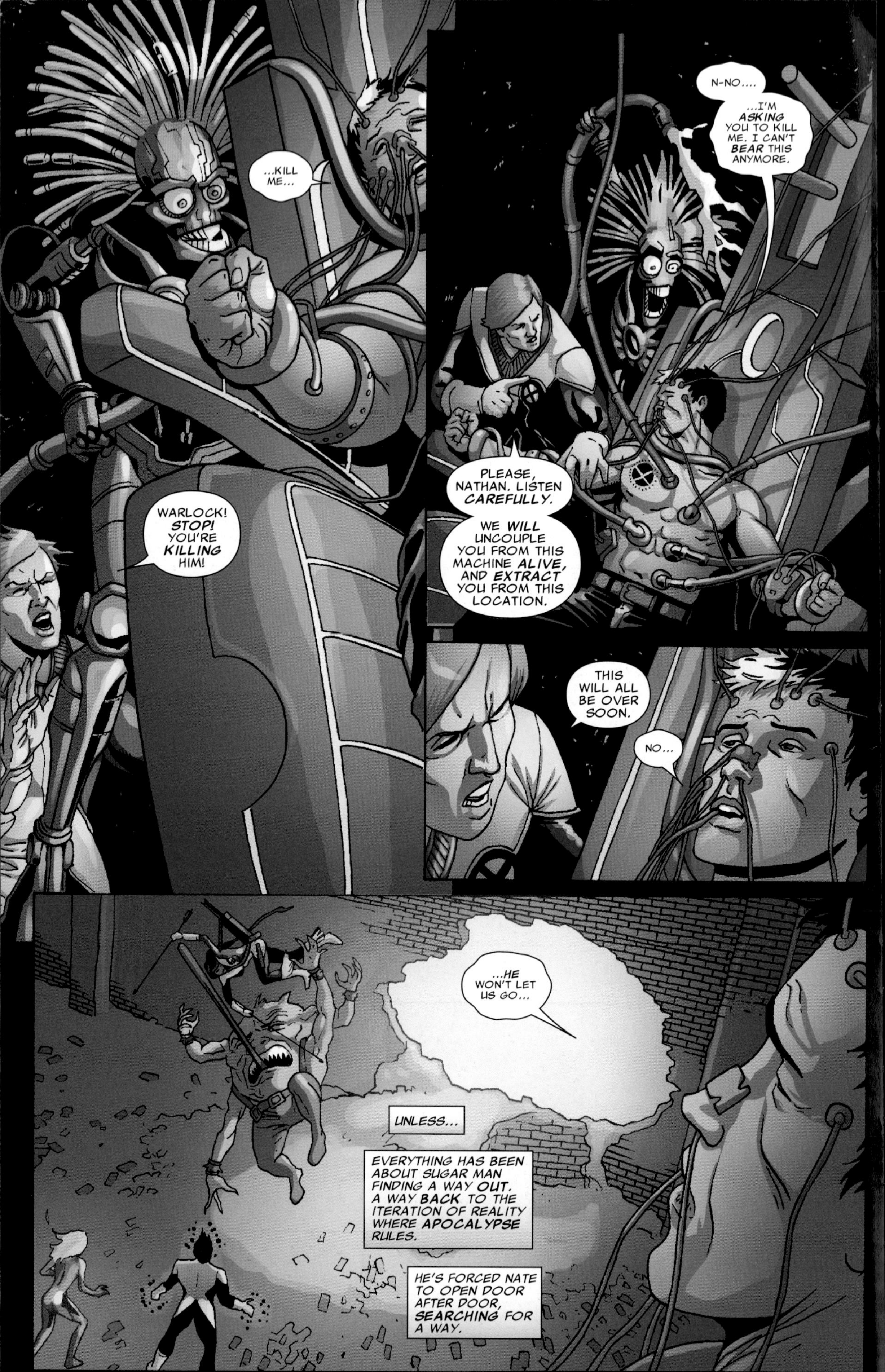

...KILL ME...
WARLOCK! STOP! YOU'RE KILLING HIM!
N-NO....
...I'M ASKING YOU TO KILL ME. I CAN'T BEAR THIS ANYMORE.
PLEASE, NATHAN. LISTEN CAREFULLY.
WE WILL UNCOUPLE YOU FROM THIS MACHINE ALIVE, AND EXTRACT YOU FROM THIS LOCATION.
THIS WILL ALL BE OVER SOON.
NO...
...HE WON'T LET US GO...
UNLESS...
EVERYTHING HAS BEEN ABOUT SUGAR MAN FINDING A WAY OUT. A WAY BACK TO THE ITERATION OF REALITY WHERE APOCALYPSE RULES.
HE'S FORCED NATE TO OPEN DOOR AFTER DOOR, SEARCHING FOR A WAY.

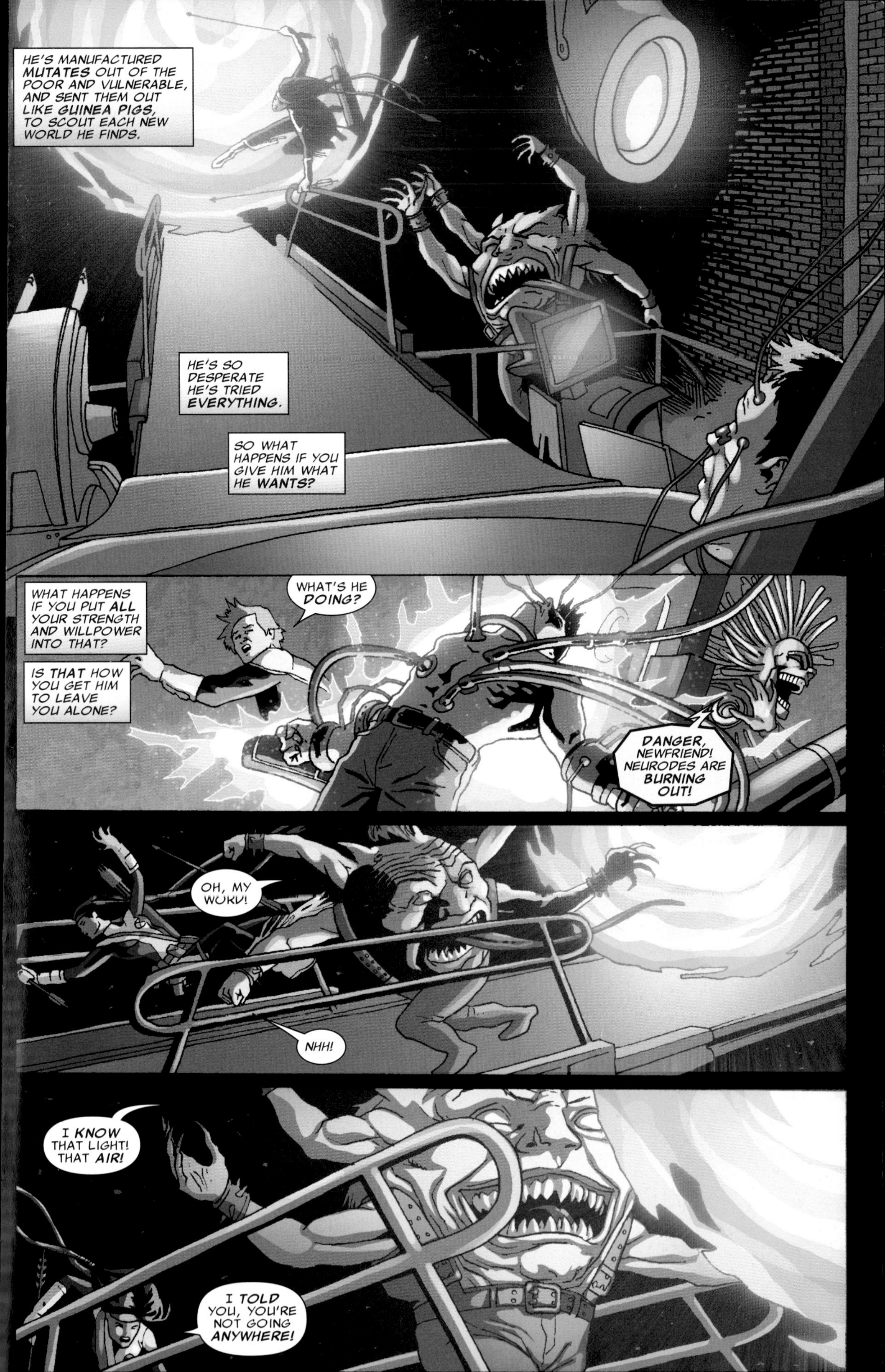
HE'S MANUFACTURED MUTATES OUT OF THE POOR AND VULNERABLE, AND SENT THEM OUT LIKE GUINEA PIGS, TO SCOUT EACH NEW WORLD HE FINDS.
HE'S SO DESPERATE HE'S TRIED EVERYTHING.
SO WHAT HAPPENS IF YOU GIVE HIM WHAT HE WANTS?
WHAT HAPPENS IF YOU PUT ALL YOUR STRENGTH AND WILLPOWER INTO THAT?
WHAT'S HE DOING?
IS THAT HOW YOU GET HIM TO LEAVE YOU ALONE?
DANGER, NEWFRIEND! NEURODES ARE BURNING OUT!
OH, MY WORD!
NHH!
I KNOW THAT LIGHT! THAT AIR!
I TOLD YOU, YOU'RE NOT GOING ANYWHERE!

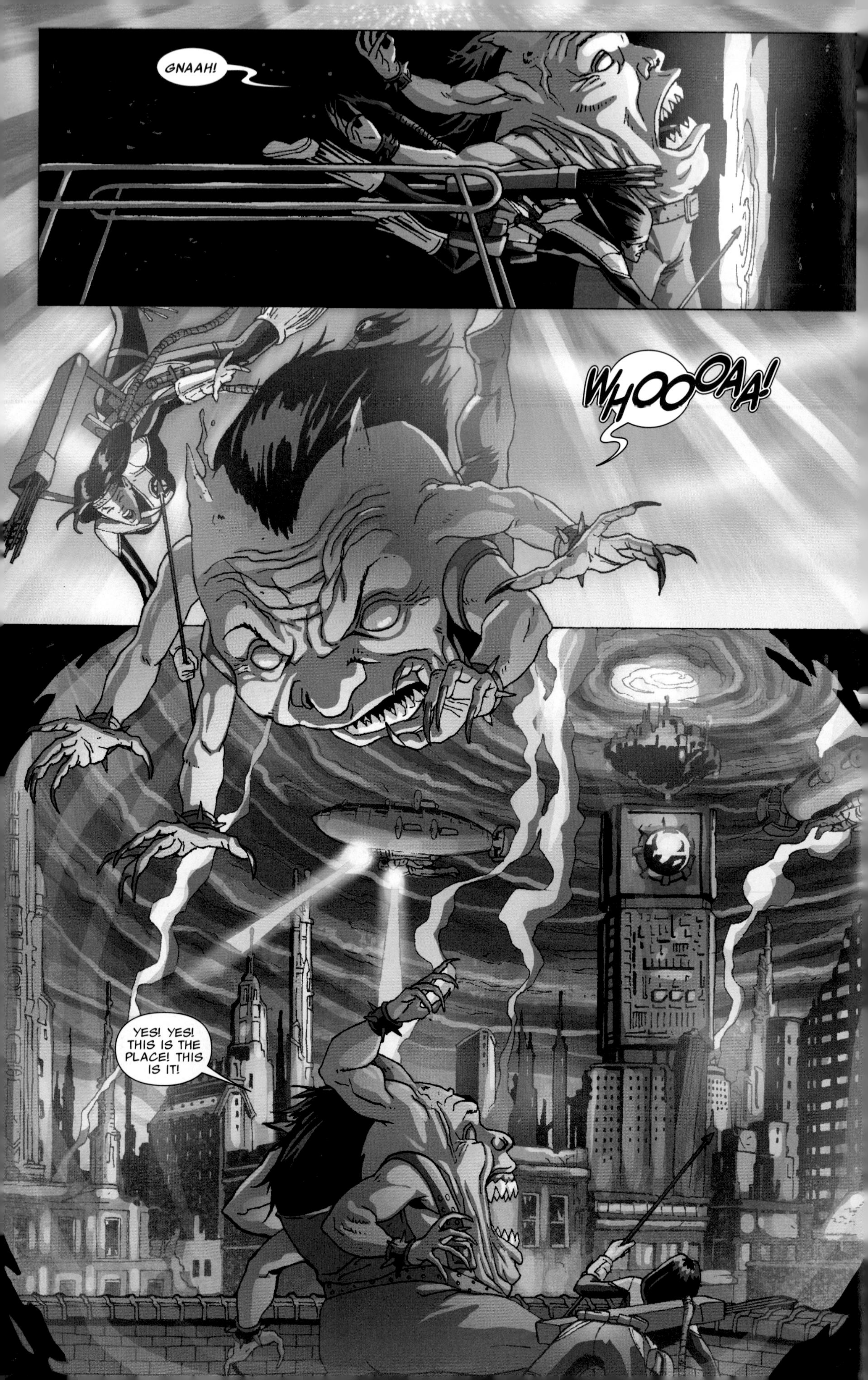
GNAAH!
WHOOOOAA!
YES! YES! THIS IS THE PLACE! THIS IS IT!

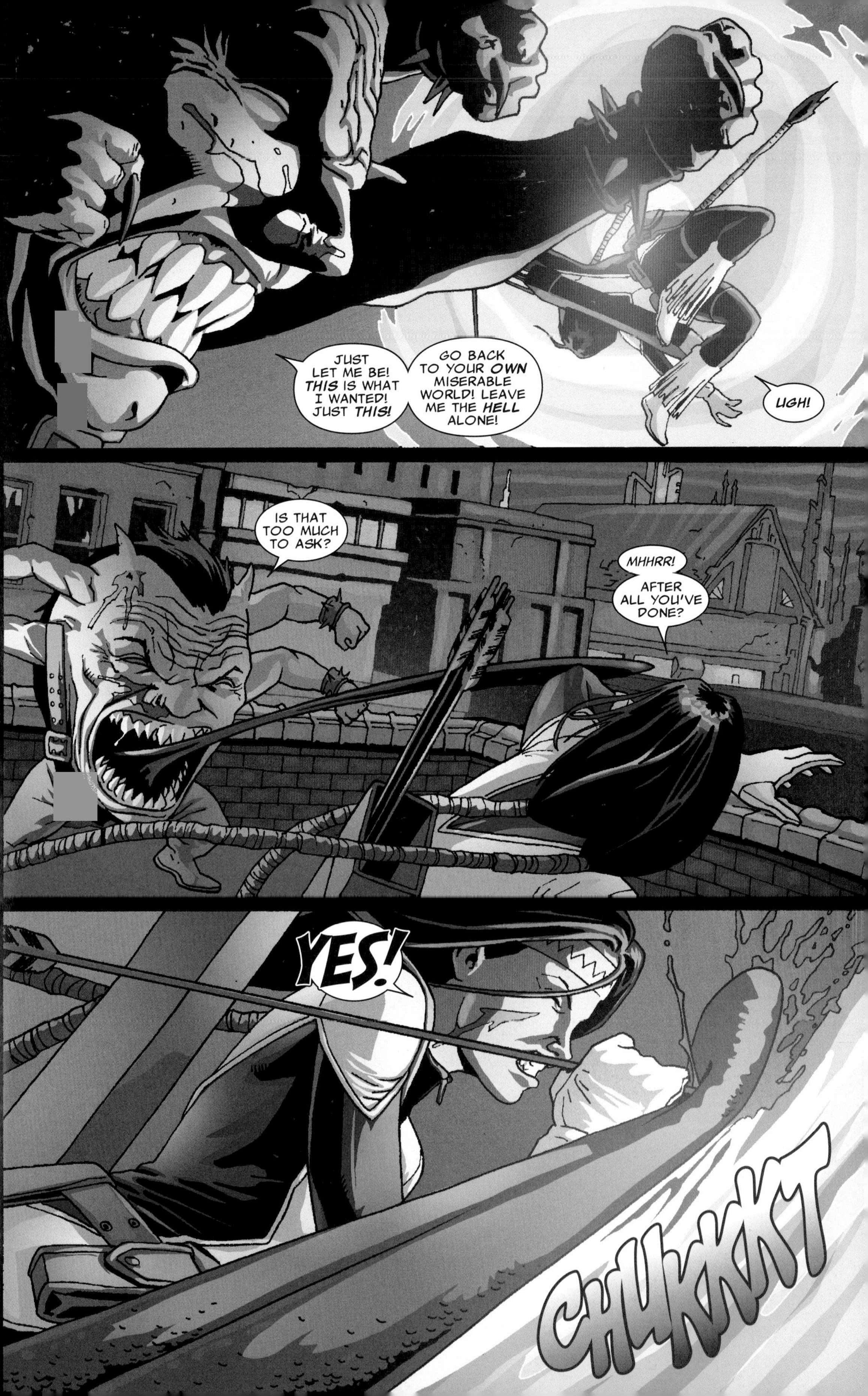
JUST LET ME BE! THIS IS WHAT I WANTED! JUST THIS!
GO BACK TO YOUR OWN MISERABLE WORLD! LEAVE ME THE HELL ALONE!
UGH!
IS THAT TOO MUCH TO ASK?
MHHRR! AFTER ALL YOU'VE DONE?
YES!
CHUKKKKT

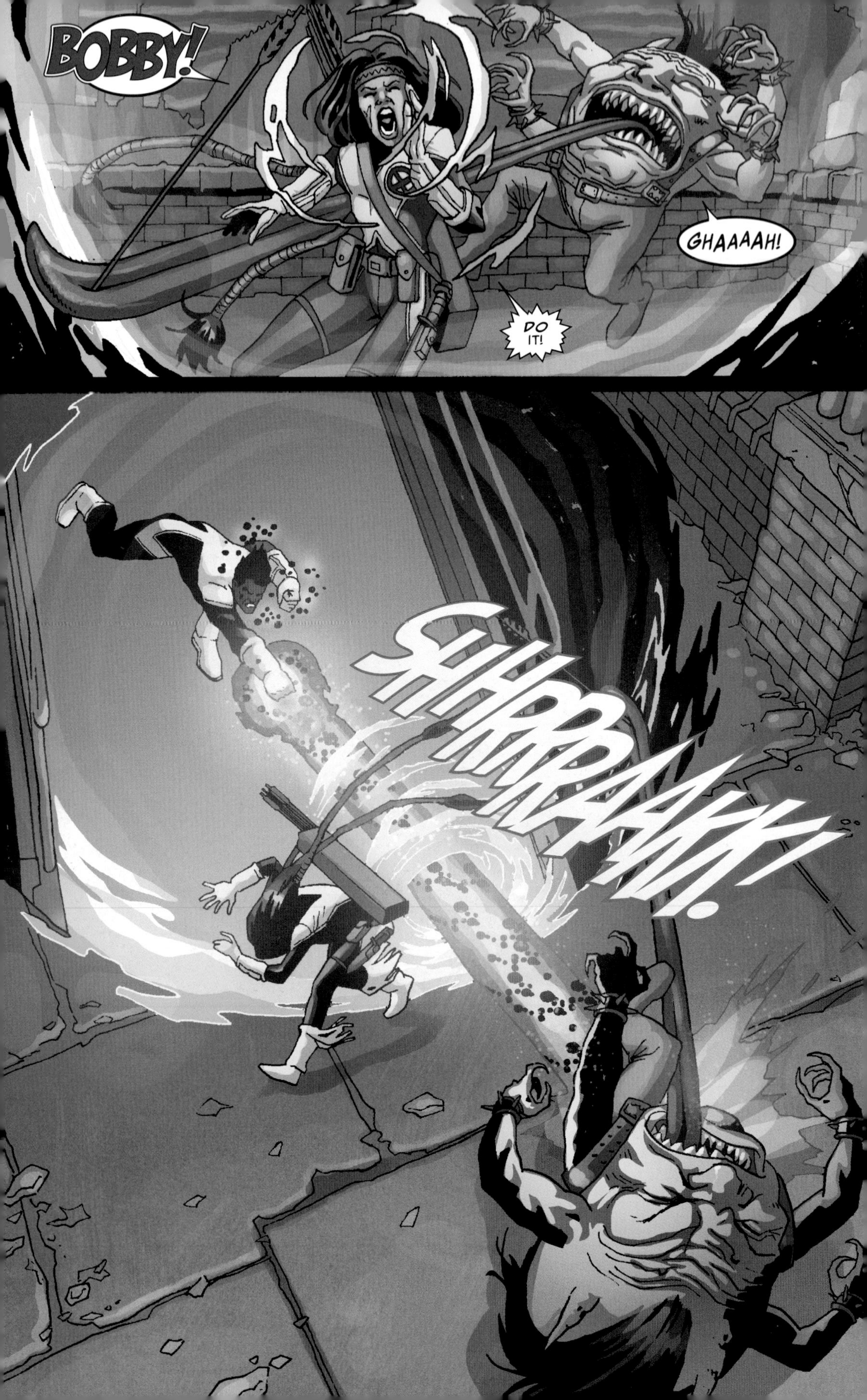
BOBBY!
GHAAAAH!
DO IT!
SHHRRAAKK!

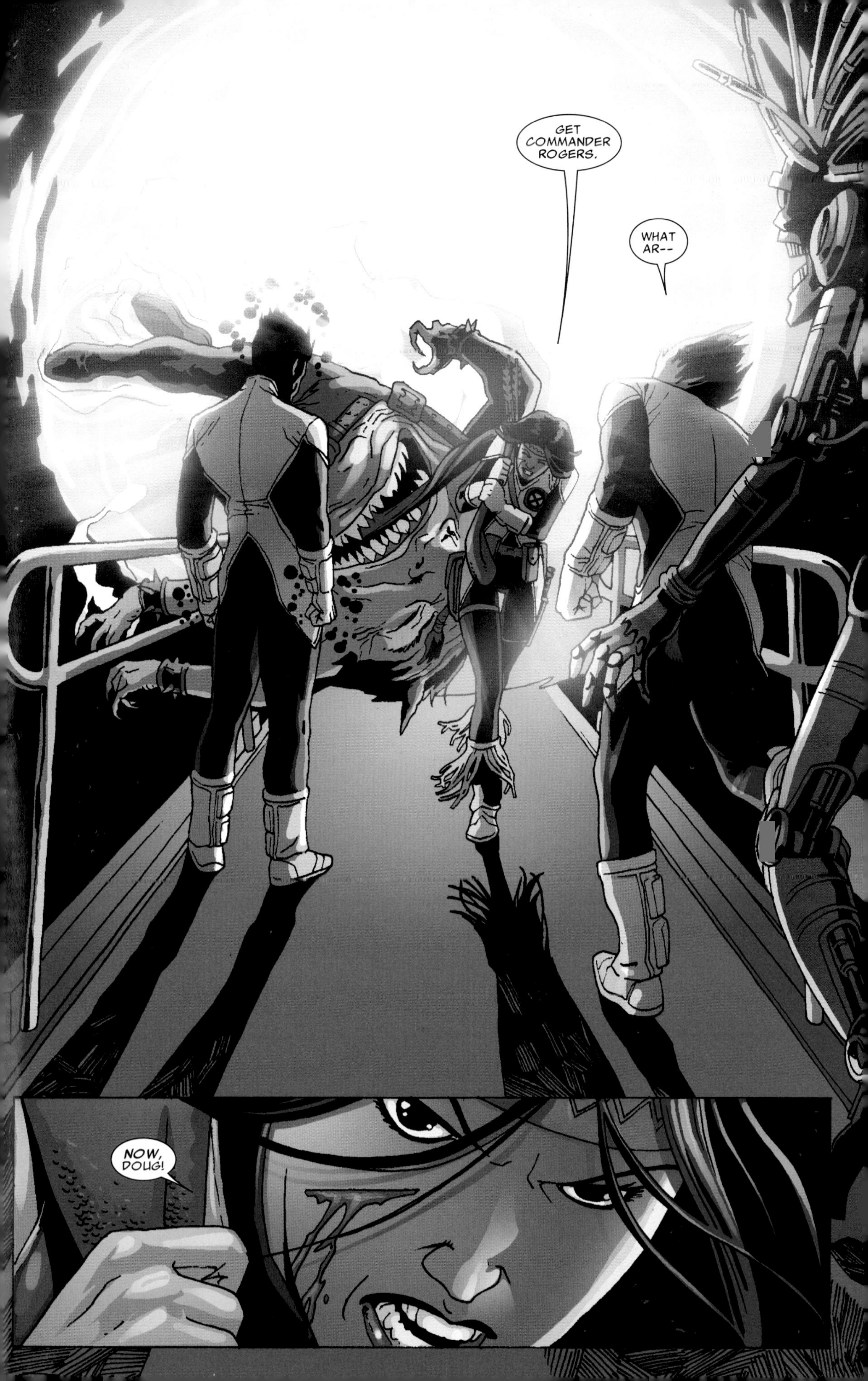
GET COMMANDER ROGERS.
WHAT AR--
NOW, DOUG!

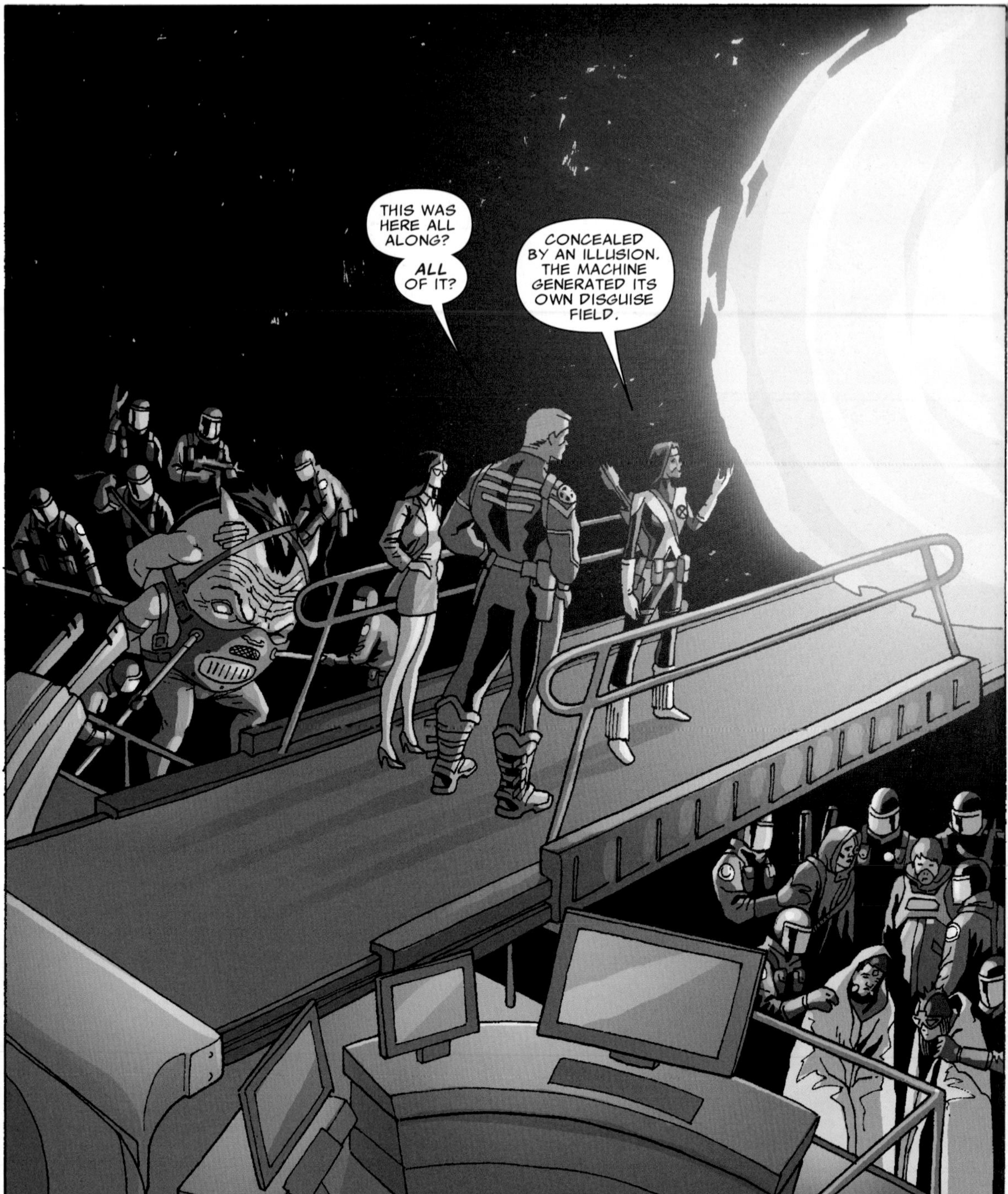
THIS WAS HERE ALL ALONG? ALL OF IT?
CONCEALED BY AN ILLUSION. THE MACHINE GENERATED ITS OWN DISGUISE FIELD.

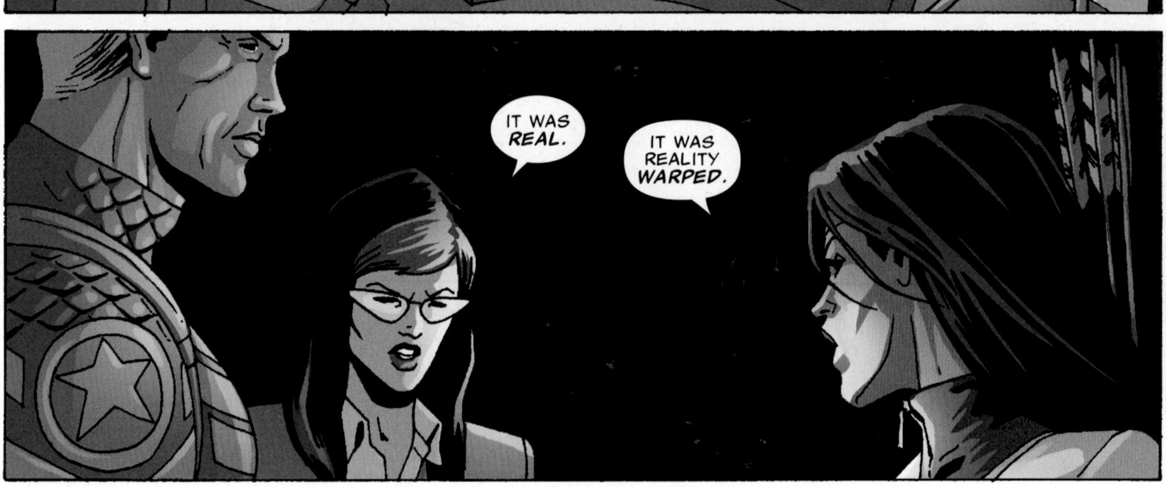
IT WAS REAL.
IT WAS REALITY WARPED.

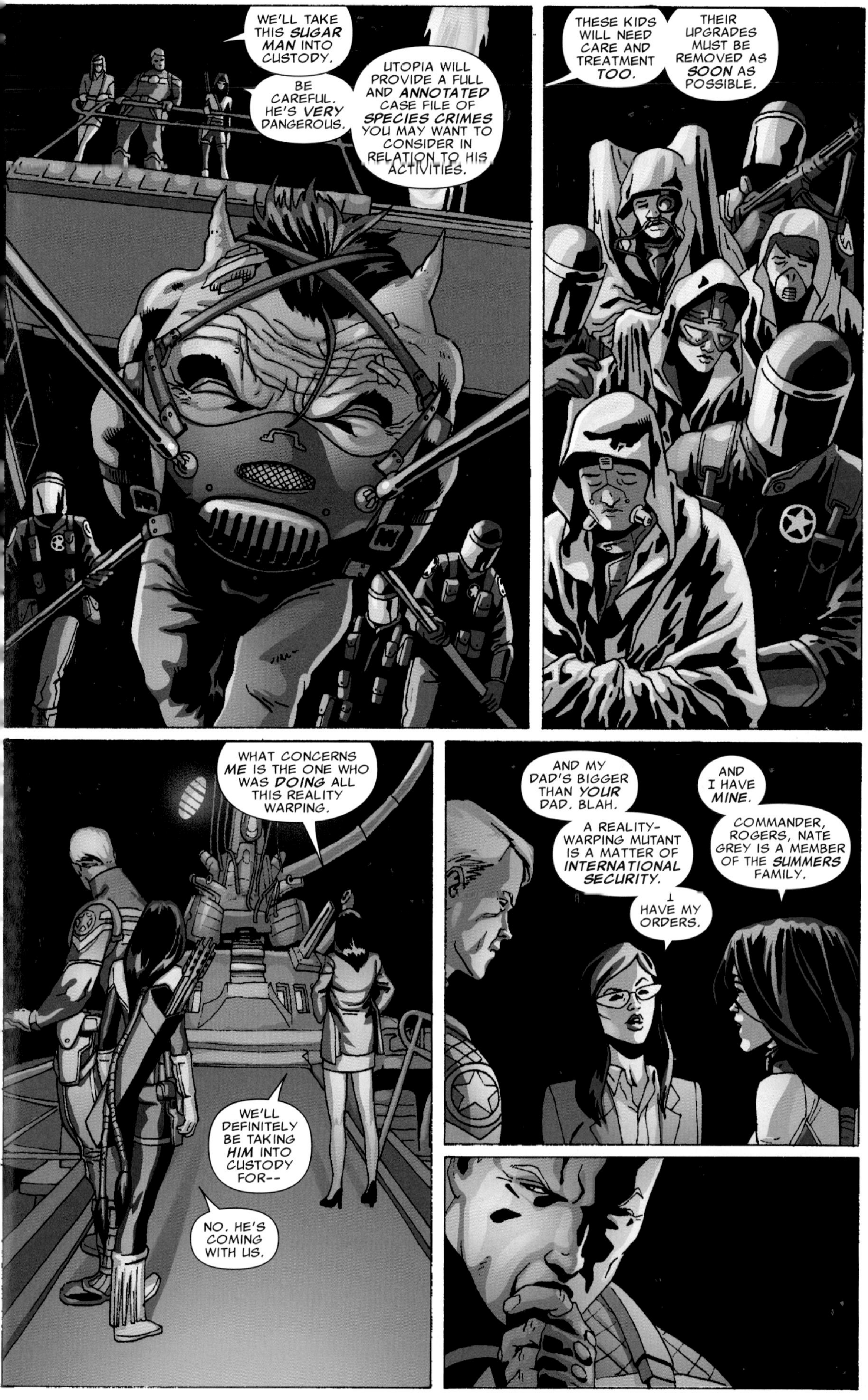
WE'LL TAKE THIS SUGAR MAN INTO CUSTODY.
BE CAREFUL. HE'S VERY DANGEROUS.
UTOPIA WILL PROVIDE A FULL AND ANNOTATED CASE FILE OF SPECIES CRIMES YOU MAY WANT TO CONSIDER IN RELATION TO HIS ACTIVITIES.
THESE KIDS WILL NEED CARE AND TREATMENT TOO.
THEIR UPGRADES MUST BE REMOVED AS SOON AS POSSIBLE.
WHAT CONCERNS ME IS THE ONE WHO WAS DOING ALL THIS REALITY WARPING.
WE'LL DEFINITELY BE TAKING HIM INTO CUSTODY FOR--
NO. HE'S COMING WITH US.
AND MY DAD'S BIGGER THAN YOUR DAD. BLAH.
A REALITY-WARPING MUTANT IS A MATTER OF INTERNATIONAL SECURITY.
I HAVE MY ORDERS.
AND I HAVE MINE.
COMMANDER, ROGERS, NATE GREY IS A MEMBER OF THE SUMMERS FAMILY.

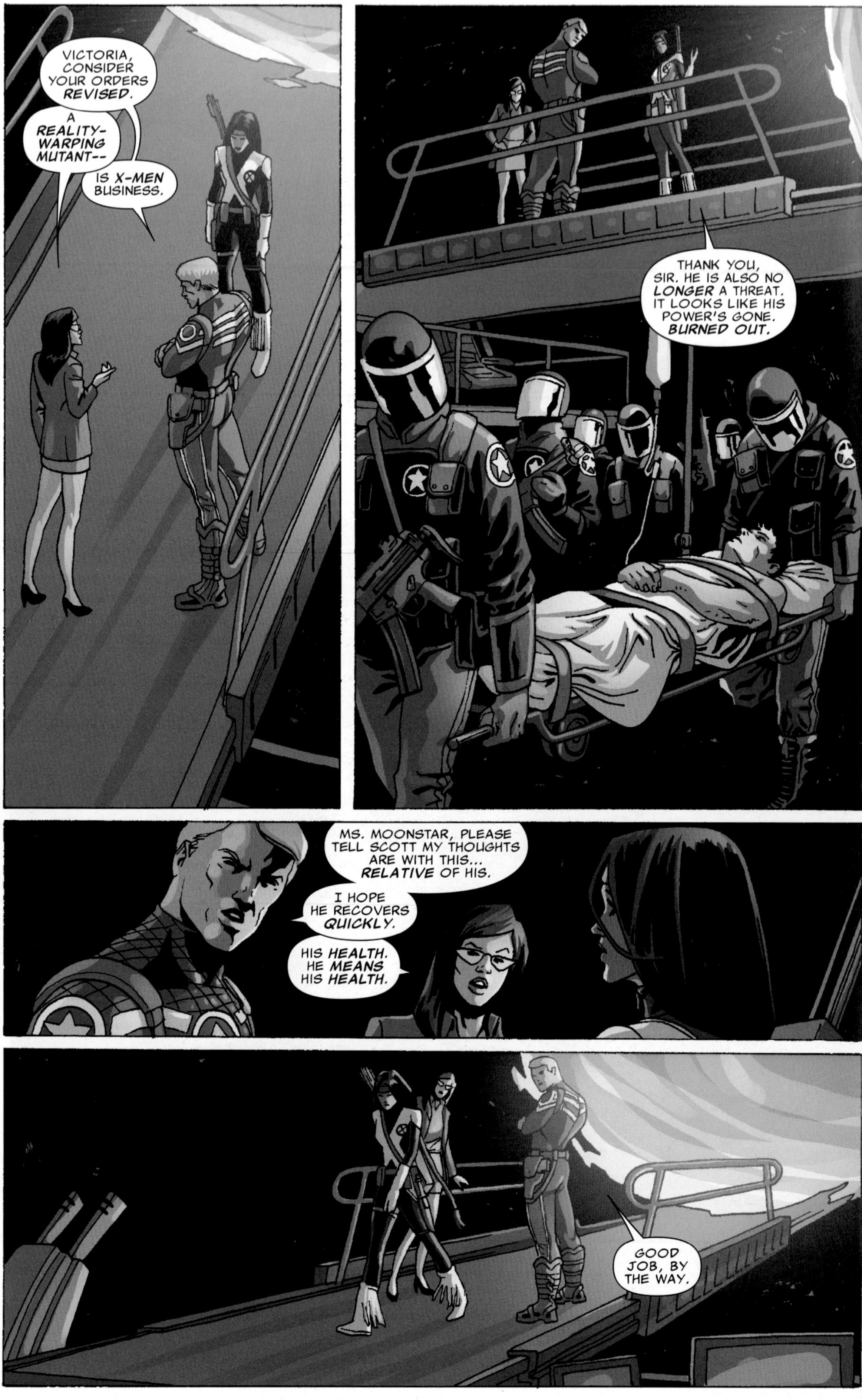
VICTORIA, CONSIDER YOUR ORDERS REVISED.
A REALITY-WARPING MUTANT--
IS X-MEN BUSINESS.
THANK YOU, SIR. HE IS ALSO NO LONGER A THREAT. IT LOOKS LIKE HIS POWER'S GONE. BURNED OUT.
MS. MOONSTAR, PLEASE TELL SCOTT MY THOUGHTS ARE WITH THIS... RELATIVE OF HIS.
I HOPE HE RECOVERS QUICKLY.
HIS HEALTH. HE MEANS HIS HEALTH.
GOOD JOB, BY THE WAY.

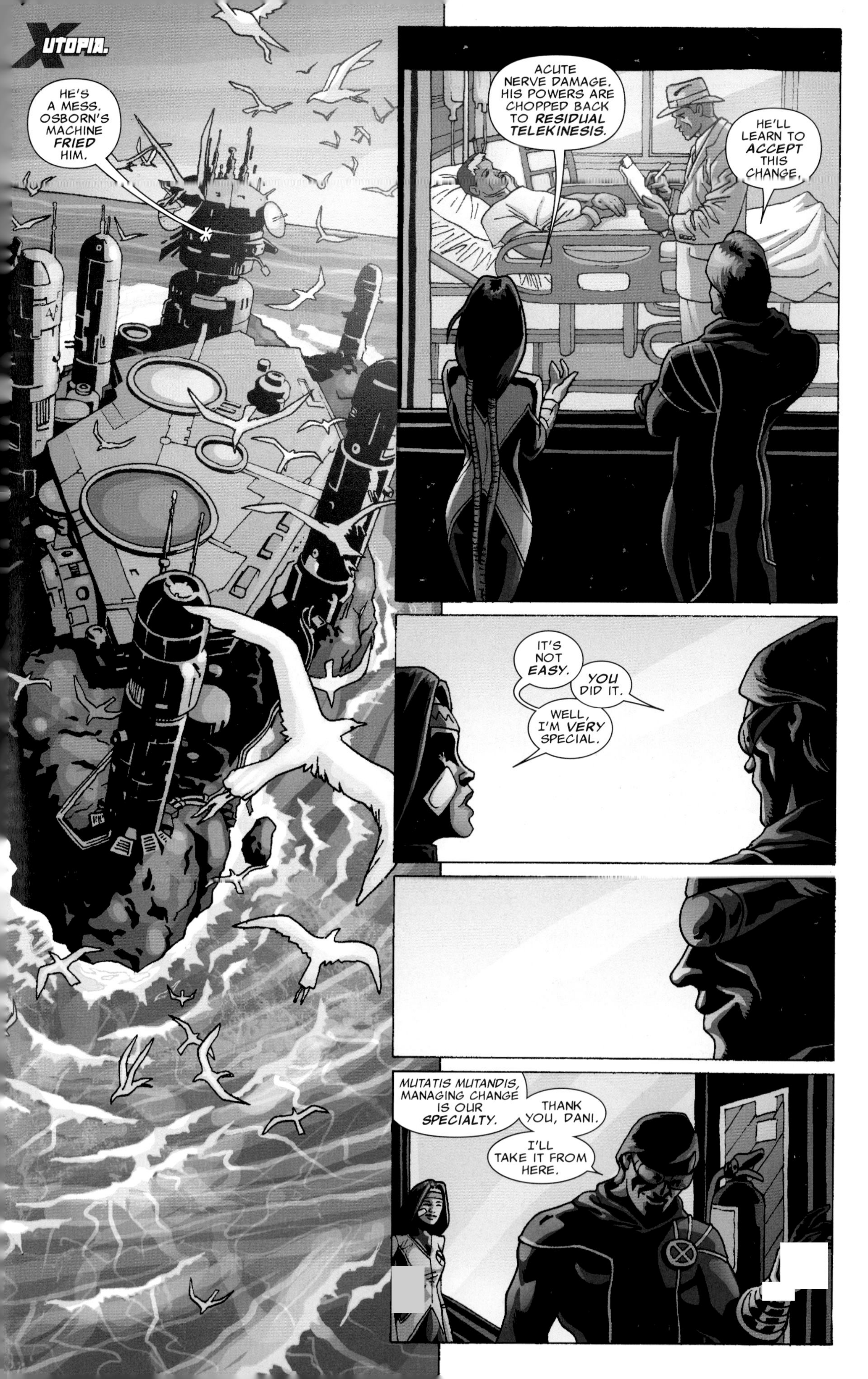
X UTOPIA.
HE'S A MESS. OSBORN'S MACHINE FRIED HIM.
ACUTE NERVE DAMAGE. HIS POWERS ARE CHOPPED BACK TO RESIDUAL TELEKINESIS.
HE'LL LEARN TO ACCEPT THIS CHANGE.
IT'S NOT EASY.
YOU DID IT.
WELL, I'M VERY SPECIAL.
MUTATIS MUTANDIS, MANAGING CHANGE IS OUR SPECIALTY.
THANK YOU, DANI.
I'LL TAKE IT FROM HERE.

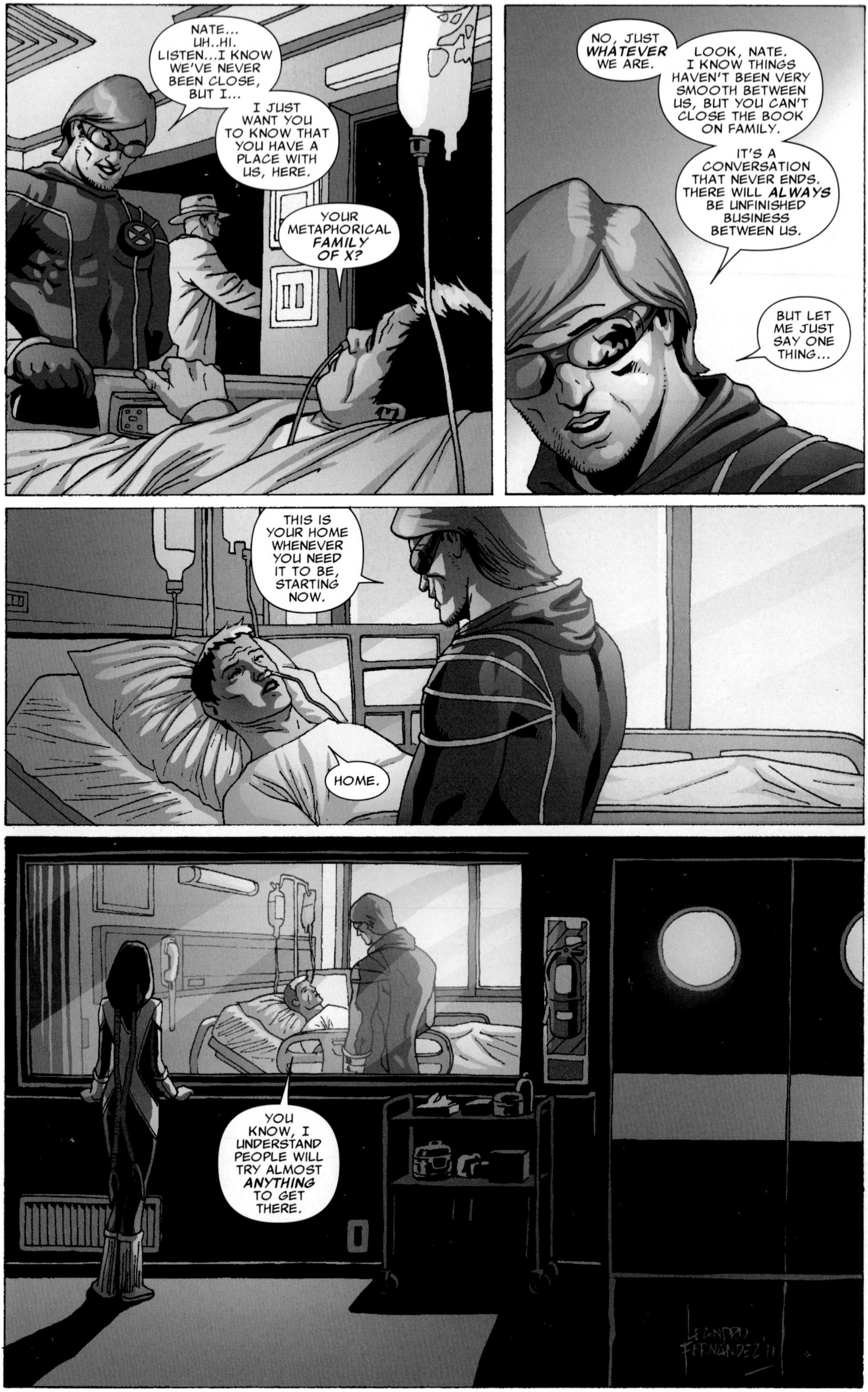
NATE... UH..HI. LISTEN...I KNOW WE'VE NEVER BEEN CLOSE, BUT I...
I JUST WANT YOU TO KNOW THAT YOU HAVE A PLACE WITH US, HERE.
YOUR METAPHORICAL FAMILY OF X?
NO, JUST WHATEVER WE ARE.
LOOK, NATE. I KNOW THINGS HAVEN'T BEEN VERY SMOOTH BETWEEN US, BUT YOU CAN'T CLOSE THE BOOK ON FAMILY.
IT'S A CONVERSATION THAT NEVER ENDS. THERE WILL ALWAYS BE UNFINISHED BUSINESS BETWEEN US.
BUT LET ME JUST SAY ONE THING...
THIS IS YOUR HOME WHENEVER YOU NEED IT TO BE, STARTING NOW.
HOME.
YOU KNOW, I UNDERSTAND PEOPLE WILL TRY ALMOST ANYTHING TO GET THERE.
LEANDRO FERNANDEZ '11

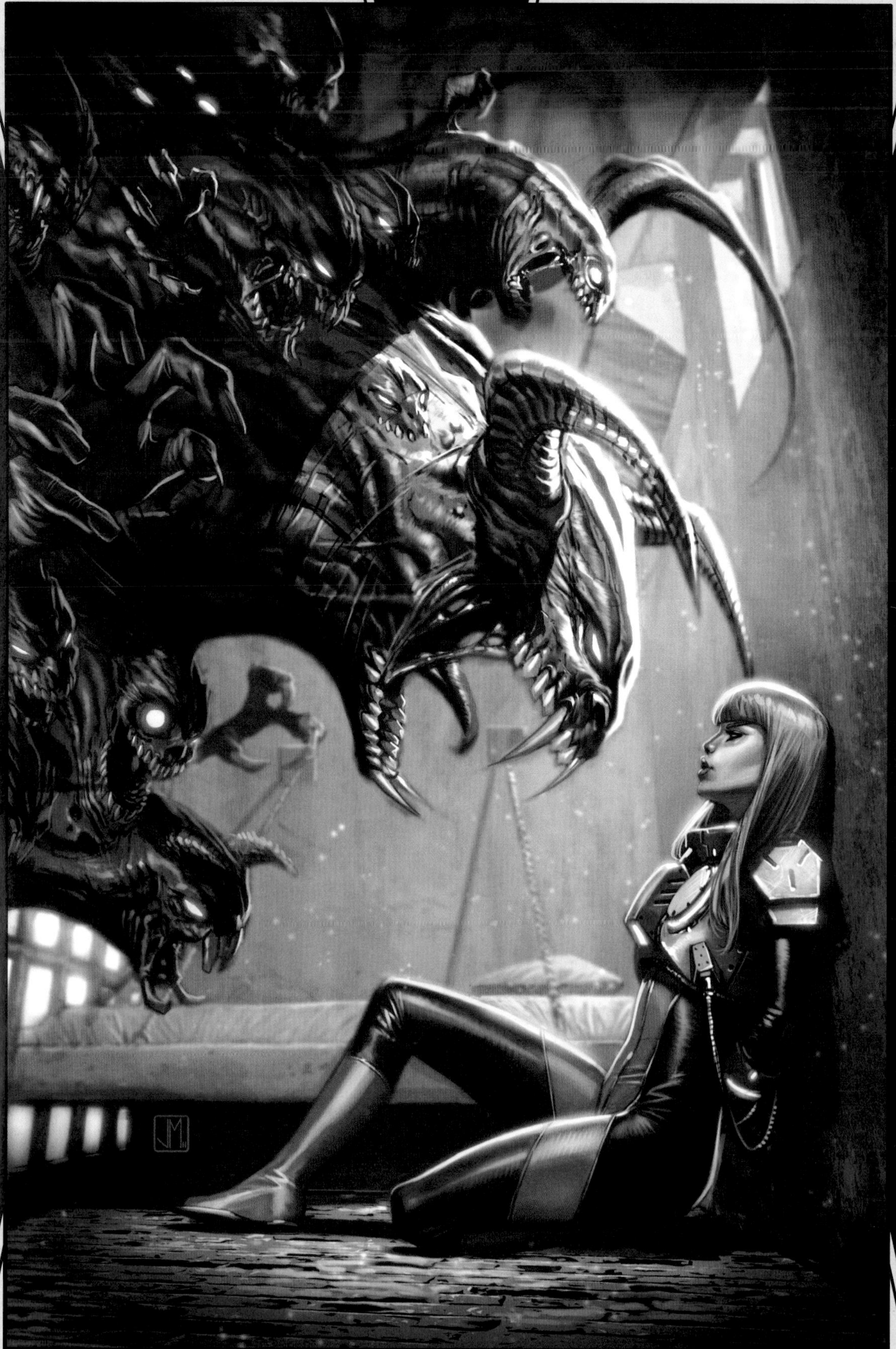

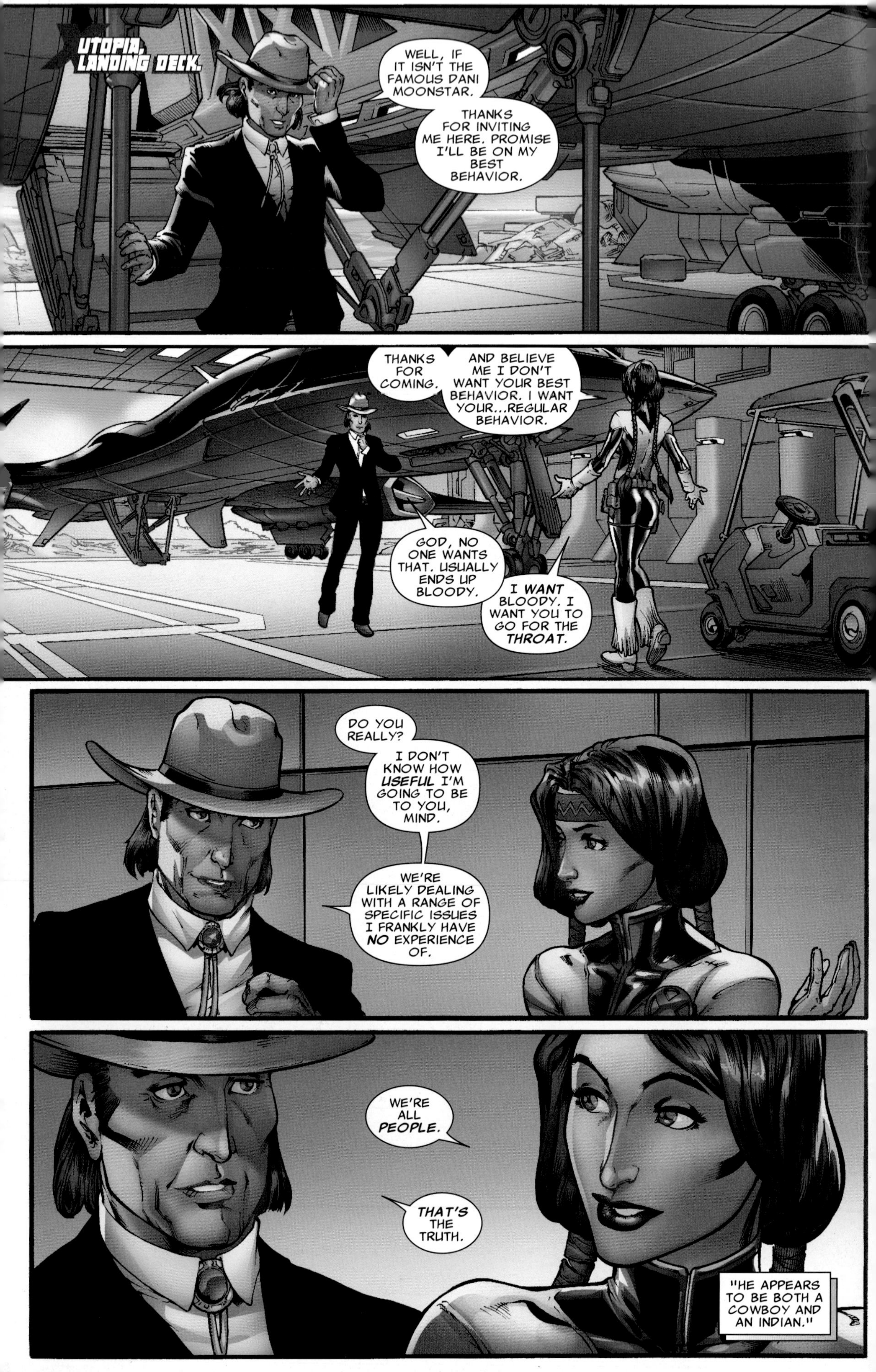
UTOPIA, LANDING DECK.
WELL, IF IT ISN'T THE FAMOUS DANI MOONSTAR.
THANKS FOR INVITING ME HERE. PROMISE I'LL BE ON MY BEST BEHAVIOR.
THANKS FOR COMING.
AND BELIEVE ME I DON'T WANT YOUR BEST BEHAVIOR. I WANT YOUR...REGULAR BEHAVIOR.
GOD, NO ONE WANTS THAT. USUALLY ENDS UP BLOODY.
I WANT BLOODY. I WANT YOU TO GO FOR THE THROAT.
DO YOU REALLY?
I DON'T KNOW HOW USEFUL I'M GOING TO BE TO YOU, MIND.
WE'RE LIKELY DEALING WITH A RANGE OF SPECIFIC ISSUES I FRANKLY HAVE NO EXPERIENCE OF.
WE'RE ALL PEOPLE.
THAT'S THE TRUTH.
"HE APPEARS TO BE BOTH A COWBOY AND AN INDIAN."

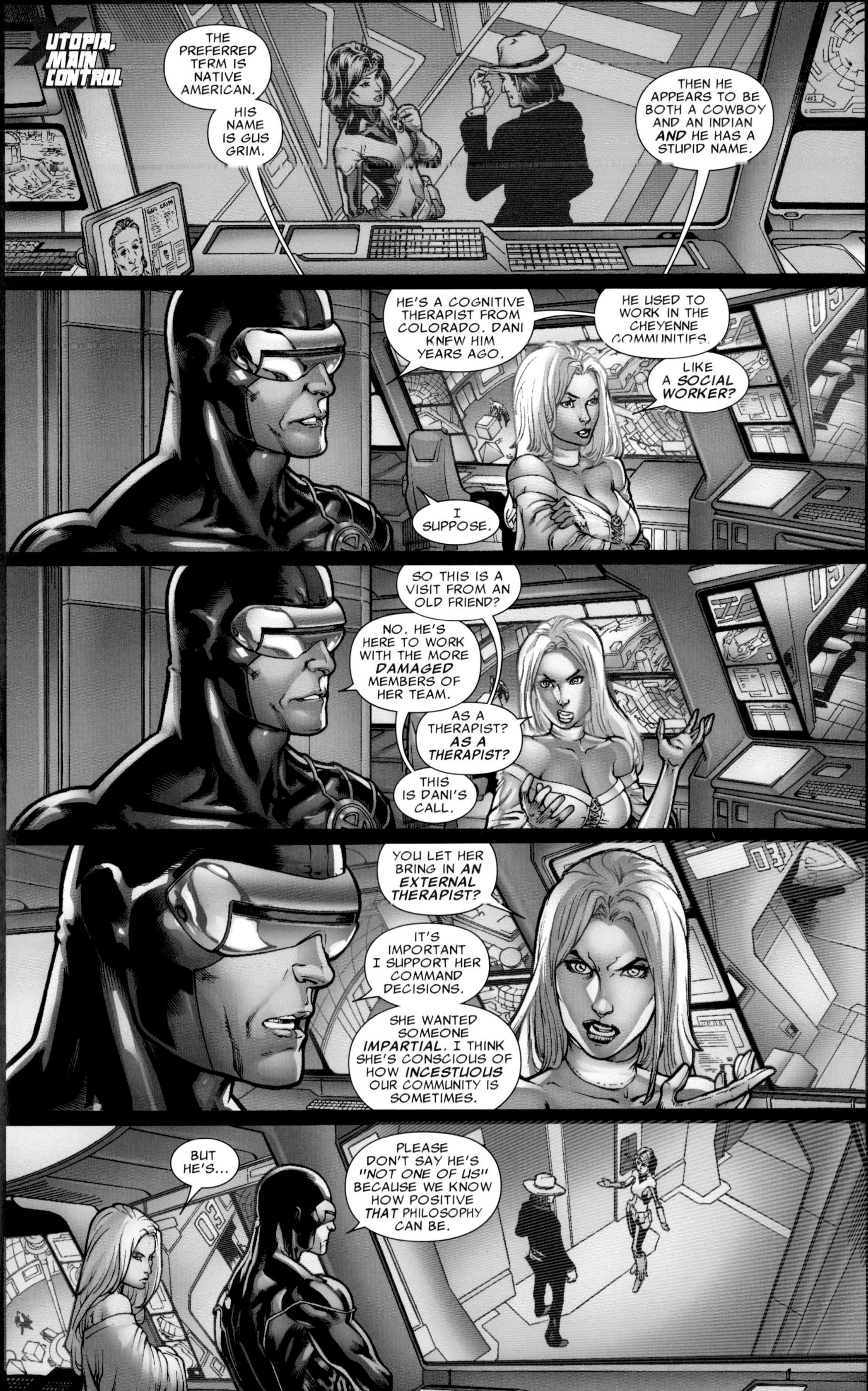
UTOPIA, MAIN CONTROL
THE PREFERRED TERM IS NATIVE AMERICAN.
HIS NAME IS GUS GRIM.
THEN HE APPEARS TO BE BOTH A COWBOY AND AN INDIAN AND HE HAS A STUPID NAME.
HE'S A COGNITIVE THERAPIST FROM COLORADO. DANI KNEW HIM YEARS AGO.
HE USED TO WORK IN THE CHEYENNE COMMUNITIES.
LIKE A SOCIAL WORKER?
I SUPPOSE.
SO THIS IS A VISIT FROM AN OLD FRIEND?
NO. HE'S HERE TO WORK WITH THE MORE DAMAGED MEMBERS OF HER TEAM.
AS A THERAPIST? AS A THERAPIST?
THIS IS DANI'S CALL.
YOU LET HER BRING IN AN EXTERNAL THERAPIST?
IT'S IMPORTANT I SUPPORT HER COMMAND DECISIONS.
SHE WANTED SOMEONE IMPARTIAL. I THINK SHE'S CONSCIOUS OF HOW INCESTUOUS OUR COMMUNITY IS SOMETIMES.
BUT HE'S...
PLEASE DON'T SAY HE'S "NOT ONE OF US" BECAUSE WE KNOW HOW POSITIVE THAT PHILOSOPHY CAN BE.

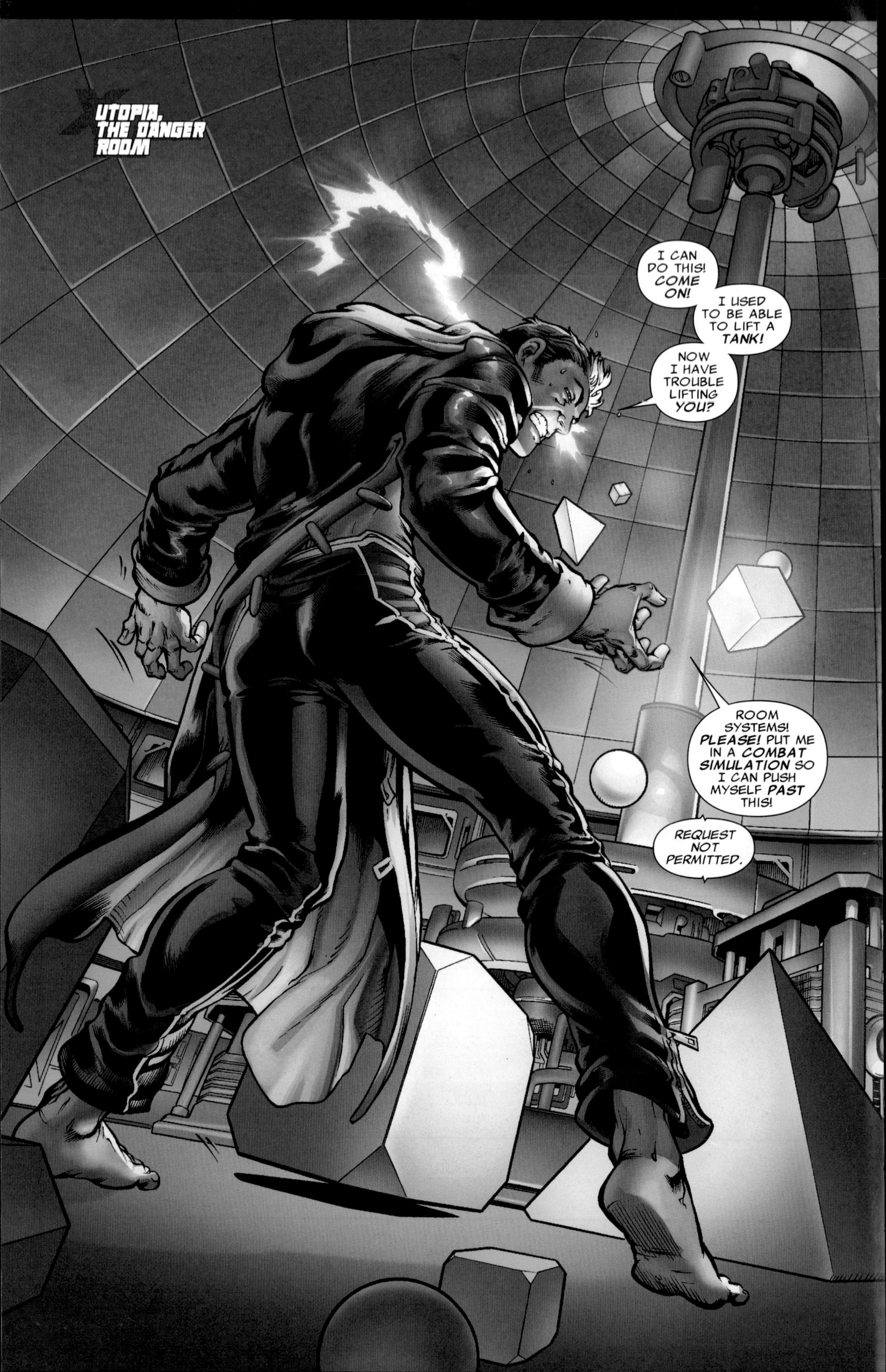
UTOPIA, THE DANGER ROOM
I CAN DO THIS! COME ON!
I USED TO BE ABLE TO LIFT A TANK!
NOW I HAVE TROUBLE LIFTING YOU?
ROOM SYSTEMS! PLEASE! PUT ME IN A COMBAT SIMULATION SO I CAN PUSH MYSELF PAST THIS!
REQUEST NOT PERMITTED.

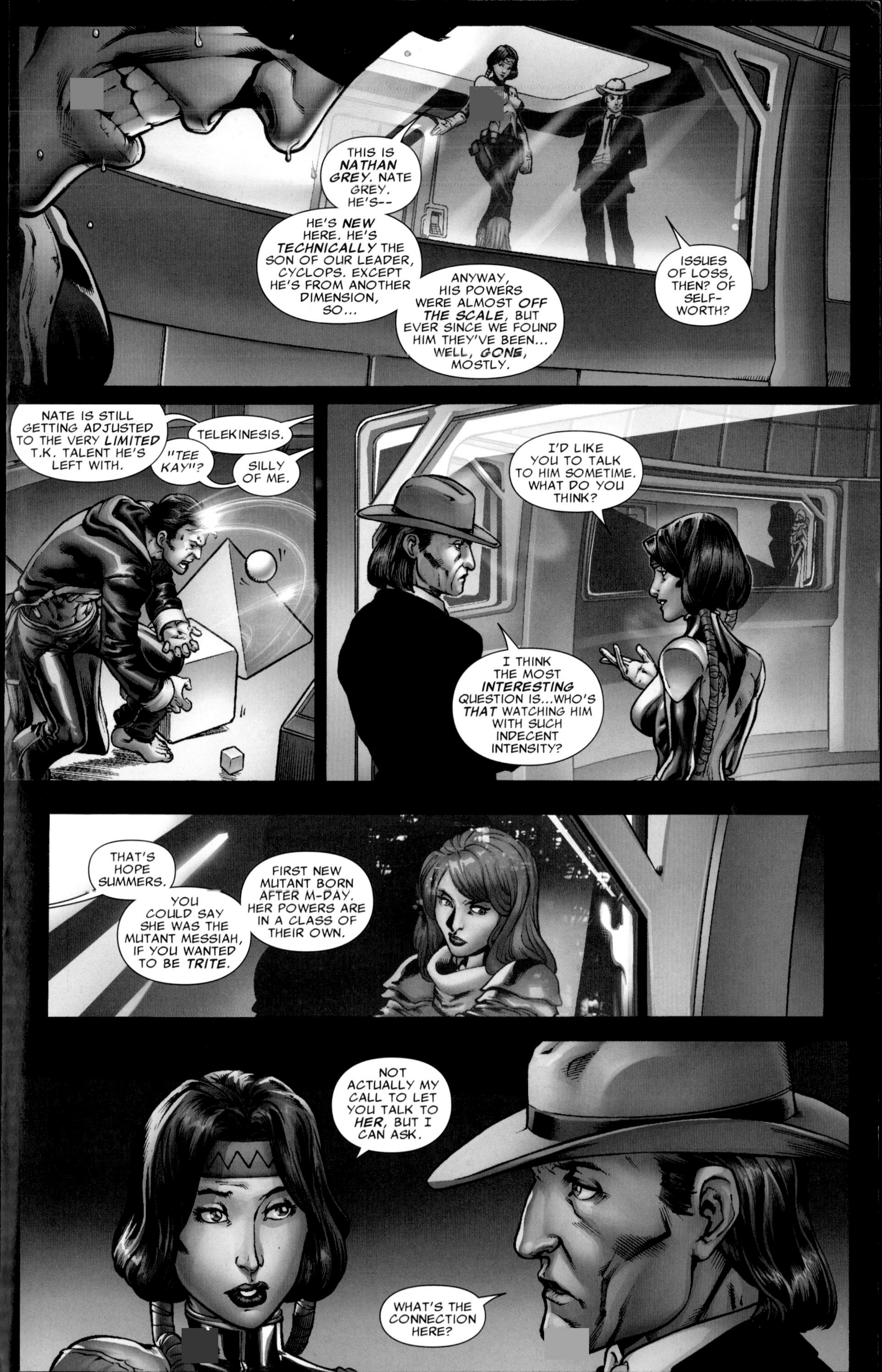
THIS IS NATHAN GREY. NATE GREY. HE'S--
HE'S NEW HERE. HE'S TECHNICALLY THE SON OF OUR LEADER, CYCLOPS. EXCEPT HE'S FROM ANOTHER DIMENSION, SO...
ANYWAY, HIS POWERS WERE ALMOST OFF THE SCALE, BUT EVER SINCE WE FOUND HIM THEY'VE BEEN... WELL, GONE, MOSTLY.
ISSUES OF LOSS, THEN? OF SELF-WORTH?
NATE IS STILL GETTING ADJUSTED TO THE VERY LIMITED T.K. TALENT HE'S LEFT WITH.
TELEKINESIS.
"TEE KAY"?
SILLY OF ME.
I'D LIKE YOU TO TALK TO HIM SOMETIME. WHAT DO YOU THINK?
I THINK THE MOST INTERESTING QUESTION IS...WHO'S THAT WATCHING HIM WITH SUCH INDECENT INTENSITY?
THAT'S HOPE SUMMERS.
YOU COULD SAY SHE WAS THE MUTANT MESSIAH, IF YOU WANTED TO BE TRITE.
FIRST NEW MUTANT BORN AFTER M-DAY. HER POWERS ARE IN A CLASS OF THEIR OWN.
NOT ACTUALLY MY CALL TO LET YOU TALK TO HER, BUT I CAN ASK.
WHAT'S THE CONNECTION HERE?

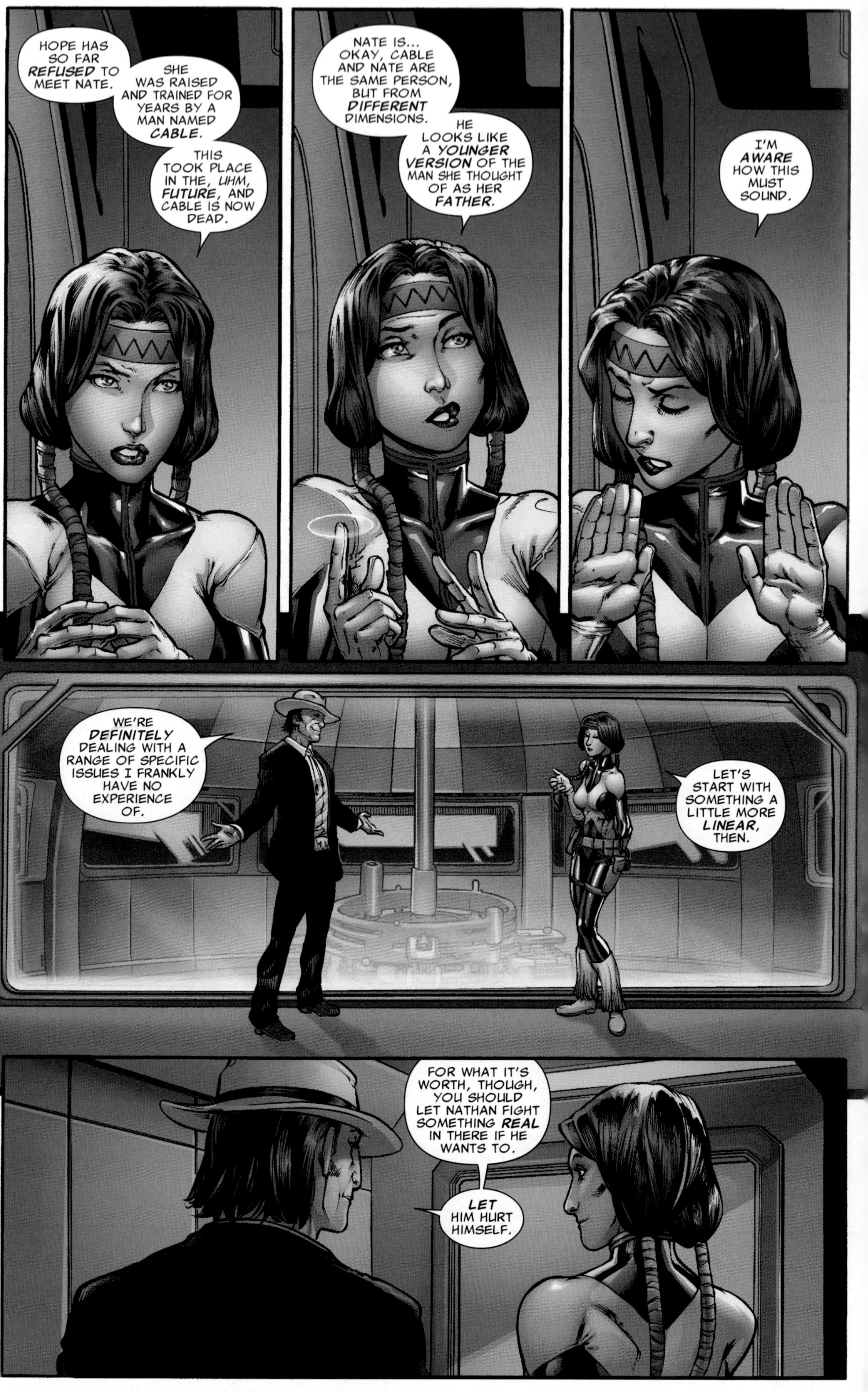
HOPE HAS SO FAR REFUSED TO MEET NATE.
SHE WAS RAISED AND TRAINED FOR YEARS BY A MAN NAMED CABLE.
THIS TOOK PLACE IN THE, UHM, FUTURE, AND CABLE IS NOW DEAD.
NATE IS... OKAY, CABLE AND NATE ARE THE SAME PERSON, BUT FROM DIFFERENT DIMENSIONS.
HE LOOKS LIKE A YOUNGER VERSION OF THE MAN SHE THOUGHT OF AS HER FATHER.
I'M AWARE HOW THIS MUST SOUND.
WE'RE DEFINITELY DEALING WITH A RANGE OF SPECIFIC ISSUES I FRANKLY HAVE NO EXPERIENCE OF.
LET'S START WITH SOMETHING A LITTLE MORE LINEAR, THEN.
FOR WHAT IT'S WORTH, THOUGH, YOU SHOULD LET NATHAN FIGHT SOMETHING REAL IN THERE IF HE WANTS TO.
LET HIM HURT HIMSELF.

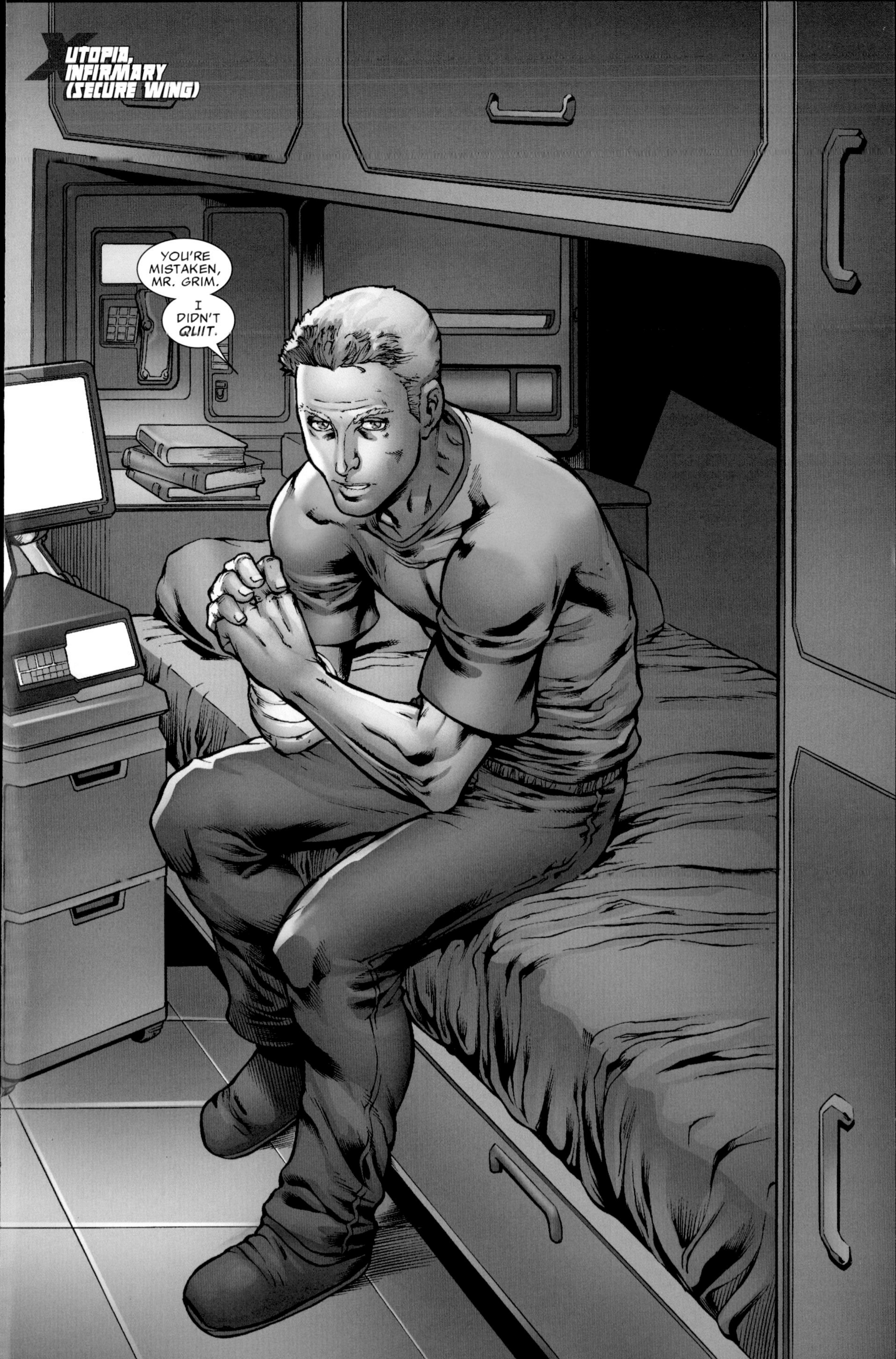
UTOPIA, INFIRMARY (SECURE WING)
YOU'RE MISTAKEN, MR. GRIM.
I DIDN'T QUIT.

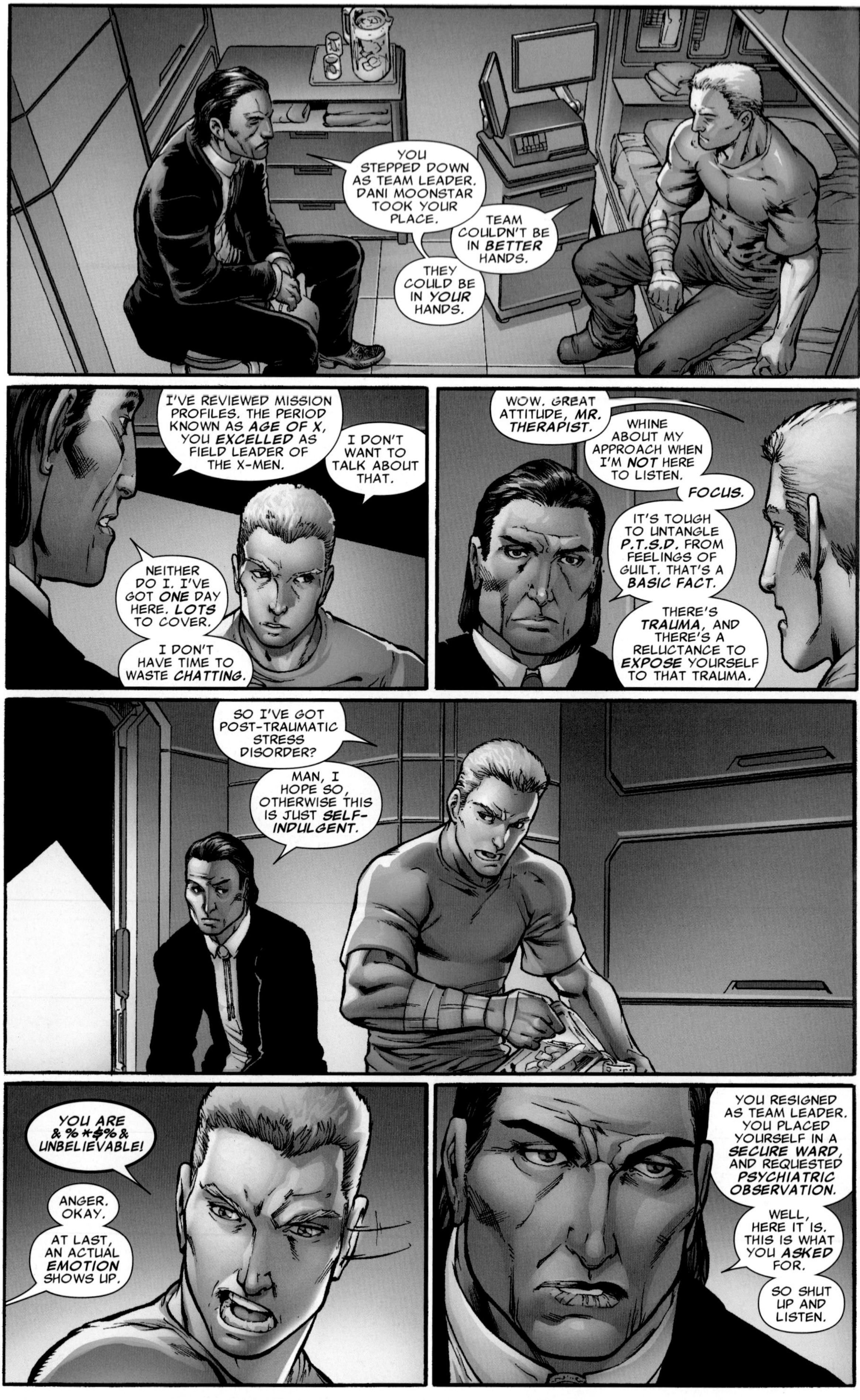
YOU STEPPED DOWN AS TEAM LEADER. DANI MOONSTAR TOOK YOUR PLACE.
TEAM COULDN'T BE IN BETTER HANDS.
THEY COULD BE IN YOUR HANDS.
I'VE REVIEWED MISSION PROFILES. THE PERIOD KNOWN AS AGE OF X, YOU EXCELLED AS FIELD LEADER OF THE X-MEN.
I DON'T WANT TO TALK ABOUT THAT.
NEITHER DO I. I'VE GOT ONE DAY HERE. LOTS TO COVER.
I DON'T HAVE TIME TO WASTE CHATTING.
WOW. GREAT ATTITUDE, MR. THERAPIST.
WHINE ABOUT MY APPROACH WHEN I'M NOT HERE TO LISTEN.
FOCUS.
IT'S TOUGH TO UNTANGLE P.T.S.D. FROM FEELINGS OF GUILT. THAT'S A BASIC FACT.
THERE'S TRAUMA, AND THERE'S A RELUCTANCE TO EXPOSE YOURSELF TO THAT TRAUMA.
SO I'VE GOT POST-TRAUMATIC STRESS DISORDER?
MAN, I HOPE SO, OTHERWISE THIS IS JUST SELF-INDULGENT.
YOU ARE &%*$%& UNBELIEVABLE!
ANGER. OKAY.
AT LAST, AN ACTUAL EMOTION SHOWS UP.
YOU RESIGNED AS TEAM LEADER. YOU PLACED YOURSELF IN A SECURE WARD, AND REQUESTED PSYCHIATRIC OBSERVATION.
WELL, HERE IT IS. THIS IS WHAT YOU ASKED FOR.
SO SHUT UP AND LISTEN.

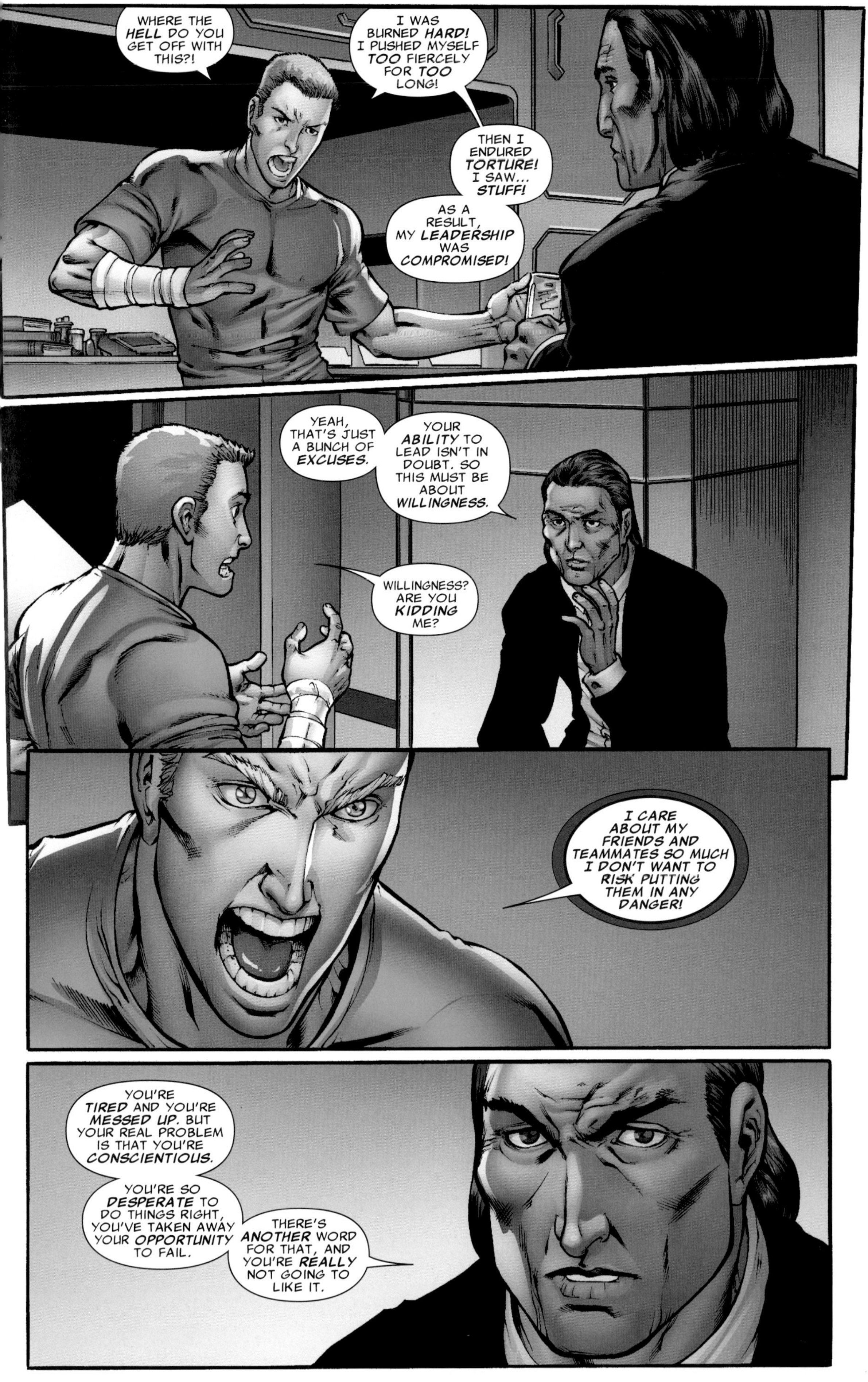
WHERE THE HELL DO YOU GET OFF WITH THIS?!
I WAS BURNED HARD! I PUSHED MYSELF TOO FIERCELY FOR TOO LONG!
THEN I ENDURED TORTURE! I SAW... STUFF!
AS A RESULT, MY LEADERSHIP WAS COMPROMISED!
YEAH, THAT'S JUST A BUNCH OF EXCUSES.
YOUR ABILITY TO LEAD ISN'T IN DOUBT. SO THIS MUST BE ABOUT WILLINGNESS.
WILLINGNESS? ARE YOU KIDDING ME?
I CARE ABOUT MY FRIENDS AND TEAMMATES SO MUCH I DON'T WANT TO RISK PUTTING THEM IN ANY DANGER!
YOU'RE TIRED AND YOU'RE MESSED UP. BUT YOUR REAL PROBLEM IS THAT YOU'RE CONSCIENTIOUS.
YOU'RE SO DESPERATE TO DO THINGS RIGHT, YOU'VE TAKEN AWAY YOUR OPPORTUNITY TO FAIL.
THERE'S ANOTHER WORD FOR THAT, AND YOU'RE REALLY NOT GOING TO LIKE IT.

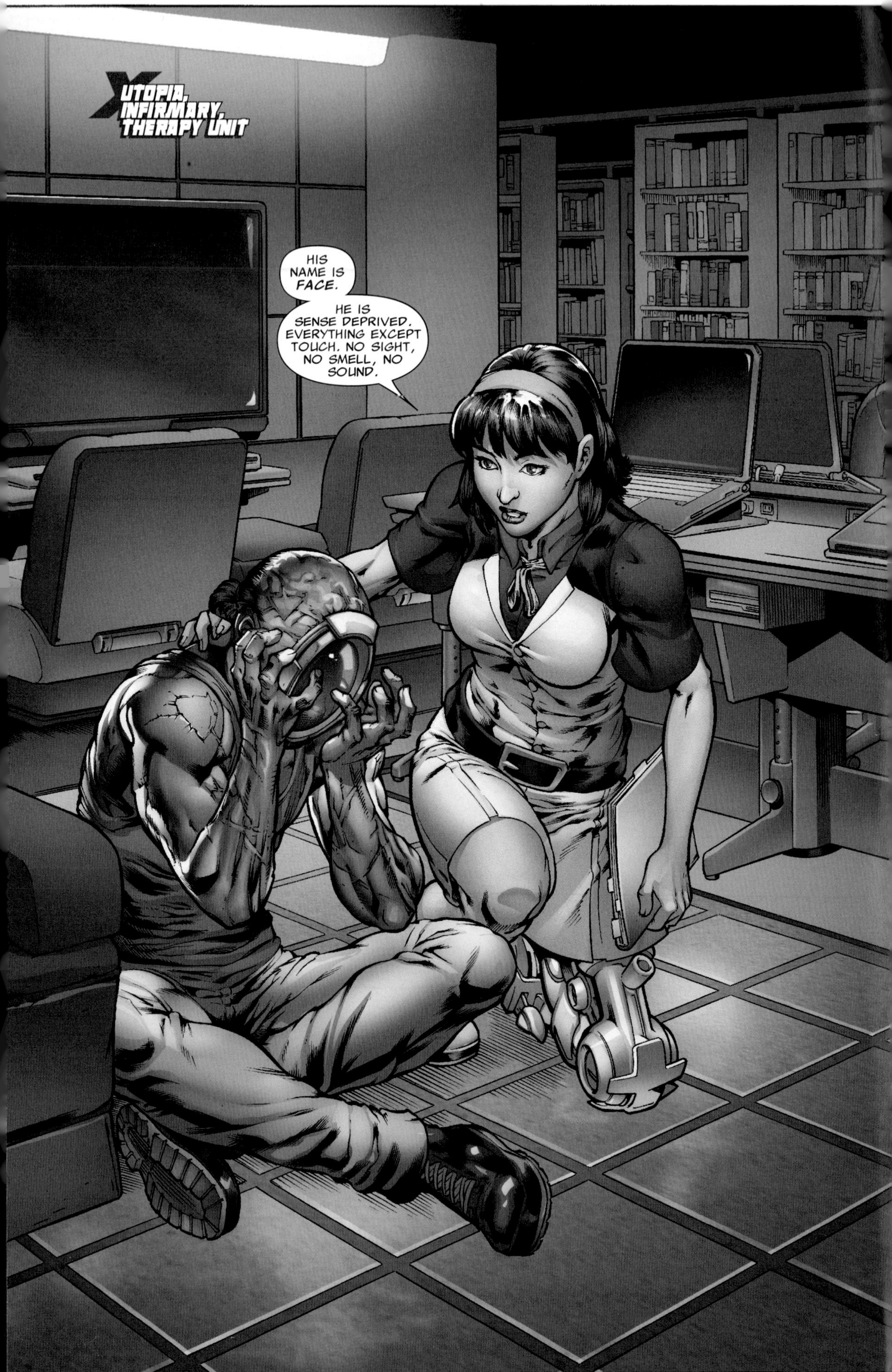
UTOPIA, INFIRMARY, THERAPY UNIT
HIS NAME IS FACE.
HE IS SENSE DEPRIVED. EVERYTHING EXCEPT TOUCH. NO SIGHT, NO SMELL, NO SOUND.

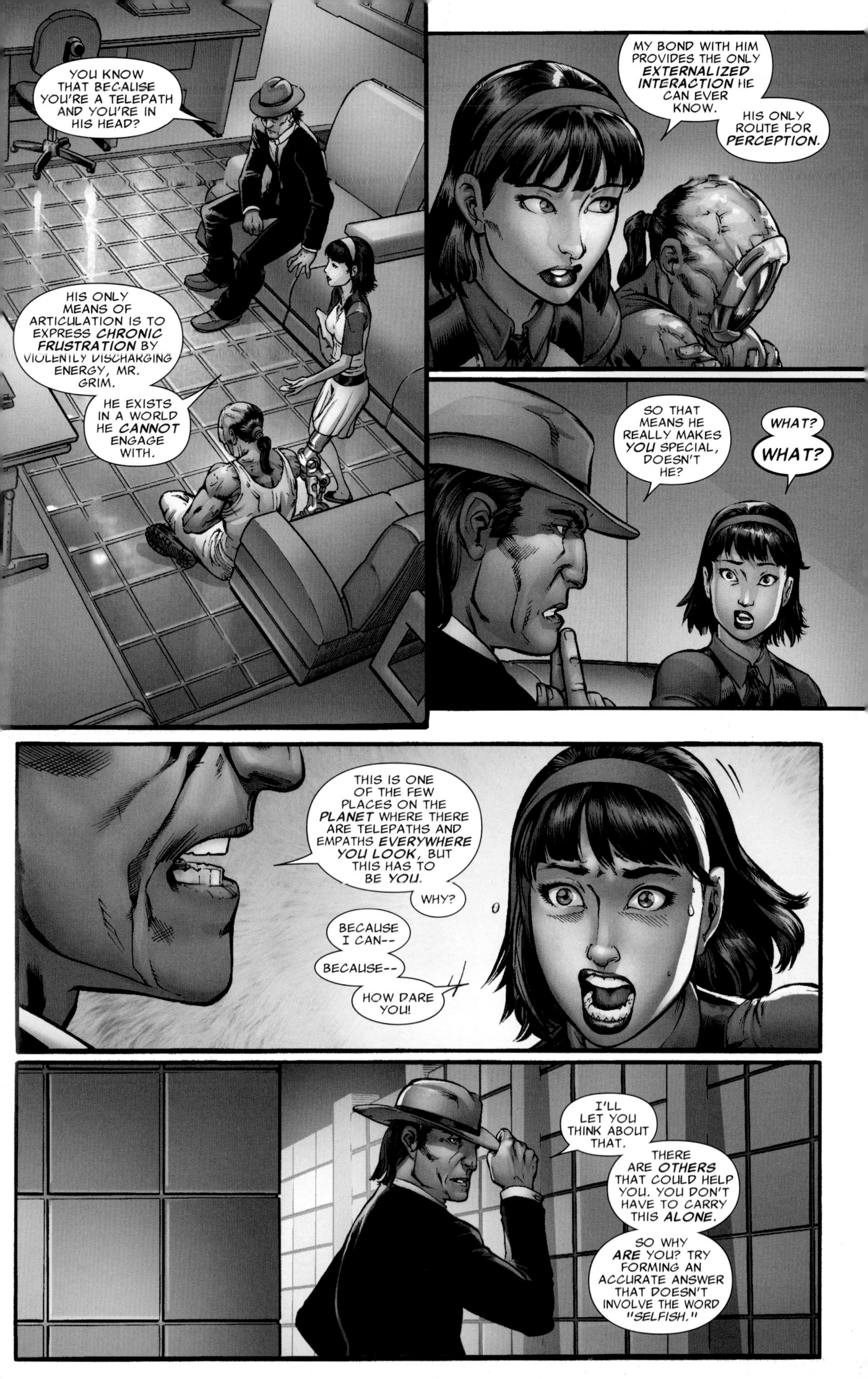
YOU KNOW THAT BECAUSE YOU'RE A TELEPATH AND YOU'RE IN HIS HEAD?
HIS ONLY MEANS OF ARTICULATION IS TO EXPRESS CHRONIC FRUSTRATION BY VIOLENTLY DISCHARGING ENERGY, MR. GRIM.
HE EXISTS IN A WORLD HE CANNOT ENGAGE WITH.
MY BOND WITH HIM PROVIDES THE ONLY EXTERNALIZED INTERACTION HE CAN EVER KNOW.
HIS ONLY ROUTE FOR PERCEPTION.
SO THAT MEANS HE REALLY MAKES YOU SPECIAL, DOESN'T HE?
WHAT?
WHAT?
THIS IS ONE OF THE FEW PLACES ON THE PLANET WHERE THERE ARE TELEPATHS AND EMPATHS EVERYWHERE YOU LOOK, BUT THIS HAS TO BE YOU.
WHY?
BECAUSE I CAN--
BECAUSE--
HOW DARE YOU!
I'LL LET YOU THINK ABOUT THAT.
THERE ARE OTHERS THAT COULD HELP YOU. YOU DON'T HAVE TO CARRY THIS ALONE.
SO WHY ARE YOU? TRY FORMING AN ACCURATE ANSWER THAT DOESN'T INVOLVE THE WORD "SELFISH."

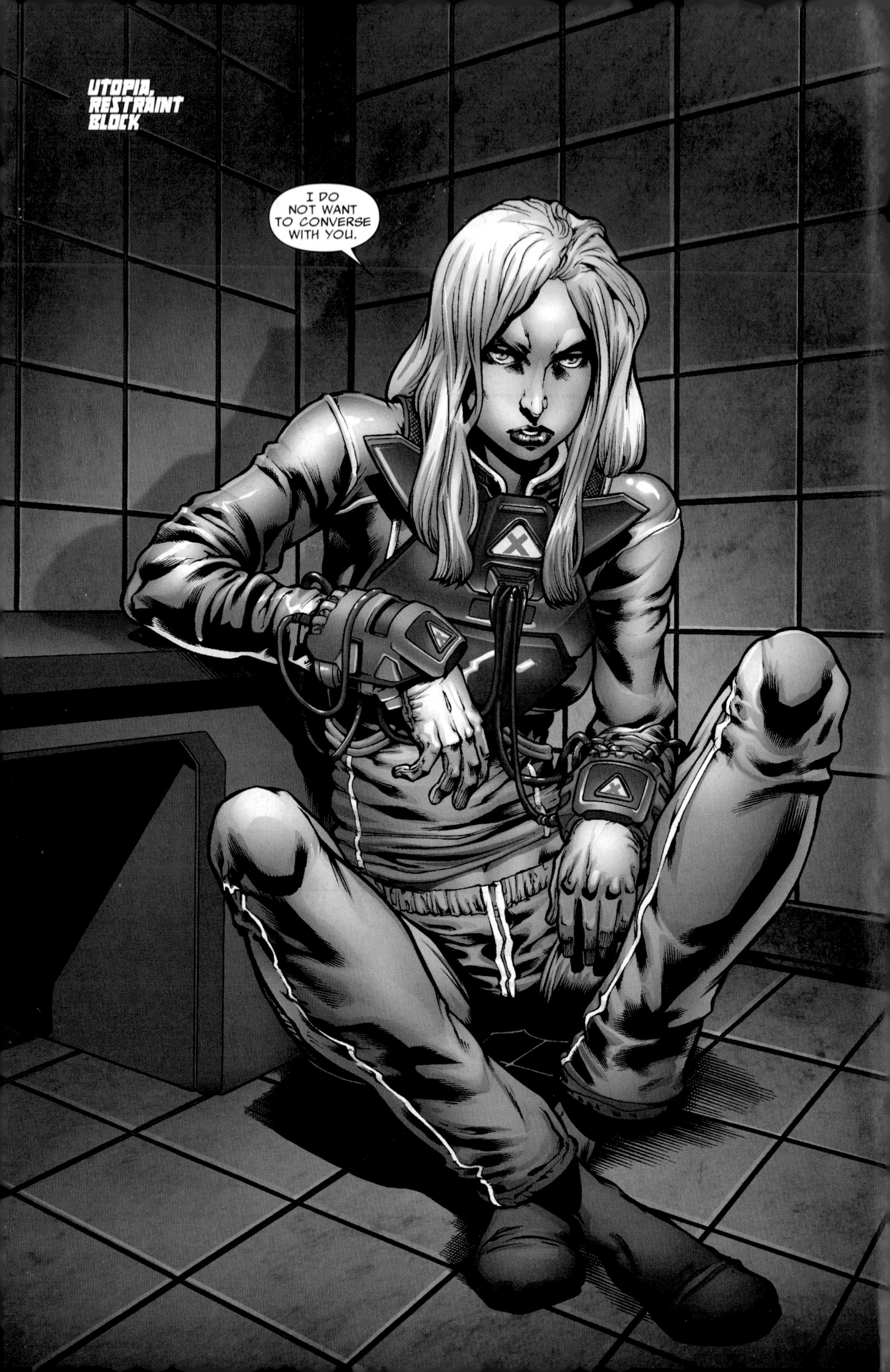
UTOPIA, RESTRAINT BLOCK
I DO NOT WANT TO CONVERSE WITH YOU.

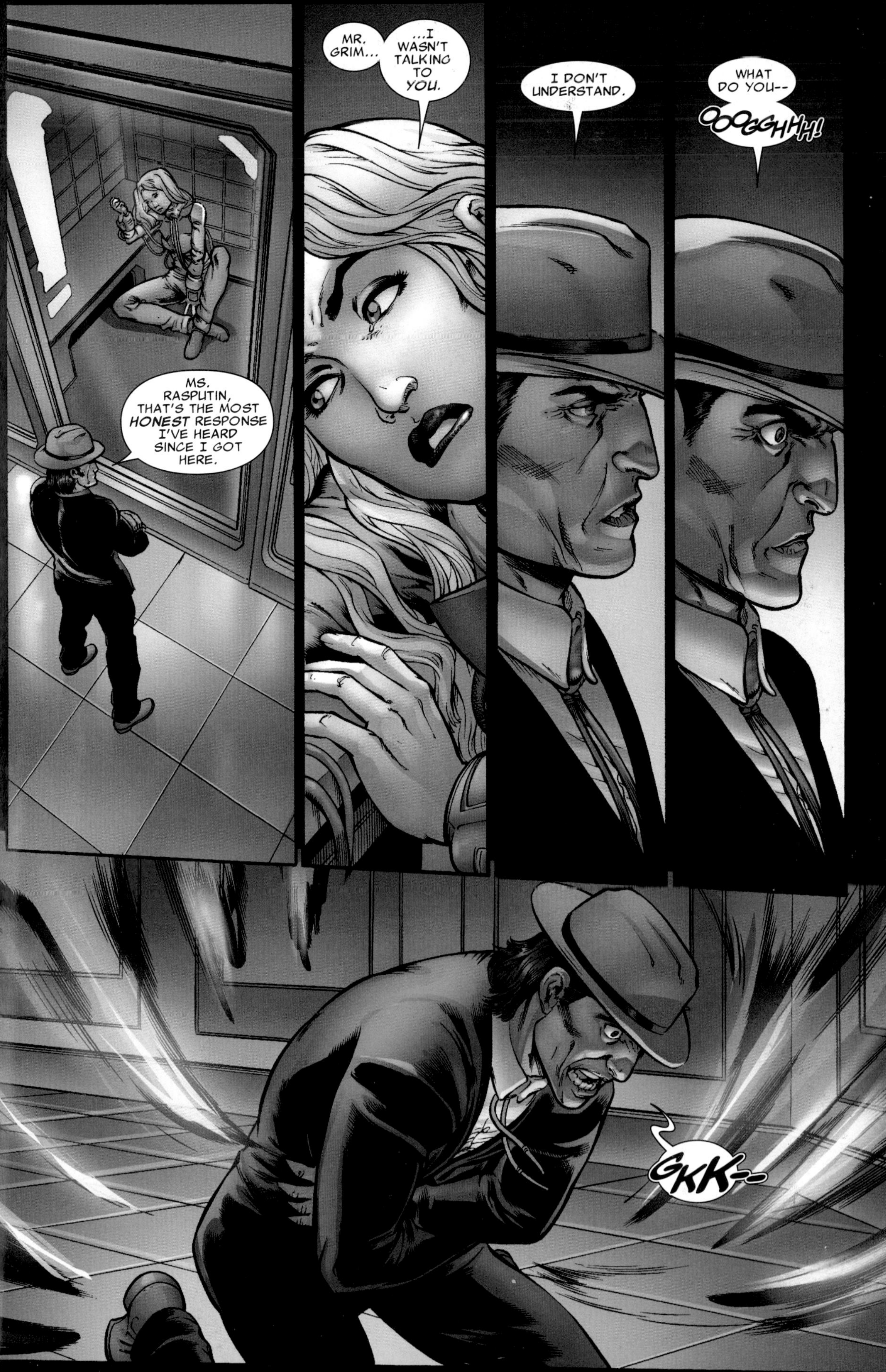
MS. RASPUTIN, THAT'S THE MOST HONEST RESPONSE I'VE HEARD SINCE I GOT HERE.
MR. GRIM...
...I WASN'T TALKING TO YOU.
I DON'T UNDERSTAND.
WHAT DO YOU--
OOOGGHHH!
GKK--

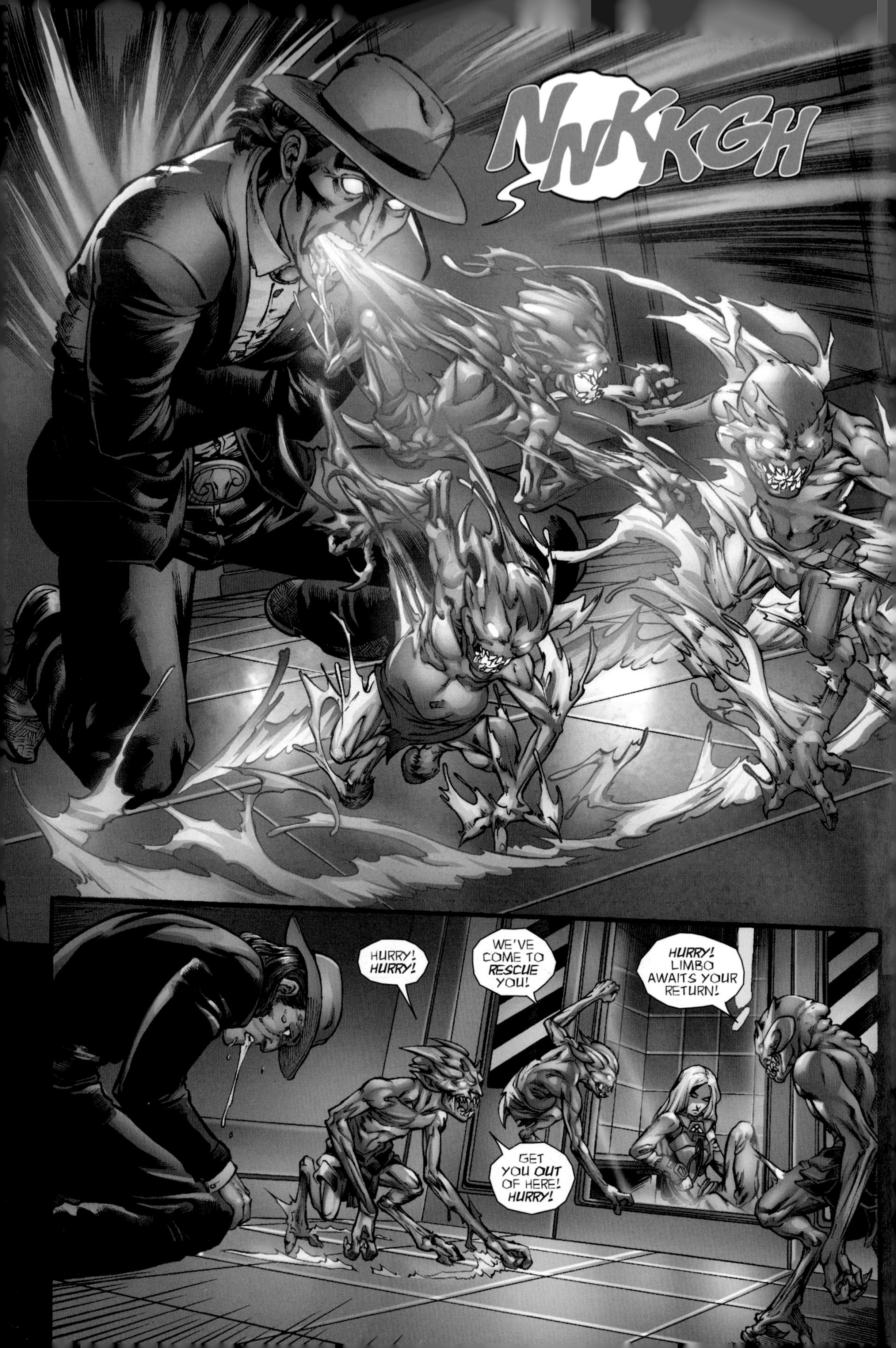
NNKKGH
HURRY! HURRY!
WE'VE COME TO RESCUE YOU!
HURRY! LIMBO AWAITS YOUR RETURN!
GET YOU OUT OF HERE! HURRY!

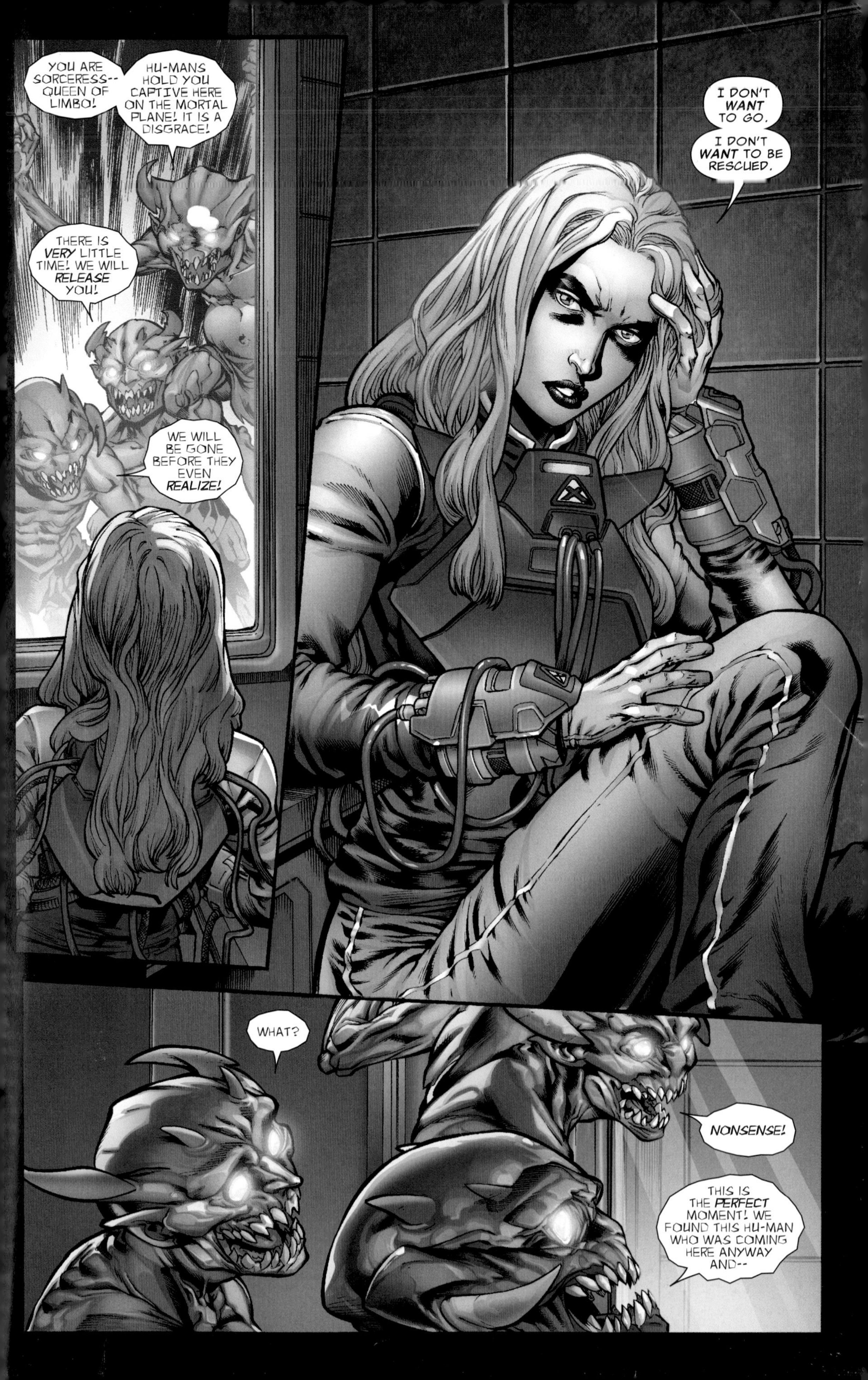
YOU ARE SORCERESS-- QUEEN OF LIMBO!
HU-MANS HOLD YOU CAPTIVE HERE ON THE MORTAL PLANE! IT IS A DISGRACE!
THERE IS *VERY* LITTLE TIME! WE WILL *RELEASE* YOU!
WE WILL BE GONE BEFORE THEY EVEN *REALIZE!*
I DON'T *WANT* TO GO.
I DON'T *WANT* TO BE RESCUED.
WHAT?
NONSENSE!
THIS IS THE *PERFECT* MOMENT! WE FOUND THIS HU-MAN WHO WAS COMING HERE ANYWAY AND--

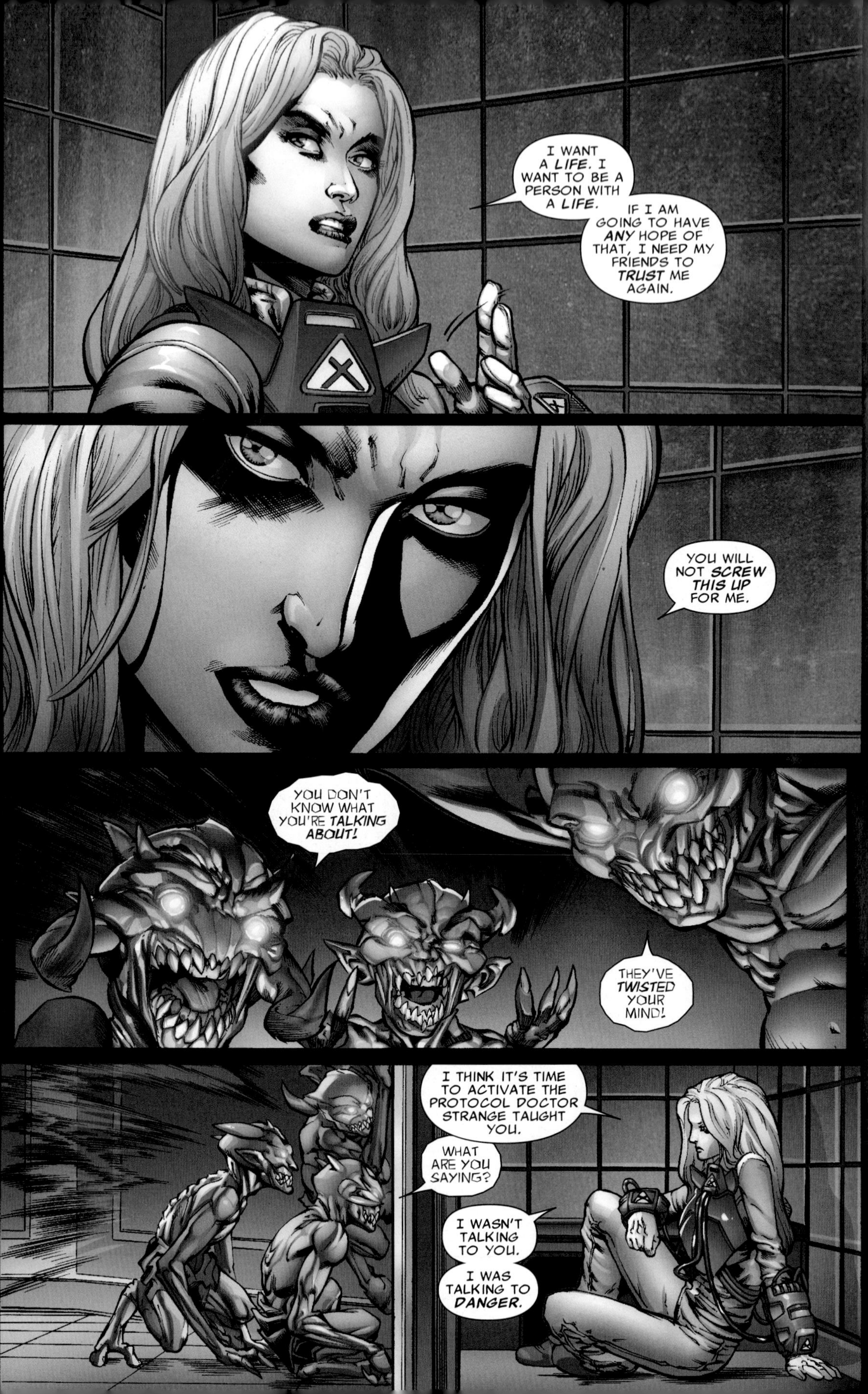
I WANT A LIFE. I WANT TO BE A PERSON WITH A LIFE.
IF I AM GOING TO HAVE ANY HOPE OF THAT, I NEED MY FRIENDS TO TRUST ME AGAIN.
YOU WILL NOT SCREW THIS UP FOR ME.
YOU DON'T KNOW WHAT YOU'RE TALKING ABOUT!
THEY'VE TWISTED YOUR MIND!
I THINK IT'S TIME TO ACTIVATE THE PROTOCOL DOCTOR STRANGE TAUGHT YOU.
WHAT ARE YOU SAYING?
I WASN'T TALKING TO YOU.
I WAS TALKING TO DANGER.

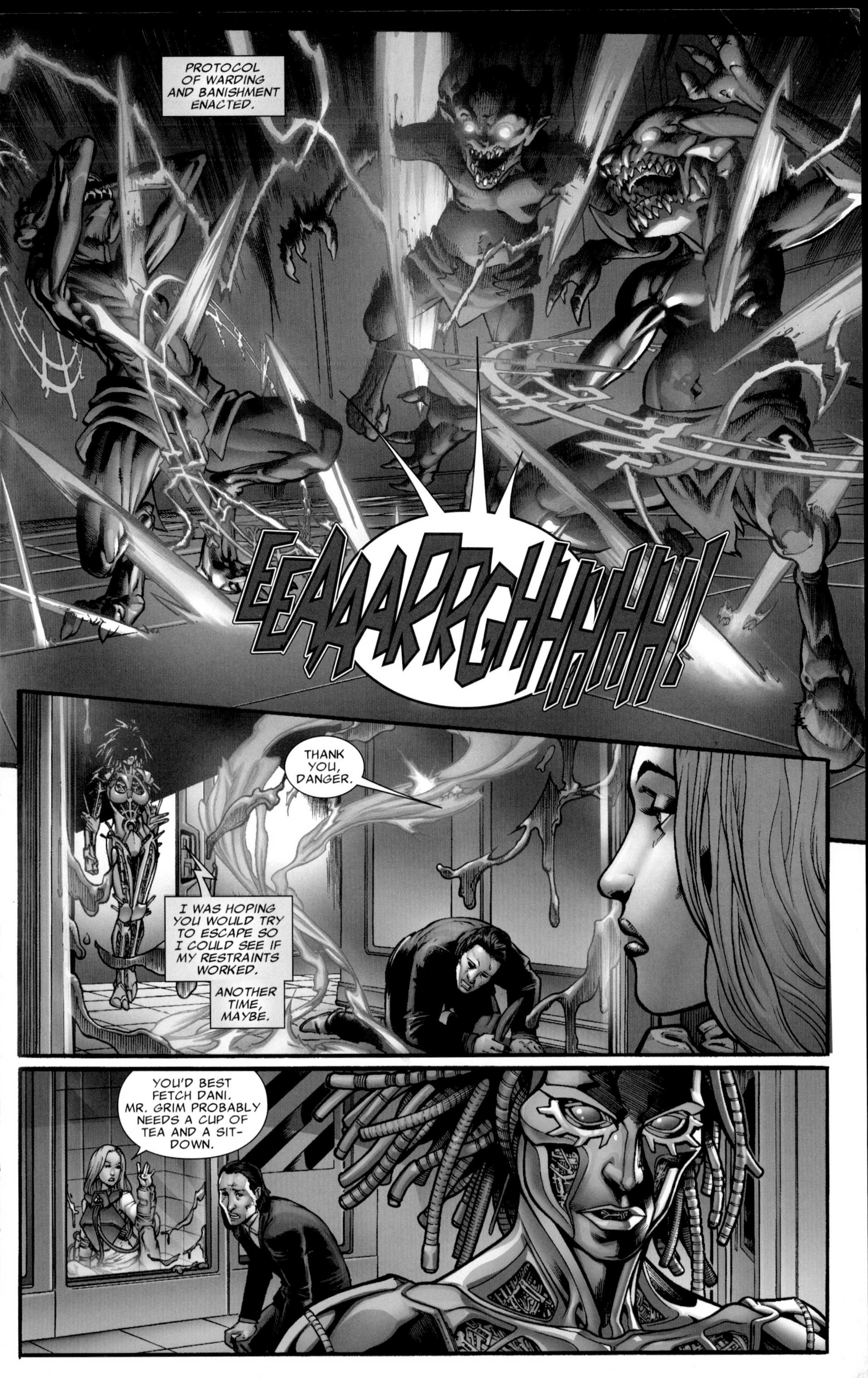

PROTOCOL OF WARDING AND BANISHMENT ENACTED.
EEAAAARRGHHHHH!
THANK YOU, DANGER.
I WAS HOPING YOU WOULD TRY TO ESCAPE SO I COULD SEE IF MY RESTRAINTS WORKED.
ANOTHER TIME, MAYBE.
YOU'D BEST FETCH DANI. MR. GRIM PROBABLY NEEDS A CUP OF TEA AND A SIT-DOWN.

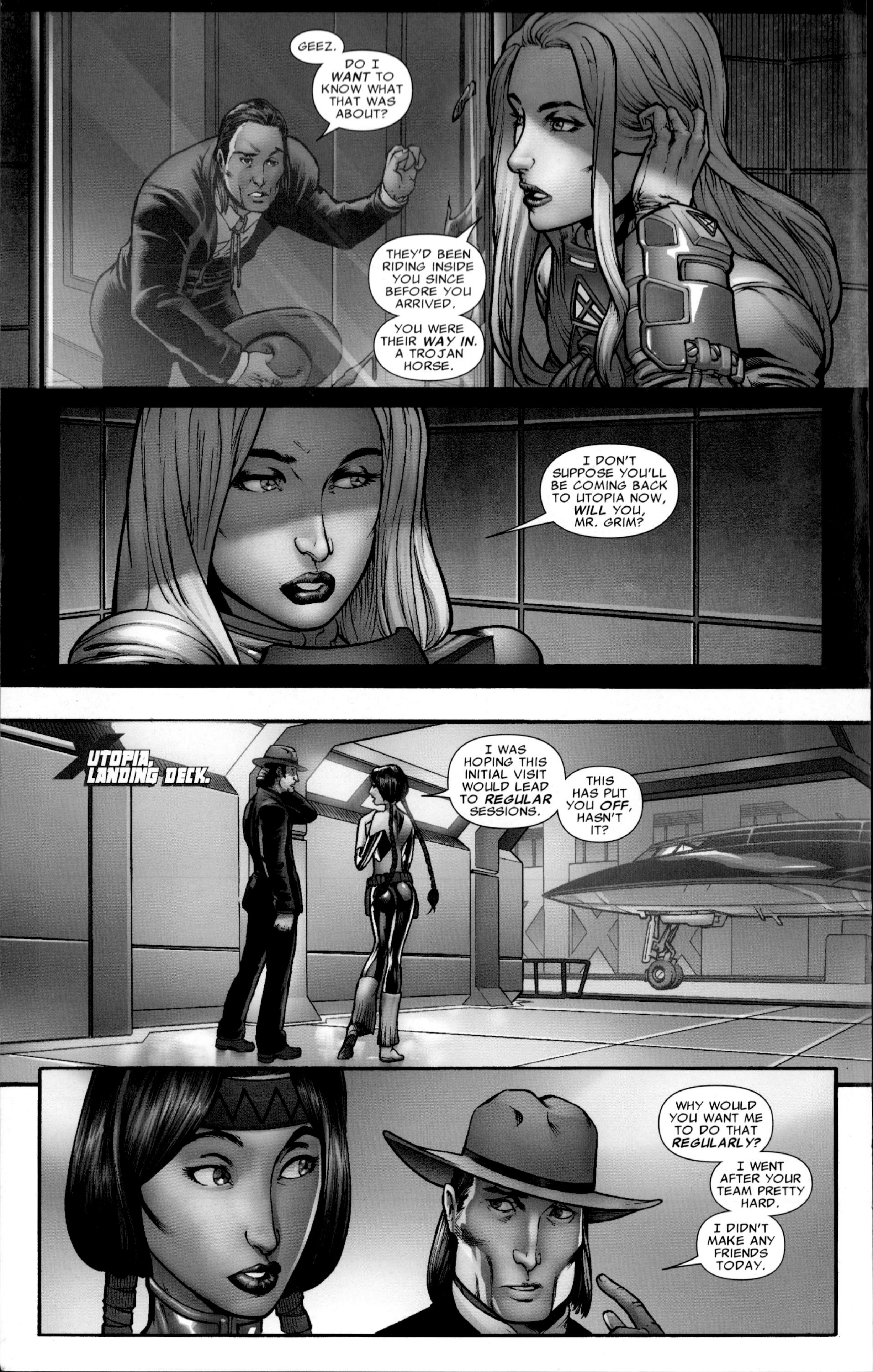
GEEZ.
DO I *WANT* TO KNOW WHAT THAT WAS ABOUT?
THEY'D BEEN RIDING INSIDE YOU SINCE BEFORE YOU ARRIVED.
YOU WERE THEIR *WAY IN.* A TROJAN HORSE.
I DON'T SUPPOSE YOU'LL BE COMING BACK TO UTOPIA NOW, *WILL* YOU, MR. GRIM?
UTOPIA. LANDING DECK.
I WAS HOPING THIS INITIAL VISIT WOULD LEAD TO *REGULAR* SESSIONS.
THIS HAS PUT YOU *OFF*, HASN'T IT?
WHY WOULD YOU WANT ME TO DO THAT *REGULARLY?*
I WENT AFTER YOUR TEAM PRETTY HARD.
I DIDN'T MAKE ANY FRIENDS TODAY.

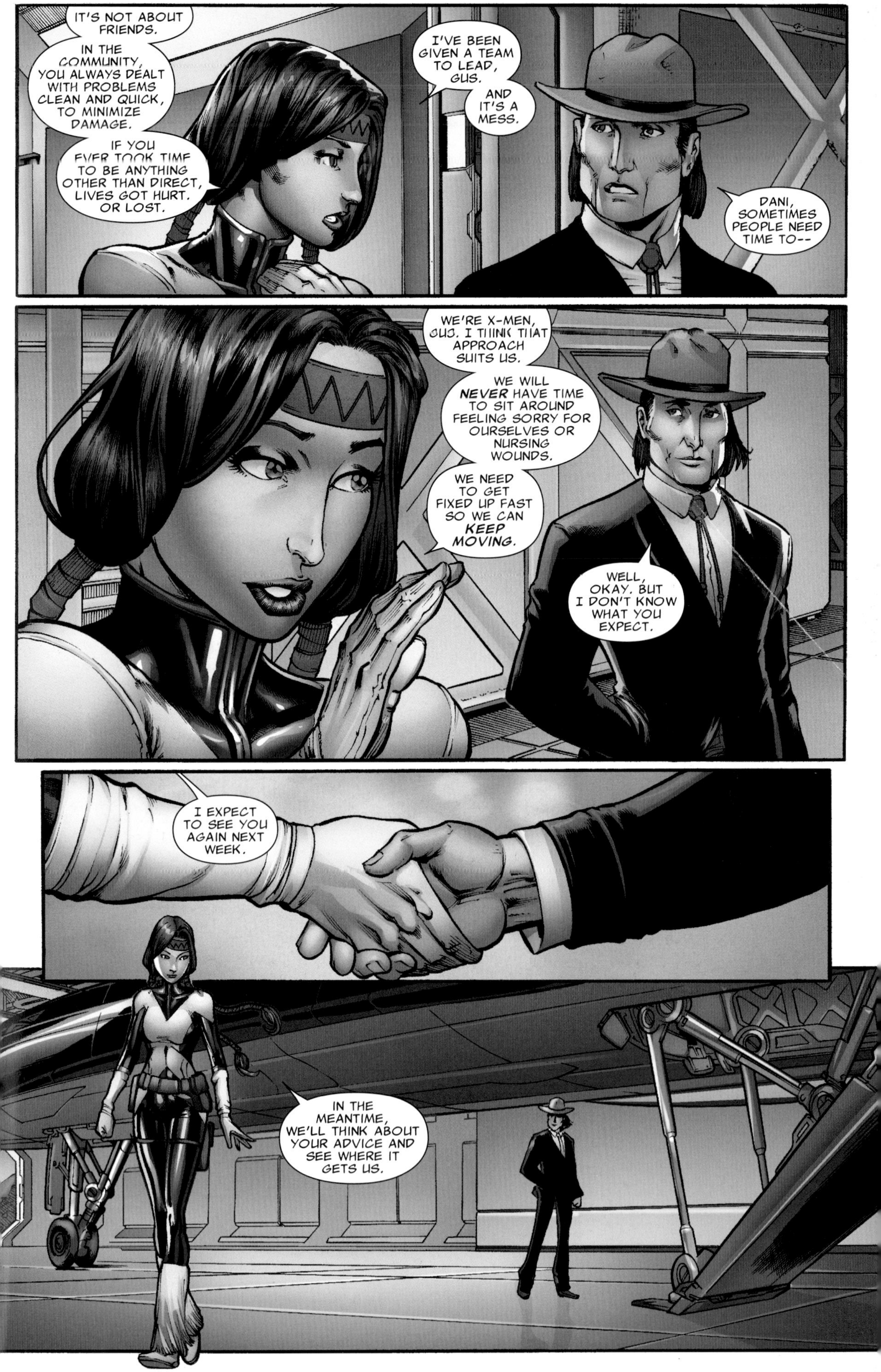
IT'S NOT ABOUT FRIENDS.
IN THE COMMUNITY, YOU ALWAYS DEALT WITH PROBLEMS CLEAN AND QUICK, TO MINIMIZE DAMAGE.
IF YOU EVER TOOK TIME TO BE ANYTHING OTHER THAN DIRECT, LIVES GOT HURT. OR LOST.
I'VE BEEN GIVEN A TEAM TO LEAD, GUS.
AND IT'S A MESS.
DANI, SOMETIMES PEOPLE NEED TIME TO--
WE'RE X-MEN, GUS. I THINK THAT APPROACH SUITS US.
WE WILL NEVER HAVE TIME TO SIT AROUND FEELING SORRY FOR OURSELVES OR NURSING WOUNDS.
WE NEED TO GET FIXED UP FAST SO WE CAN KEEP MOVING.
WELL, OKAY. BUT I DON'T KNOW WHAT YOU EXPECT.
I EXPECT TO SEE YOU AGAIN NEXT WEEK.
IN THE MEANTIME, WE'LL THINK ABOUT YOUR ADVICE AND SEE WHERE IT GETS US.

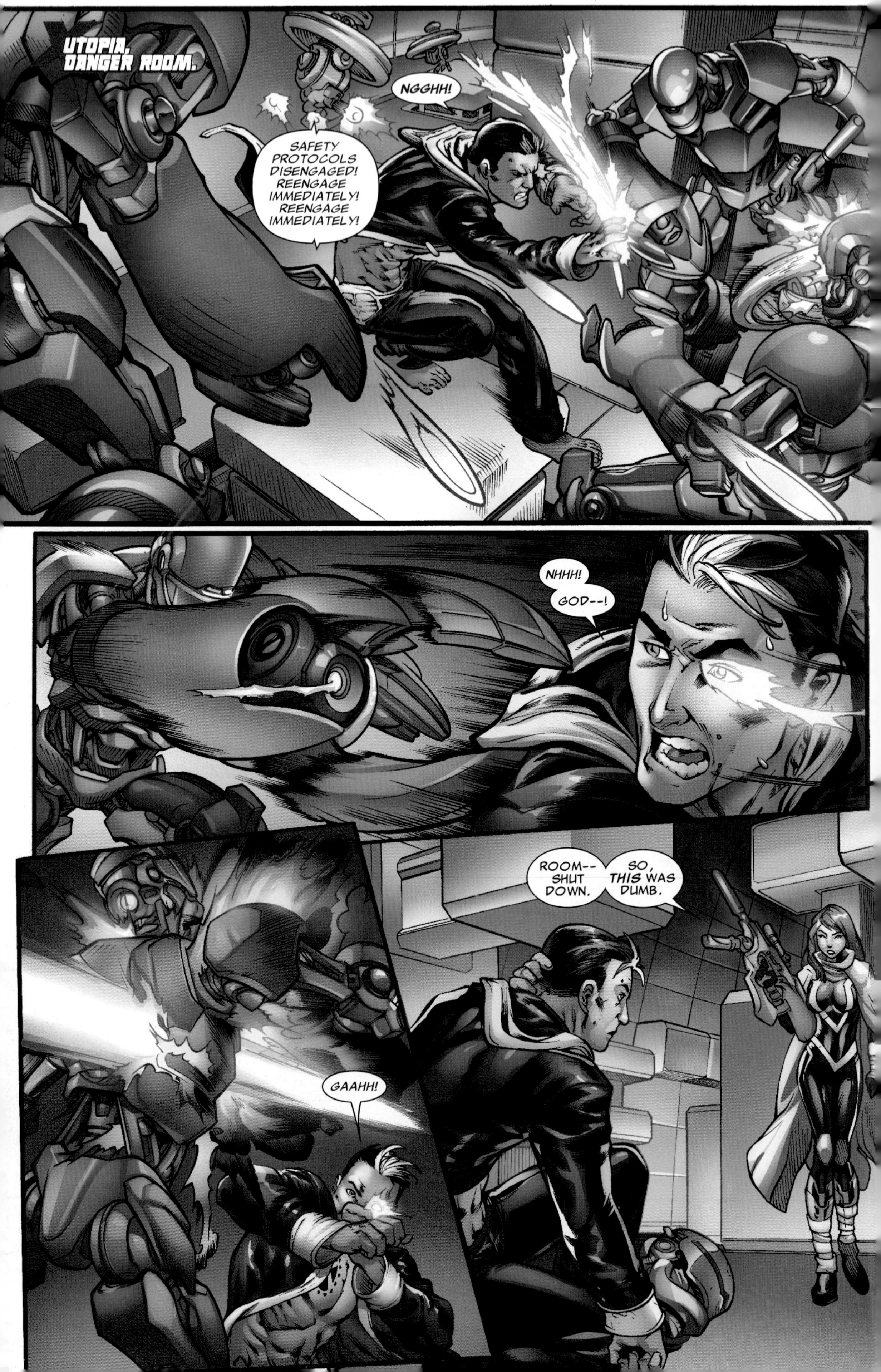
UTOPIA, DANGER ROOM.
NGGHH!
SAFETY PROTOCOLS DISENGAGED! REENGAGE IMMEDIATELY! REENGAGE IMMEDIATELY!
NHHH!
GOD--!
GAAHH!
ROOM-- SHUT DOWN.
SO, THIS WAS DUMB.

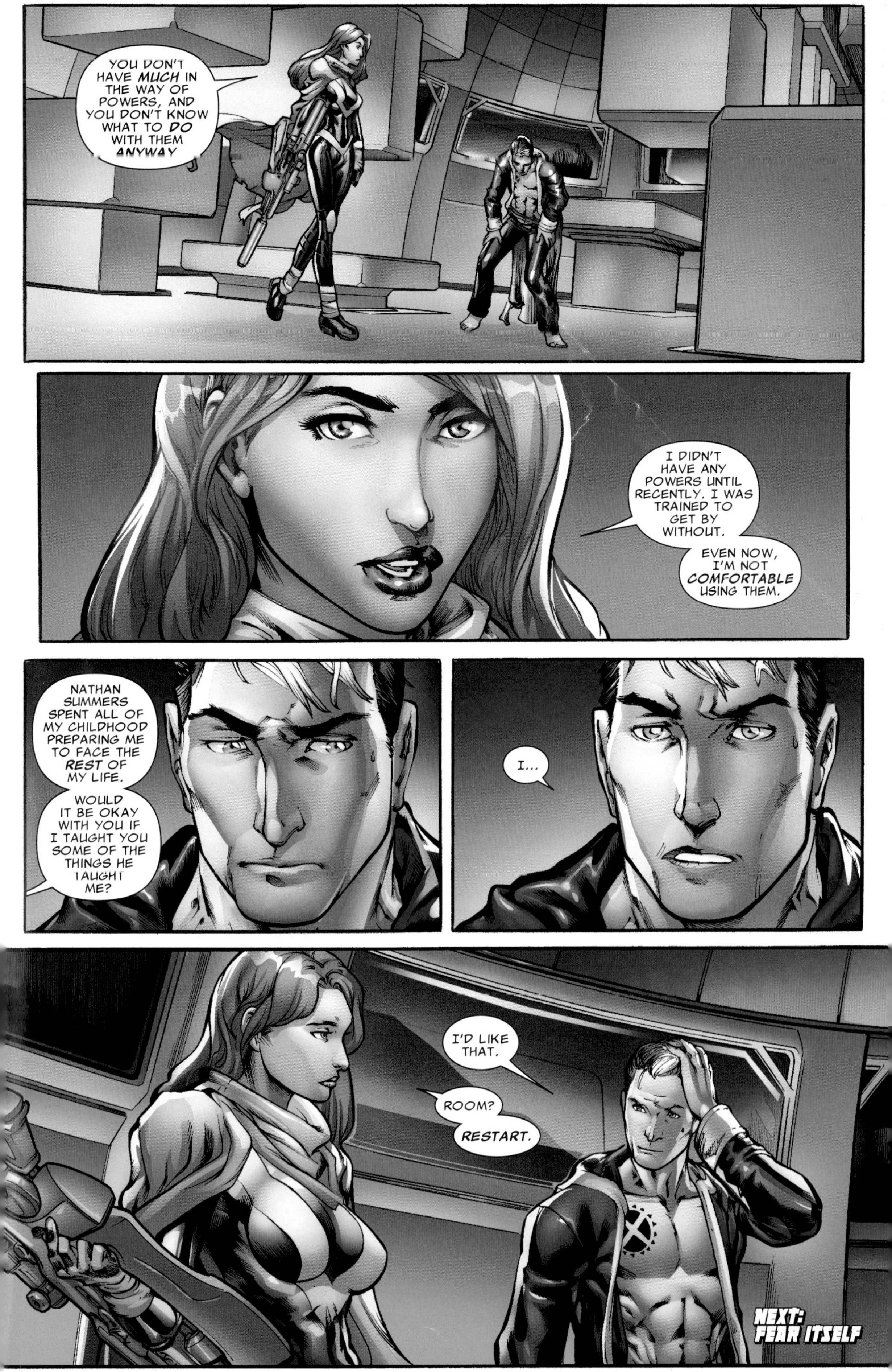
YOU DON'T HAVE MUCH IN THE WAY OF POWERS, AND YOU DON'T KNOW WHAT TO DO WITH THEM ANYWAY
I DIDN'T HAVE ANY POWERS UNTIL RECENTLY. I WAS TRAINED TO GET BY WITHOUT.
EVEN NOW, I'M NOT COMFORTABLE USING THEM.
NATHAN SUMMERS SPENT ALL OF MY CHILDHOOD PREPARING ME TO FACE THE REST OF MY LIFE.
WOULD IT BE OKAY WITH YOU IF I TAUGHT YOU SOME OF THE THINGS HE TAUGHT ME?
I...
I'D LIKE THAT.
ROOM?
RESTART.
NEXT: FEAR ITSELF

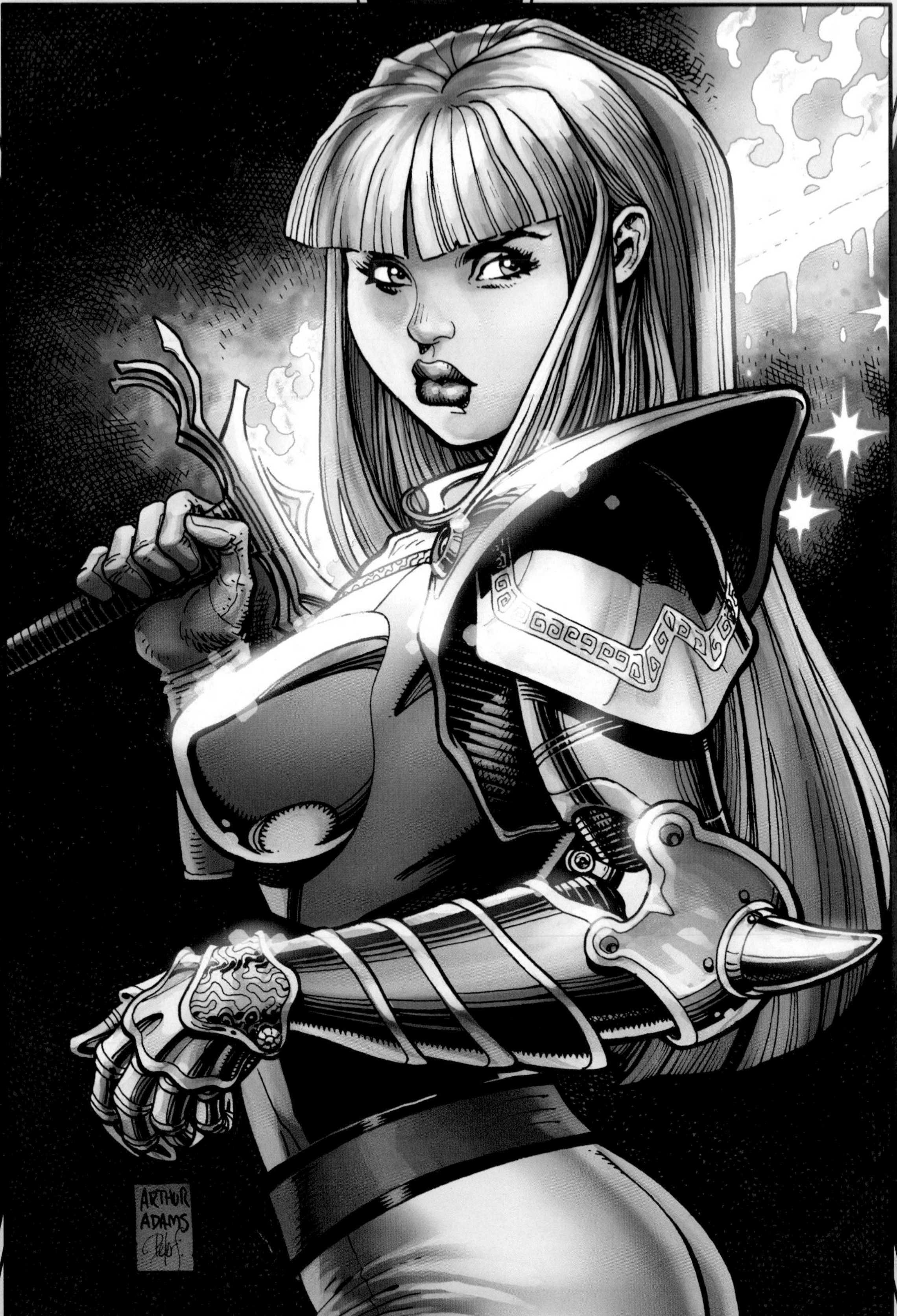
ARTHUR ADAMS

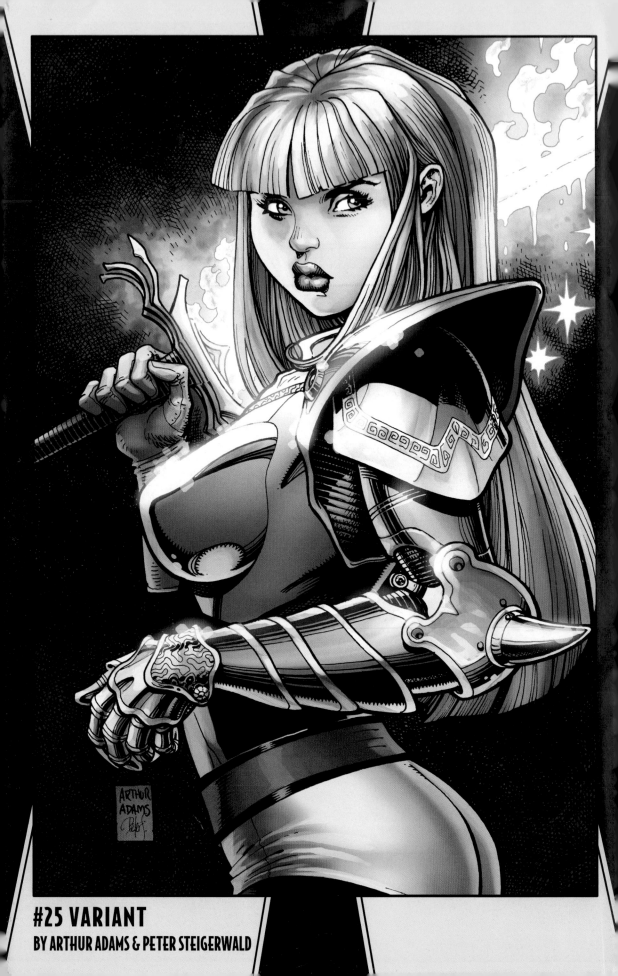

#25 VARIANT

BY ARTHUR ADAMS & PETER STEIGERWALD

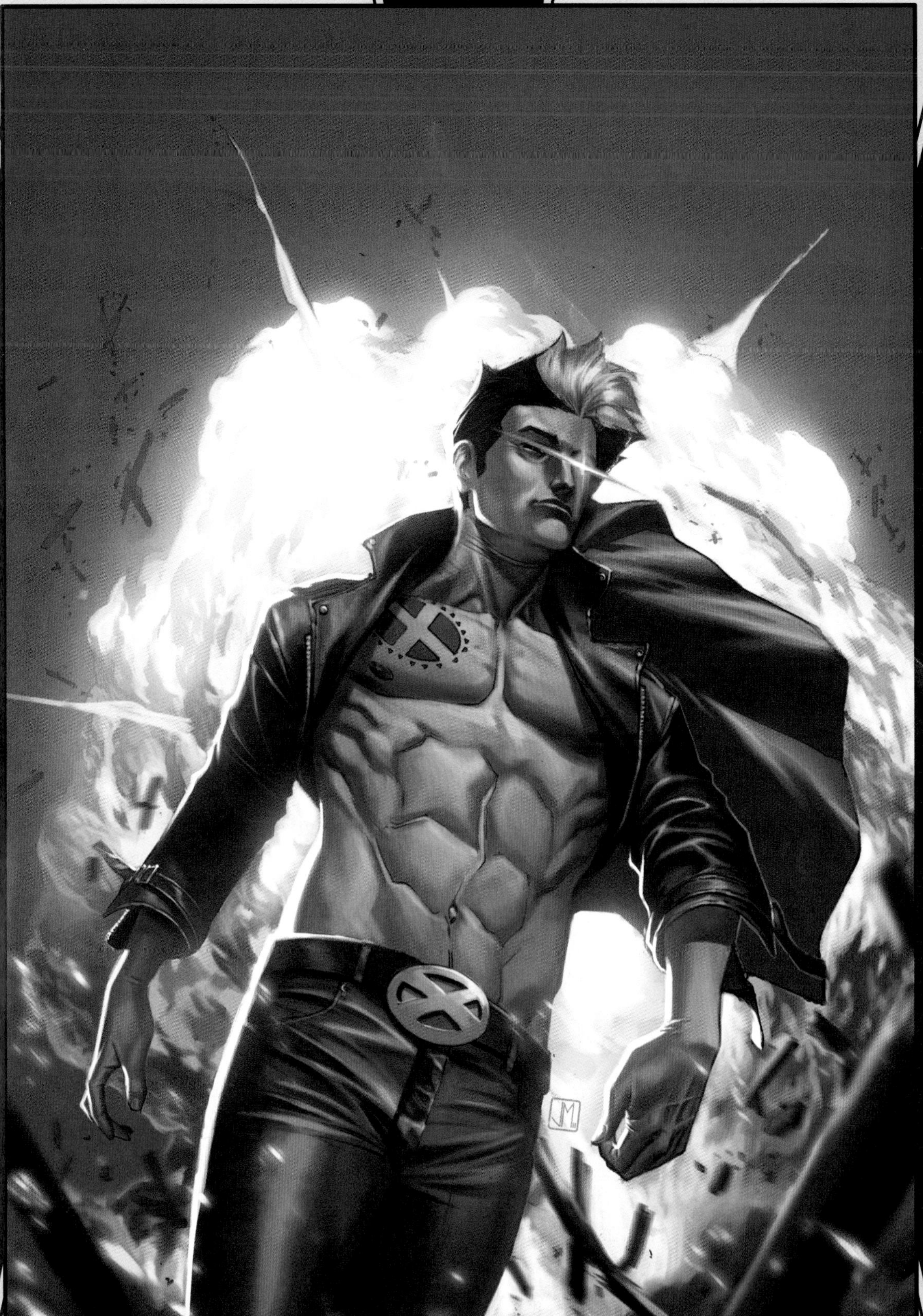

#25 VARIANT
BY JORGE MOLINA

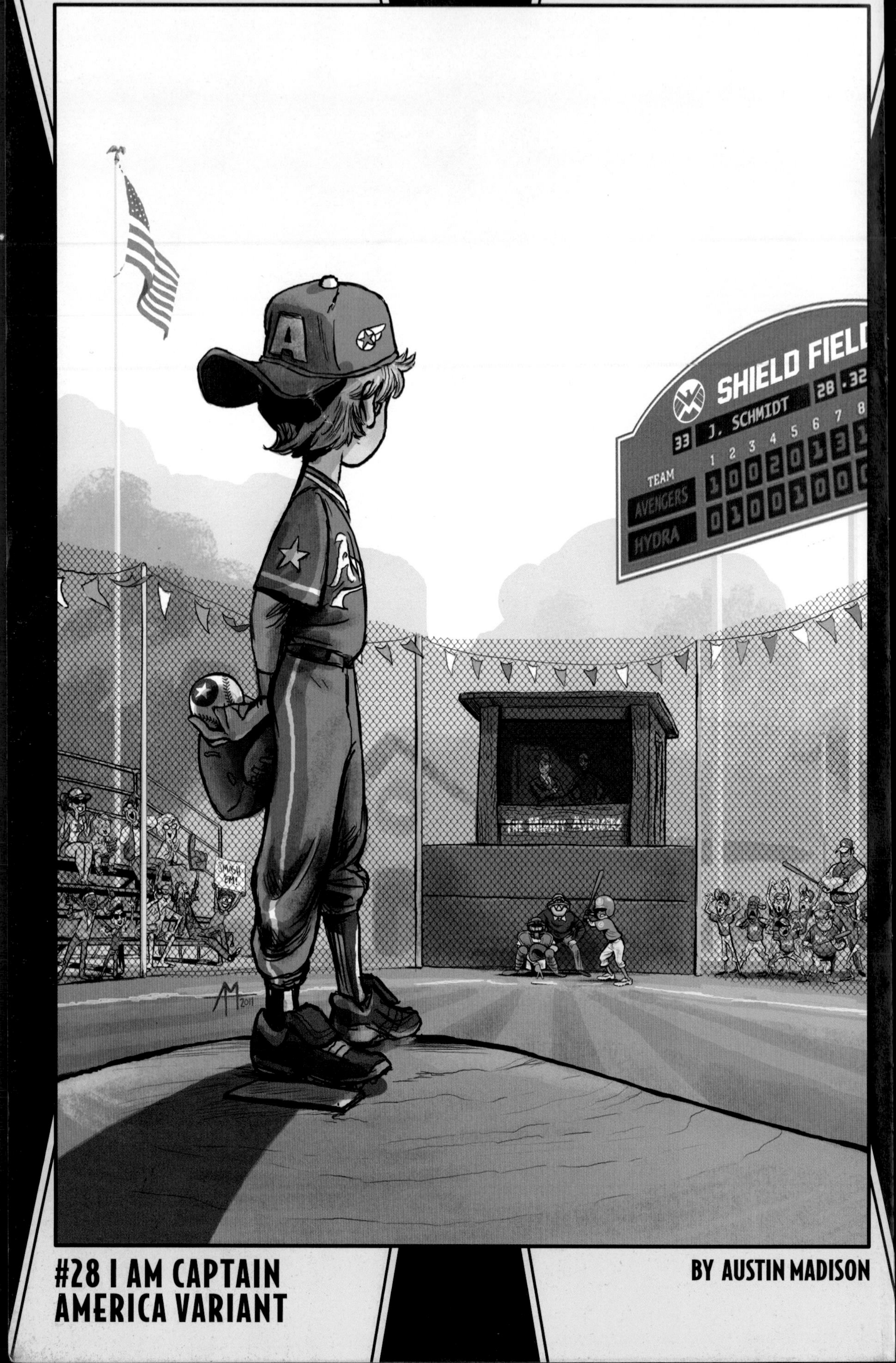
SHIELD FIEL
J. SCHMIDT
TEAM
AVENGERS
HYDRA

#28 I AM CAPTAIN AMERICA VARIANT

BY AUSTIN MADISON

CHARACTER SKETCHES

BY LEANDRO FERNANDEZ

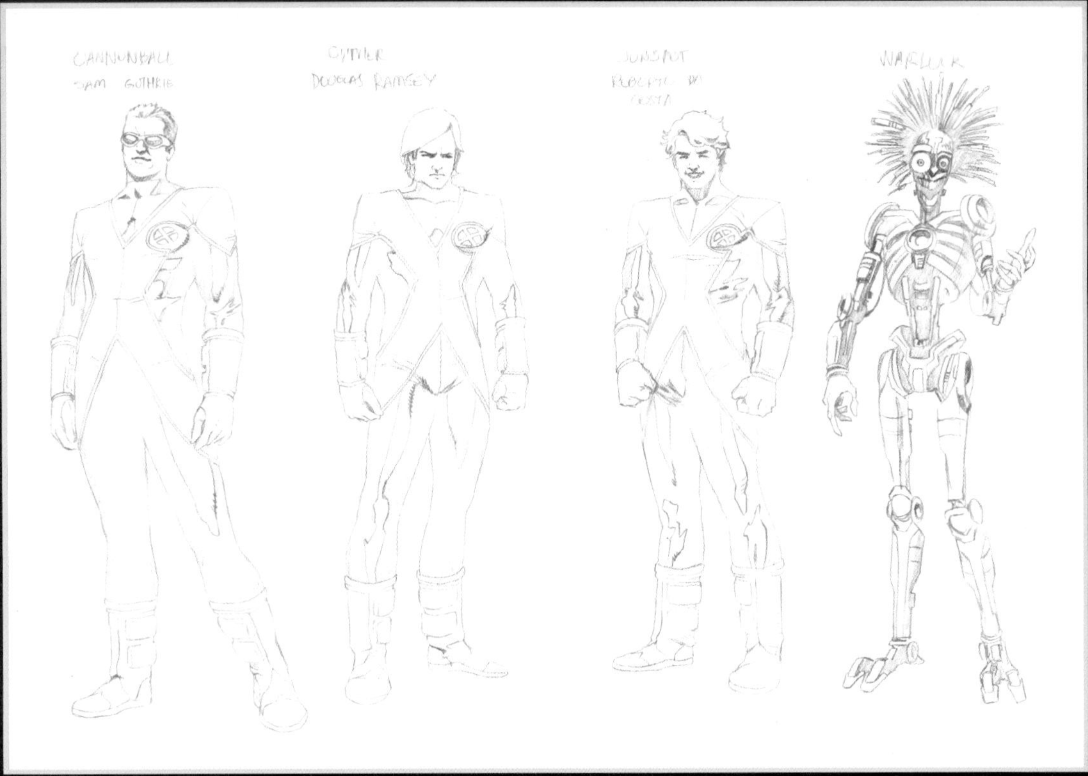
CANNONBALL
SAM GUTHRIE
CYPHER
DOUGLAS RAMSEY
SUNSPOT
WARLOCK

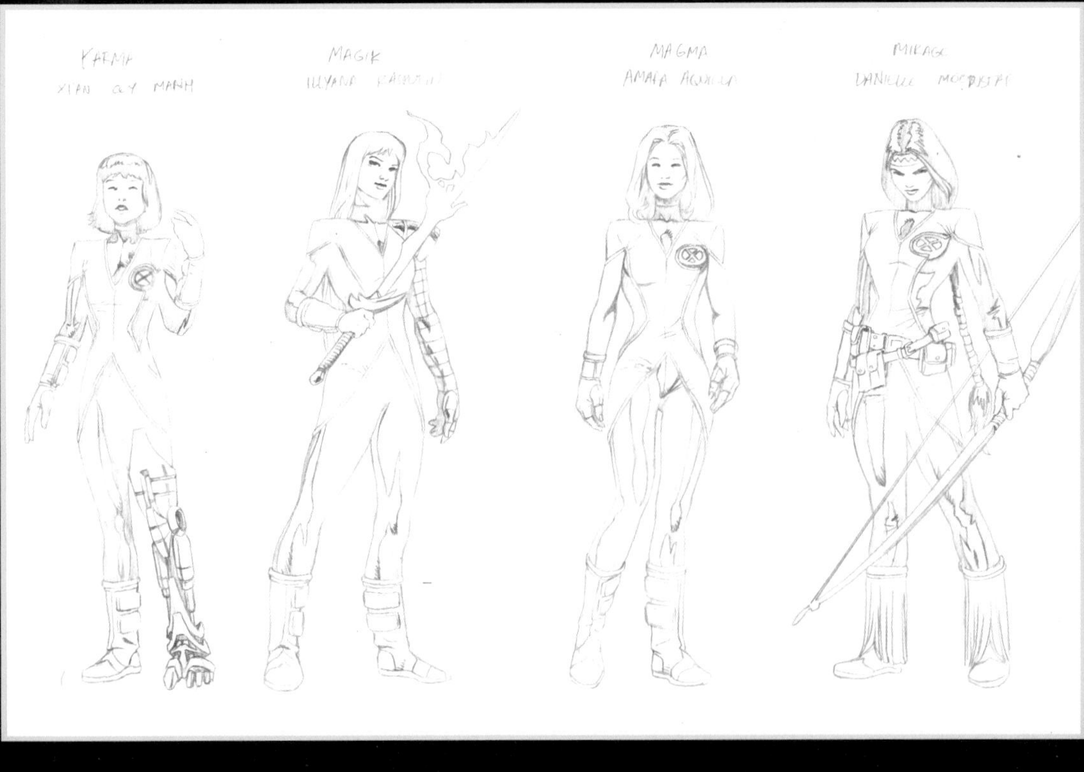
KARMA
XIAN COY MANH
MAGIK
MAGMA
AMARA AQUILLA
MIRAGE

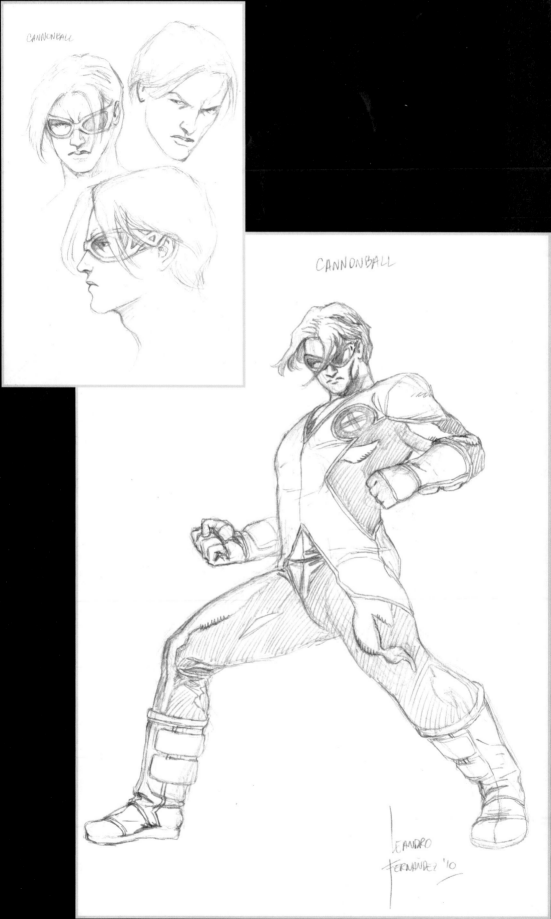

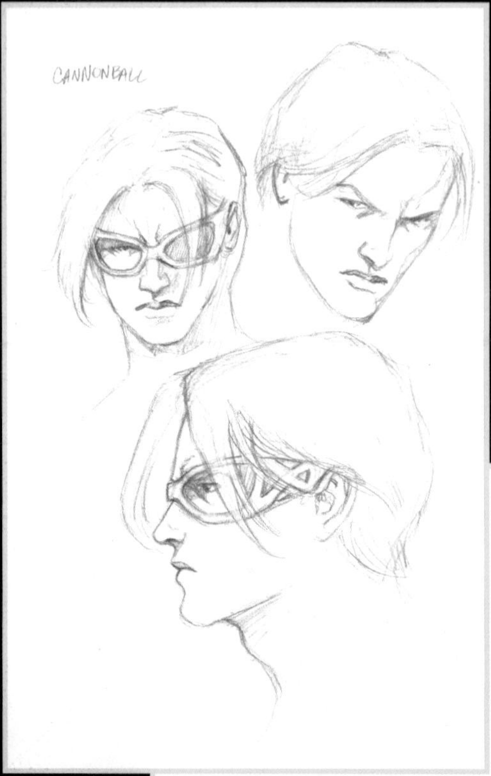
CANNONBALL

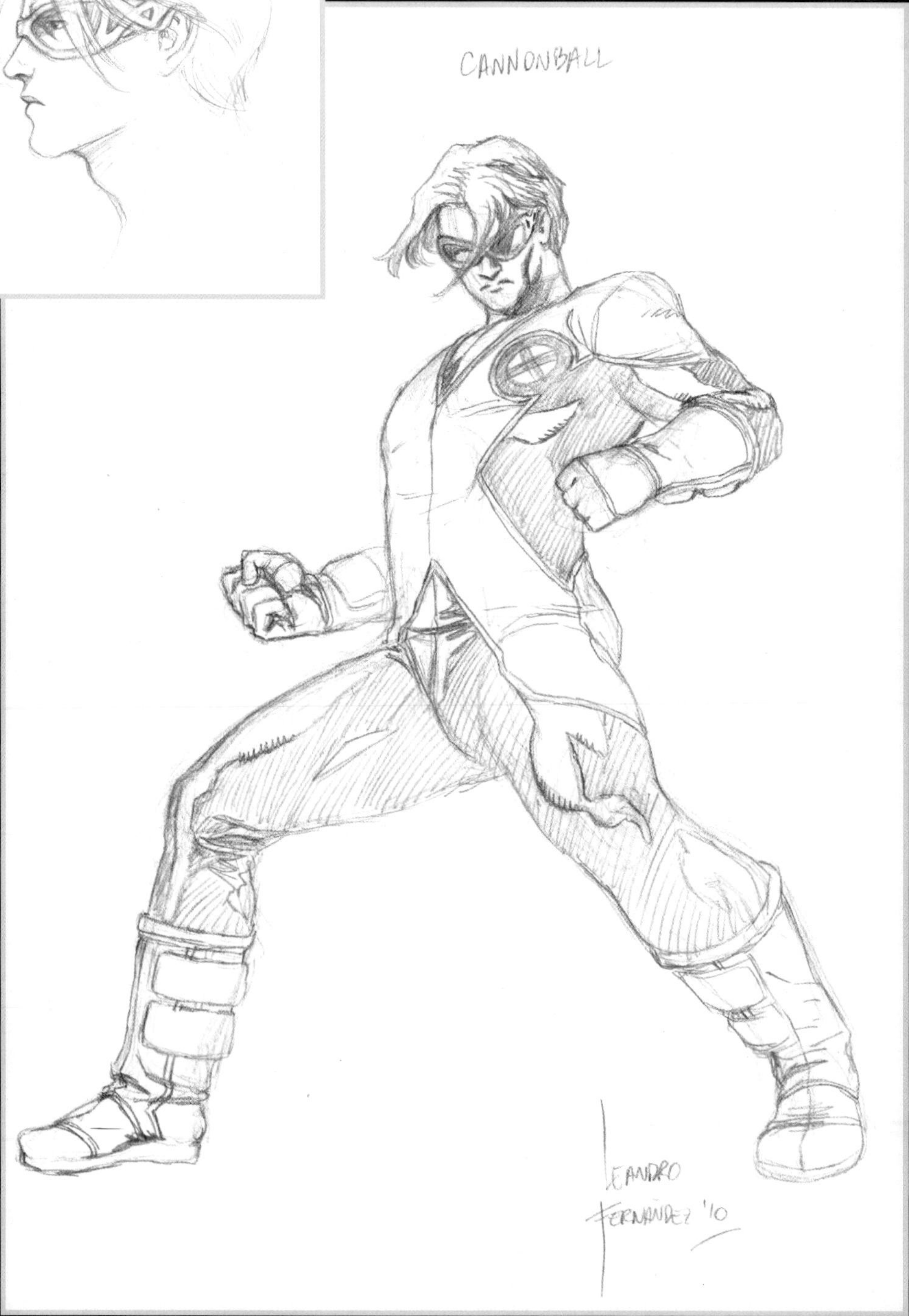
CANNONBALL
LEANDRO
FERNANDEZ '10

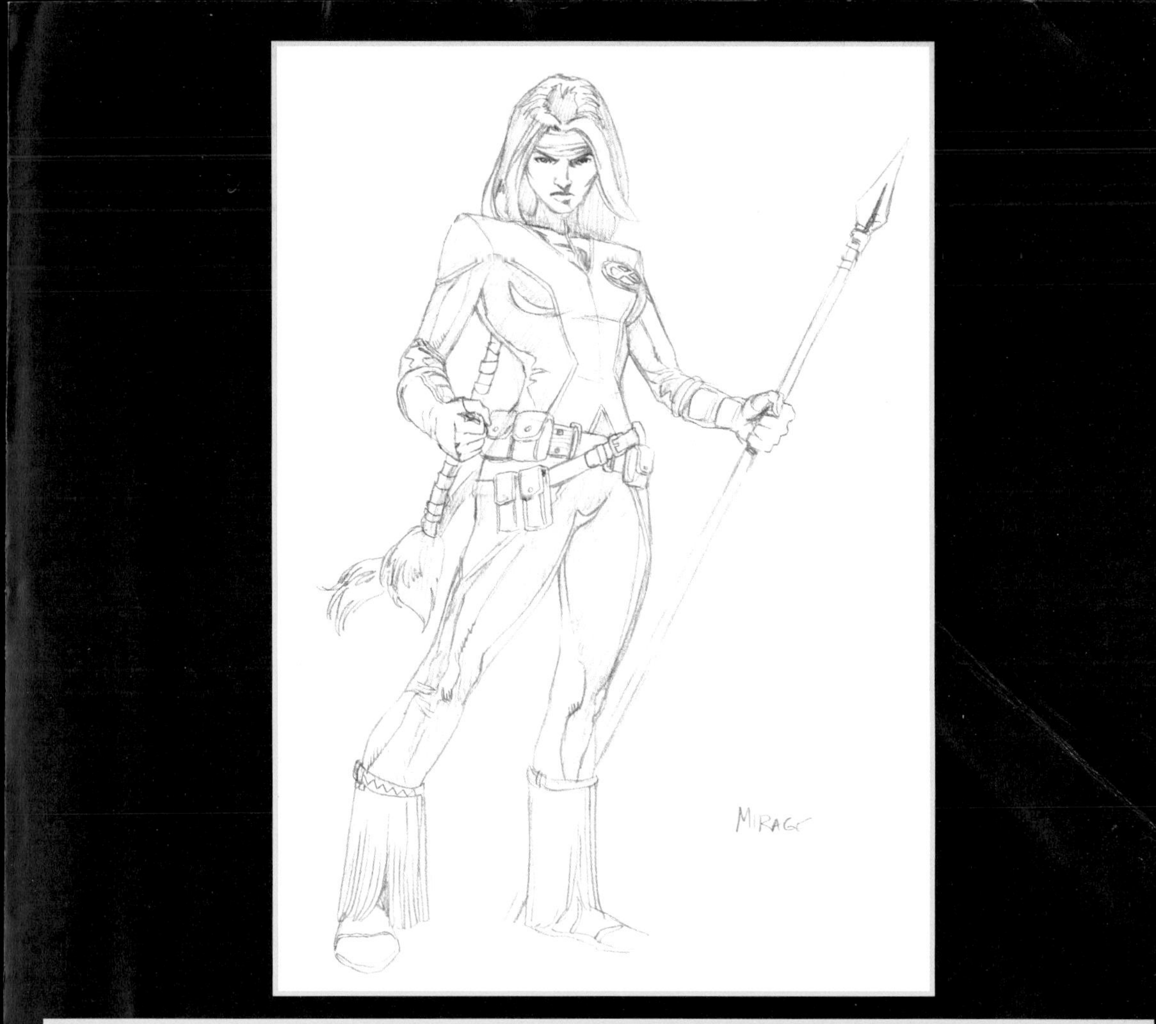
MIRAGE

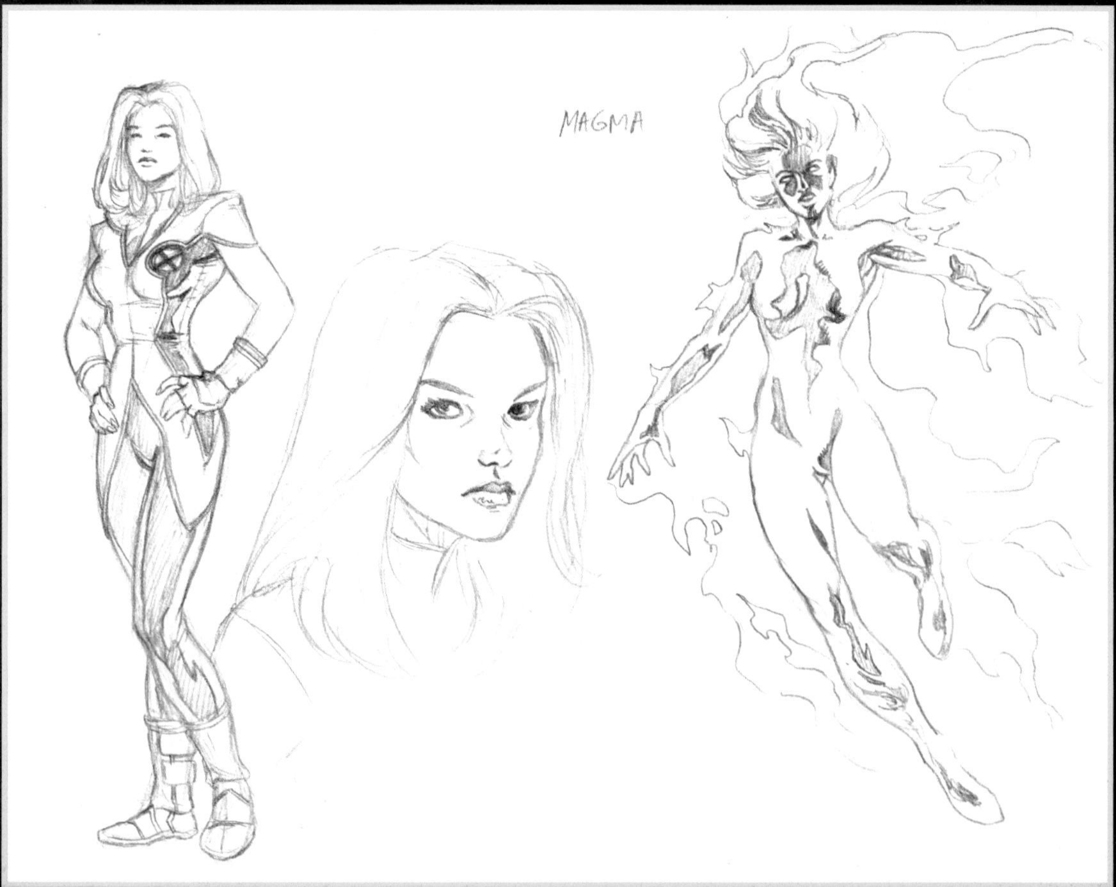
MAGMA

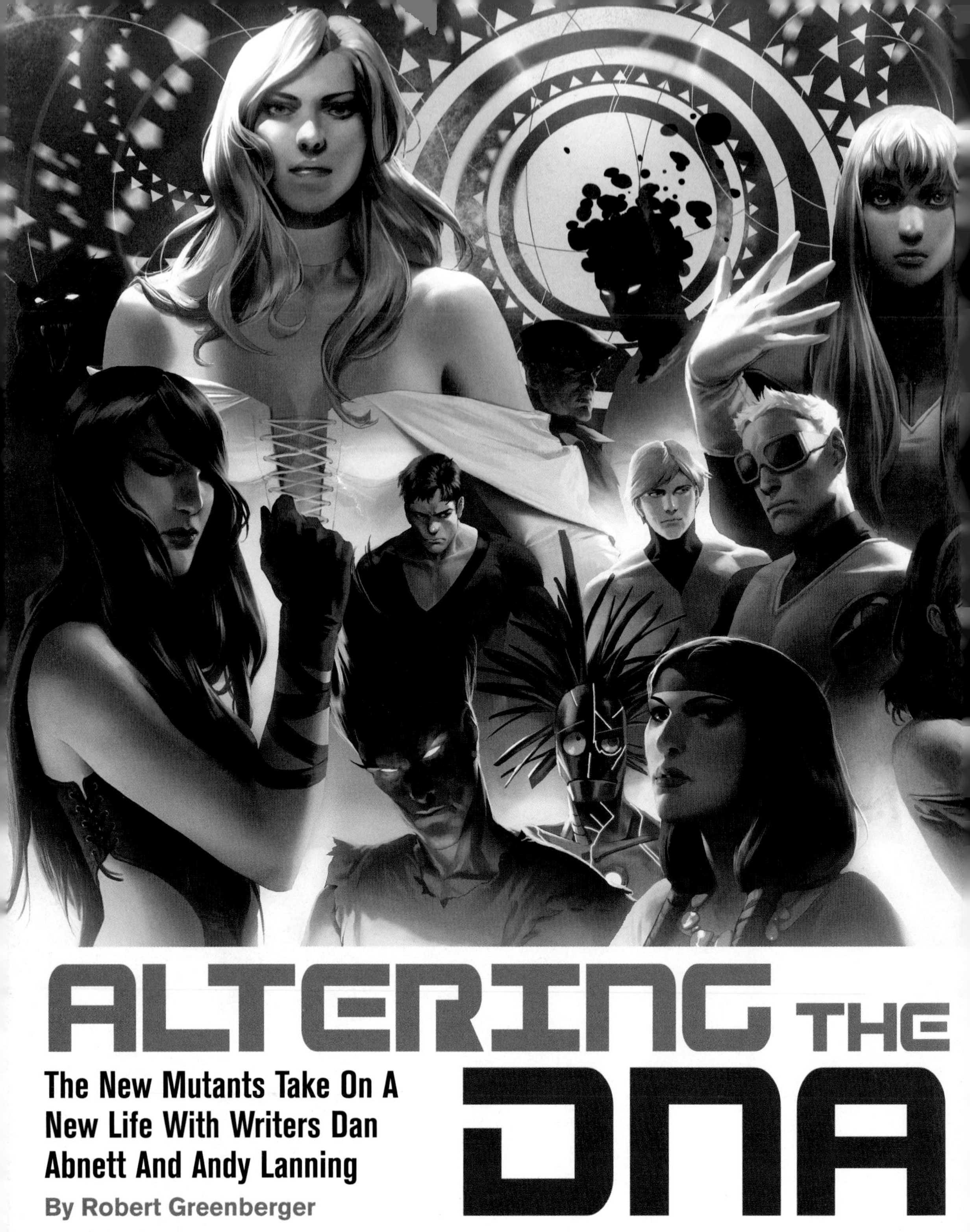

ALTERING THE DNA

The New Mutants Take On A New Life With Writers Dan Abnett And Andy Lanning

By Robert Greenberger

New Mutants returned with a bang in 2009 when Zeb Wells and Diogenes Neves gave readers a fresh look at the younger members of the X-Men's cast. Amid returning friends and foes, the team has struggled to find its place in a world of barely 200 mutants.

The series will get a shot in the arm this spring with the arrival of new writers Dan Abnett and Andy Lanning. The two have been prolific through the years since their collaboration began during the 1990s, both together and on their own. Abnett is an accomplished novelist, exploring fantasy worlds for Black Flame Library; he recently sold his first original novels to the UK's Angry Robot press. As an inker, Lanning remains in demand with a lengthy list of credits over the field's biggest pencilers.

Abnett and Lanning are no strangers to epic-scale super heroics – beginning in 2000 with DC Comics' *Legion of Super-Heroes*, followed by a stint on

New Mutants #25 cover by
Marko Djurdjevic.

WildStorm's *The Authority*.
But since 2008, they've made
their reputations working on
their largest canvas yet on
Marvel's *Annihilation* cycle of
titles, a revived *Guardians of
the Galaxy* and more.

Abnett and Lanning
explained why teams hold
such appeal. "We particularly
enjoy the interaction of the
character dynamics. Everything
is character-driven for us. It
sounds like an insult, but there's
a soap-opera quality that is
delicious to weave."

The move to *New
Mutants*, then, suits the pair
just fine. "We were both kids
who read and adored the
classic Claremont/Byrne run,
and the X-books remained
favorite reads from that point."

When interviewed, Abnett
and Lanning prefer to speak
in one voice, as they write.
"There's a particular dynamic
of shared character continuity
that the X-books do so well.
When we first started to
consider the *New Mutants*
characters from a writing
point of view, we found they
were bizarrely familiar to us,
like friends we'd known for a long time."

Wells' saga ended with issue #21, the conclusion to
his "Fall of the/Rise of the New Mutants" storyline. The
team was left licking its wounds after ending the threat
of Project Purgatory and preventing the Elder Gods from
destroying the world. The following three issues detoured
into the "Age of X" crossover with *X-Men: Legacy,* and
Abnett and Lanning took over with May's issue #25.

What happens when a new creative team arrives on
a title? Do they start over from scratch? Build on their
predecessors' work? Or just take direction from the editor?
"Can we say all three? Zeb's built a great foundation for us
with his run. It's like a relay race where we're taking the baton
from him. We don't want to demolish everything he's set
up, so there are character points and the repercussions of
recent stories to deal with. Even if our style's a little different,
the character linkage should be seamless from the readers'
point of view. That's where (editor) Nick (Lowe) comes in.
He knows what he wants, and the oversight he brings is

genuinely impressive. He's properly orchestrating the efforts
of all the creative teams and can help the books – and the
crisscrossing characters within them – operate without
contradiction. But...he's also hired us to bring new thoughts
and new ideas with us. New characters, too."

But before they could begin, they needed to make
familiarize themselves with all the recent the goings-on
in both the X-titles and the broader Marvel Universe. And
that means "lots of reading, lots of fact-checking, lots
of research. On the plus side, lots of audience, lots of
invested love for these characters."

As conceived by writer Chris Claremont and artist Bob
McLeod in 1982, the New Mutants were a group of teens
studying to one day become X-Men. But a fair amount of
Marvel time has passed since the team's first appearance,
and the age gap between the New Mutants and X-Men is
less of a factor today than in those original stories.

"There's not so much difference anymore," Abnett
and Lanning said. "These guys don't call themselves
the New Mutants. That's just the book's title. Nick was
keen to stress that they are grownup, proven, graduated
characters – fully one of the X-Men teams."

Having done their homework, Abnett and Lanning
recognized that Wells left plenty of dangling threads for
them to play with – leading them to name their opening
arc "Unfinished Business." And there's plenty for the New
Mutants to do. "Cyclops charges them with this specific
task: to tidy loose ends that the X-Men often have no time
to clean up, and which then end up biting them on the

Logan, Colossus and Kitty team up with the New Mutants
squad in DnA's first issue. (Art from *NM #25* by Leandro
Fernandez.)

TAKING THE OFFENSIVE: Dani Moonstar is looking badder than ever! (Art from *NM #25* by Fernandez.)

behind. It's a systematic effort to close cases and clean house, to get rid of any lingering nasty surprises. First order of business: Find Nate Grey."

Since his introduction in 1995's "Age of Apocalypse" saga, the son of Earth-295's Scott Summers and Jean Grey has struggled to find a place for himself in the Marvel Universe. He resurfaced during last year's *Siege* epic, psychically tortured within Norman Osborn's mind, which left him powerless in the corporeal world. Nate was last seen being dragged off panel during *Dark X-Men #5*, and it now falls to Abnett and Lanning to figure out what happened.

"It's hard to define Nate," they said. "Nate probably has a hard time defining himself. That's what we're going to do in this story: find out how he ticks, what he needs, where

he's going. He learns about himself as we learn about him."

Nate's fate is not the only thing the team will be confronting in the opening months of Abnett and Lanning's run. Another thread to be explored is what it means to be a young teen mutant in a world with under 200 mutants. "There's a real feeling of community — or a family reduced in a time of peril who know they have to work extra hard, together, through lean years, so that the family can rebuild and thrive. There is a sense of determination," the writers said.

Any community sees people coming and going, and members stepping into the spotlight based on circumstances. As a result, Abnett and Lanning foresee making "gentle modifications" to the team's lineup. "Just a little boost in prominence for some and a chance to step back for others. Nothing traumatic. And just because a character becomes 'inactive' on the team roster for a while, it doesn't mean they won't feature in the book. Some characters' stories will be about them *not* being on the team."

Given the writers' previous work, might the team find itself rocketing to the stars? "New Mutants in space? We're still working out exactly how it's going to go, but there's got to be some cool cosmic cross-continuity we can play with."

The New Mutants have plenty of earthbound business to take care of first, but the writers warned it won't be all action. "Nick wants as much kissing as possible, so pretty much anyone is fair game. We're trying to work out the most interesting, surprising, satisfying or unexpected possibilities."

Each writer took a moment to identify his favorite New Mutant and favorite New Mutant foe with Abnett answering, "I'd be hard pressed to call it between Illyana and Cypher. The Hellions." Lanning replied, "Dani or Warlock. The Demon Bear." There are other members of the New Mutants' rogues' gallery Abnett and Lanning eagerly await bringing on stage, but they won't name names. "Answering that would be giving away some big surprises. The X-books have a great villain catalogue. There aren't many we're not excited to use. Plus, we're bringing a few new ones along."

Joining them to visualize these exciting new tales is Leandro Fernandez, who previously illustrated Garth Ennis' *Punisher MAX*. The writers heaped praise on their collaborator. "His art is wonderful and he's extremely hard-working. We're just seeing the first pages come through now, and we're open to anything he sends us in terms of ideas."

Abnett and Lanning are clearly eager to get rolling, anticipating fan reaction over the summer months. "Apart from kissing and real high drama, we hope this book is going to be fun...fun and funny, when it needs to be."

New Mutants #25, *featuring the debut of DnA in Marvel's Mutant Universe, hits stores in May!* ●

"FIND X-MAN!": The New Mutants' first mission is to find out where in the world is Nate Grey. (Cover to *NM #25* by Jorge Molina.)